# SOCRATES' EDUCATION TO VIRTUE

## Learning the Love of the Noble

MARK J. LUTZ

State University
of New York
Press

Published by
State University of New York Press, Albany



Production by Susan Geraghty
Marketing by Nancy Farrell

Printed in the United States of America



For information, address State University of New York Press, State University Plaza, Albany, N.Y., 12246

**Library of Congress Cataloging-in-Publication Data**

Lutz, Mark J.
Socrates' education to virtue : learning the love of the noble / Mark J. Lutz.
p. cm.
Includes bibliographical references (p. ) and index.
ISBN 0-7914-3653-5 (alk. paper). — ISBN 0-7914-3654-3 (pbk. : alk. paper)
1. Socrates—Contributions in doctrine of virtue. 2. Socrates--Contributions in doctrine of virtues. 3. Virtue. 4. Virtues. 5. Plato. Dialogues. I. Title.
B318.V57L88 1998
179'.9'092—dc21 97-16696
CIP

10 9 8 7 6 5 4 3 2 1

# SOCRATES' EDUCATION TO VIRTUE

*To my mother and father*

# CONTENTS

# ACKNOWLEDGMENTS

I am grateful for this opportunity to thank those whose guidance, questions, and examples enabled me to write this book. I owe a particular debt to Thomas L. Pangle, who has been a constant source of useful advice, trenchant criticism, and encouragement. Similarly, I owe Clifford Orwin for his good counsel and for serving as a model of scholarship. They are two of the most generous and inspiring teachers one could hope to find. I am also pleased to thank Michael Rosano for reading and helping to improve the whole manuscript. In addition, I wish to thank Robert Goldberg, Peter Ahrensdorf, David Bolotin, John Koritansky, Patrick Powers, and Walter Nicgorski for their assistance at various stages of my thinking and writing. Finally, I am especially grateful to my wife, Kelly, for her careful, judicious, and crucial help in thinking through and formulating the arguments in this book.

The *Journal of Politics* has granted permission to reprint parts of "The Problem of the Noble and the Practicality of Platonic Political Philosophy" vol. 56, no. 1, 1994. *Polity* has granted permission to reprint parts of "Civic Virtue and Socratic Virtue," vol. 29, no. 4, 1997. The University of Wisconsin Press has granted permission to reprint parts of "Socratic Virtue in Post-Modernity," which was published in the *American Journal of Political Science*, vol. 41, no. 4, 1997.

# CHAPTER 1

# *Introduction*

One of the most serious and now most urgent questions facing liberal democracy is whether there is a place in it for virtue. We seem to founder for the lack of it and to risk losing the autonomy we cherish by taking direct steps to foster it. It is the contention of this book that the clearest account of virtue and of its place in political life is Plato's account of Socrates and that studying his account of Socrates may be our best opportunity to cultivate virtue while strengthening liberal democracy.

For many years, there was broad agreement that liberalism is a system of institutional checks and balances that functions smoothly without regard to the virtue or vice of its citizens. Perhaps the clearest statement of this view is Kant's suggestion in *Perpetual Peace* that liberal institutions could effectively govern a race of devils. But today a remarkably broad range of thinkers agrees that if liberal democracy is to survive it must undertake new efforts to cultivate its own civic virtues. There is an emerging consensus that we suffer a decline in "values," a crisis of "character," a lack of "higher purpose." In particular, we hear warnings about the absence of "personal responsibility" to family and to society, the slackening of self-discipline, the lack of tolerance, the debasement of culture, the coarsening of political debate, among other problems. It thus becomes far clearer than before that liberalism has always depended on particular qualities of character. Yet there does not appear to be complete agreement about which virtues are most important or about how we can promote particular virtues without threatening our freedom. Nor is there a solid consensus about what virtue is.

As we begin the difficult task of identifying, ranking, and fostering the virtues, we find that the models of virtue that inspired earlier generations of citizens seem to have lost much of their luster. Locke's model of the rational and industrious individual is widely considered to be petty and isolated, based on an excessively materialistic and narrow understanding of human nature. Similarly, the Kantian model of the autonomous individual who acts in accordance with universal moral categories seems abstract and rooted in dogmatic, enlightenment conceptions of reason and natural right that are no longer tenable. Seeking a model of virtue that combines independence of mind with a sense of civic responsibility, some thinkers look back behind modernity to the figure of Socrates. Long a hero to liberals such as Hume, Mill, and Dewey, Socrates is once again recognized as a paragon of citizenship. Richard Rorty identifies liberalism's civic virtues as the "Socratic virtues" of talking, listening, and deliberating about common concerns (Rorty 1982, 172; 1991, 29, 191). J. Peter Euben and Arlene Saxonhouse claim that Socrates' eagerness to consider every opinion and to reason with everyone about virtue makes him the image of democratic man (Euben 1990, 207–11; Saxonhouse 1992, 144). William Bennett's *Book of Virtues* repeatedly cites Socrates' courage, self-discipline, and sense of civic responsibility as models for contemporary moral education (Bennett 1993, 97–101, 246–51, 512–514, 657–660). While Socrates may be so appealing an example of citizenship that some will emulate him without further reflection, in order to promote his virtues as widely and as effectively as possible, it would be useful to learn what convinced him that his practices are, in fact, virtues. For how do we know that the Socratic virtues are excellences of the soul and not merely a set of habits and practices with which we could dispense at little cost? How do we know that his virtues do not merely resemble our virtues but in fact differ from them fundamentally?

While agreeing that Socrates exemplifies virtues we hope to find in liberal democrats, Leo Strauss argues that Socrates is especially useful to us because of what he can teach us about virtue. According to Strauss, liberal democracy is intended to be "an aristocracy that has broadened into a universal aristocracy" but has, instead, devolved into a narrow and spiritless "mass culture" that emphasizes security and efficiency and pays scant attention to excellence or virtue (Strauss 1968, 4, 5, 8, 19, 64). In order for liberal democracy to accomplish its original goal, we must recover the "liberal education" that Socrates practiced as he led his friends to "perfect gentlemanship," that is, to excellence and greatness. Plato indicates that in its "highest sense," this education is philosophy (7). According to Plato, a philosopher such as Socrates possesses "all the virtues or excellences of which man's mind is capable, to the highest degree" (8). As a philosopher, Socrates is a "perfect gentleman" in the highest sense (Strauss 1970, 175–176). Strauss says that since we are not philosophers and cannot acquire the highest form of education, we must strive to share in it by listening to the "great conversation" among the "greatest minds" (Strauss 1968, 8). In this sense, Socrates is not only an example of a virtuous human being, but also our best access to learning and caring about virtue. For Socrates is "that one among the greatest minds who because of his common sense is *the* mediator between us and the greatest minds" (6). Only by studying how Socrates examined and chose among the competing claims of the greatest minds can we share in the liberal education that completes the promise of liberal democracy.

Like Strauss, Thomas Pangle identifies the highest form of liberal education with a Socratic education. While Pangle agrees with Strauss that liberal democracy always needs Socratic education to help it lift its gaze above the merely practical and mundane, he places more emphasis on how we need to foster Socratic education to alleviate problems that threaten liberal democracy from within. According to Pangle, the most serious danger for liberal democracy is, not "unsettling skepticism, or revolutionary discord, or the excesses of passionate diversity," but instead "the deadening conformism to a bloodless and philistine relativism that saps the will and capacity to defend or define any principled way of life" (Pangle 1992, 213). Pangle reminds us of Tocqueville's observation that a perversion of the principle of equality often puts a powerful pressure to conform on citizens of democracies. Tocqueville argues that because we are not omniscient, we must take our bearings from some authoritative opinions about our rights and duties and goals. But as democrats, we believe that we are equal to others and should be independent of anyone else's authority. Consequently, we take as our authority opinions that are held by everyone and by no one in particular, that is to say, opinions held by "the public" at large. Because of the overwhelming reliance on the public opinion, individuals who are tempted to dissent from it are quickly isolated and overcome

(Tocqueville 1969, 254–258, 434–435). Pangle argues that this pressure to conform in democracy has become all the more powerful and dangerous now that it has embraced an especially intolerant form of "relativism." He claims that even though democratic tolerance and equality promise everyone the opportunity of attaining "a just rank in the natural hierarchy of talents and attainments, of virtue and wisdom," liberal democracy is now "haunted by the dangerous tendency to degenerate from the ideal of fertile controversy between competing moral and religious ways of life into the easygoing belief that all ways of life and all points of view are equal." Those who hold this view are prone to think that no particular ways of life or points of view are "really worthy" or "in need of profound examination and passionate defense." Moreover, they suspect that anyone who offers a substantive, principled, reasoned argument for the superiority of any one way of life, including for the superiority of liberal democracy, are for this reason "elitist" and immoral and intolerant. At this point, says Pangle, toleration and democracy begin to self-destruct (Pangle 1992, 215–216). According to Pangle, only a genuinely Socratic education can liberate us from dogmatic beliefs about the subjectivity of all values, beliefs that prevent us from experiencing true independence of mind and from rekindling the serious and free-ranging moral, religious, and political debates from which liberalism derived its original strength and purpose. He charges professors with the responsibility of helping students reenact, and thereby accept or modify, the "great reasonings" that originally "ushered in our modern civilization" (217, 194). Pangle promises that a Socratic education will be the opposite of all dogmatism to the extent that it makes us deeply aware of "the limits of our knowledge" and of "the power of the arguments that can be mustered against our beliefs" (195, 216). Without at least a taste of this Socratic education, he argues, it will be very difficult for students to develop the moral seriousness and intellectual freedom needed to practice our civic virtues.

While we may be attracted to the promise of a Socratic education, we need to know more precisely how a Socratic education differs from other kinds of education. What is it in particular about the way Socrates led his friends through books and through conversations to knowledge of the best way of life? How does a

Socratic education differ from and ultimately surpass a standard "Great Books" program? Why is it the single best antidote to our dogmatism and relativism? What evidence is there that Socrates uses reason in a way that is not reductionist or abstract but deepens our understanding of excellence and greatness?

The need to answer these questions becomes all the more urgent when we recall that making Socrates the model of our virtue runs counter to the some of the strongest currents of modern and postmodern thought. It would not be much of an exaggeration to say that one of the fundamental points of agreement among most modern and postmodern thinkers is that Socratic philosophy cannot educate us to virtue and happiness. In fact, many doubt that even Socrates hoped for such an education. Socrates is often said to have concluded that he is completely ignorant of how to be virtuous or of how to be a "perfect gentleman" (Rousseau *First Discourse* 26–30; Nietzsche *Beyond Good and Evil*, 202, 208; *Twilight of the Idols*, "The Problem of Socrates"). Many scholars now claim that it was not Socrates but Plato who established philosophy's grandiose ambition to lead us to virtue and happiness. According to Nietzsche, Socrates was a hyper-rationalist whose deafness to the instincts once permitted him the vulgar hope that reason can comprehend and even correct "Being"; but Socrates eventually recognized reason's limits, abandoned this hope, and accepted his ignorance (Nietzsche *Birth of Tragedy* 13–15, *Beyond Good and Evil* 190–191). His student Plato, however, seized on and never relinquished faith in the power of reason. He is said to have committed the "great dogmatic error" of believing that the soul is animated by a "pure" desire to know the one, permanent thing that is "good in itself" (Nietzsche *Beyond Good and Evil*, "Preface"). But in fact the soul is merely a bundle of shifting, unconscious instincts or drives that are themselves subject to historical forces. Our conscious notions of goodness and virtue are merely "values" projected on the world by our unconscious drives in order to maximize their own power (Nietzsche *Beyond Good and Evil* 1–14). Thus, Plato celebrates as true and as good only the lasting universals that are known by reason and disdains as false all the particular, changing, ineffable things that reason does not grasp. By drawing all phenomena around a "single center, principle or meaning," Plato's universal forms annihilate genuine differences and rob particulars of their identities "by forcing them to become epiphenomenal veils for a generative ontological realm" (Foucault 1984, 20). Platonic rationalism thus marginalizes alternative centers of power, silences competing voices and visions, and imposes a single, abstract notion of virtue on the world. It not only narrows the range of phenomena that we find noble or worthwhile but also prevents us from experiencing such phenomena in their fullness. According to Nietzsche and Heidegger, we experience what is truly moving or awesome only through our historically changing, sub-rational instincts or through unpredictable, historical encounters with unfathomable "Being." By grasping only what is accessible to everyone in any time or place, Platonic rationalism is able to touch only the surface of the awesome beauty known to those who experience artistic creations, political judgments, and religious revelations in the context of their particular historical settings.[1] Through Plato's universal and technological worldview, we have sunk into a "darkened world" that lacks genuine differences, creativity, and rank (Heidegger 1977 [1947] 194; 1959 [1953] 45–48; 1993 [1976] 104–105).

In particular, the Platonic teaching that politics should be guided by transcendent standards is said to vitiate civic spirit and civic virtue. According to Rorty, the belief in transcendent principles prevents us from recognizing that our particular, historically contingent communities are the actual sources of our virtues and from cherishing them as such. According to Rorty, "our identification with our community—society, political traditions, intellectual heritage—is heightened when we see that this community is *ours* rather than *nature's*, shaped rather than found, one among many which men have made" (Rorty 1982, 166). Similarly, Benjamin Barber argues that we feel the greatest civic spirit when we look only to political participation rather than to Platonic philosophy to give meaning to terms such as *freedom* and *justice* and *law* (Barber 1984). Thus, far from educating us to virtue or liberating us from intolerance, Plato appears to erect enormous barriers to experiencing authentic civic virtue.

Because Plato's admirers and critics make powerful cases for their respective sides, we might be tempted to abandon hope of deciding between them. Except that Plato's greatest critics allow that the brunt of their assault is aimed less at Plato's authentic thinking than at the "Platonism" into which that thinking devolved in the hands of subsequent thinkers and scholars. Nietzsche allows that his Socrates is an exaggeration and his Plato, a caricature (*Will to Power* 374, 432). As Heidegger observes, Nietzsche "protects" Plato by identifying his chief target as "Platonism" (Heidegger 1979 [1961] 205; cf. Nietzsche *Beyond Good and Evil* "Preface"; *Twilight of the Idols* "How the True World Became a Myth"). In his own name, Heidegger warns against interpreting Plato in light of the language and thought of subsequent interpreters (Heidegger 1979 [1961] 190–191). In fact, a growing number of contemporary scholars, ranging from Strauss and his students to thinkers such as Hans-Georg Gadamer, J. Peter Euben, and Martha Nussbaum, have raised long-neglected questions about Plato's thinking by paying serious attention to the drama of his dialogues. By reading Platonic dialogues non-dogmatically, by considering the context of Socrates' words and actions, and by observing what Plato teaches about the variety of human types in his portrayals of Socrates' interlocutors, we may be able to determine for ourselves whether a Socratic education expands or contracts our political, religious, and moral horizon.

## SOCRATES' EDUCATION IN THE LOVE OF THE NOBLE

One of Plato's most revealing accounts of Socratic education to virtue is contained in the *Symposium*, for this dialogue recounts how Socrates himself became educated in "erotic matters," the only positive knowledge that he ever claims to possess (Plato *Symposium* 177d7–8, 212b5–6; *Charmides* 155d4–e2; *Lysis* 204b5–c2; *Phaedrus* 257; *Theages* 128b1–4; cf. Xenophon *Memorabilia* 2.6.28). The importance of this knowledge emerges as one discovers that it includes knowledge of how to cultivate and gratify our erotic longing to be "noble and good" and to manifest "true virtue" (*Symposium* 212a). According to Socrates' teacher, Diotima, this eros animates not only love affairs but also politics and the arts. Yet it is most fully expressed and most fully gratified through philosophy (*Symposium* 203, 206, 210a, 210d ff.; *Phae-*

*drus* 243–57; *Republic* 474d–475a, 485b–c, 490b, 499c, 501d, 521b). The drama of *Symposium* indicates that upon reflecting on Diotima's teaching, Socrates recognizes that his own, youthful love of the beauty or nobility of wisdom is based on hitherto unrecognized assumptions about justice and nobility and piety. Using what he learns from Diotima to think through his own experiences and beliefs about these things, Socrates concludes that he can learn what is truly "noble and good." He finds evidence in his own soul that philosophy can comprehend the soul, gratify its needs, and perfect its virtues. But he also discovers important reasons to question what he thinks he knows about what is noble and good and just and sacred. He becomes convinced that in order for philosophy to confirm that it can know the soul and its virtue, it must become "dialectical" and must examine the widest range of political, moral, and religious beliefs on their own terms. On the whole, Socrates' education in "erotic matters" teaches him that he can complete his own education to virtue only by "turning away" from his youthful, exclusively apolitical, study of nature and by becoming the mature *political* philosopher we know from Plato's dialogues (Cicero *Tusculan Disputations* 5.10–11; *Academia* 1.15–6; *Brutus* 39).

The *Symposium* is also important for the questions it raises about Socratic education to virtue. The speech that recounts Socrates' education is preceded by five other speeches praising the god Eros. By far the most impressive and celebrated of these is made by Aristophanes, the comic poet who is Socrates' greatest and most influential critic. In the *Clouds*, Aristophanes depicts Socrates as an atheistic and amoral natural philosopher who readily teaches his students that neither Zeus nor justice exist. Plato's presentation of Aristophanes in the *Symposium* helps us understand Aristophanes' own thinking about human nature and the gods and thus helps us see more clearly the core of his critique of Socrates in the *Clouds*. After Socrates finishes his speech, Aristophanes tries to respond but is interrupted by the entrance of Alcibiades, a brilliant but corrupt statesman, who makes a famous speech in praise of Socrates. But Alcibiades' praise is ambiguous. His very presence in the *Symposium* raises decisive questions about Socrates' ability to educate others to virtue. According to Alcibiades, he was very eager to acquire a Socratic education but found Socrates unwilling to teach him. Socrates stirred Alcibiades' need to know how to be noble and good but cruelly mocked him when he asked for guidance. On the whole, Alcibiades' words and actions dramatically represent Aristophanes' critique of Socrates. By surrounding Socrates' account of his education with profound challenges to his wisdom, justice, and piety, Plato invites us to raise a dialogue among Socrates and his greatest critics so that we might learn for ourselves whether Socrates is a suitable educator to virtue.

The demonstration of Socrates' knowledge of erotic matters, or of the soul and its virtue, lies in his conversations with those who love noble virtue, such as with Alcibiades in the *Alcibiades Major* and *Symposium* and with Glaucon in the *Republic*. Socrates tries to educate both these ambitious, noble-minded young men to virtue. In both cases, he fails in some important respects to lead them to philosophy. Yet in these conversations he is able to show that his interlocutors are moved by an erotic need to know how to be both "noble" and "good." Furthermore, he is able to show that neither of them remains satisfied with his alternative account of virtue and that both admire, explicitly and implicitly, the virtues that Socrates admires and exemplifies. In addition to vindicating Socrates' knowledge and virtue, these dialogues help us understand the obstacles that prevent non-philosophers from reaching these things as well. Plato's dramatic presentation of Alcibiades shows us what can prevent ambitious people from benefiting from philosophic guidance. Plato's dramatic presentation of Glaucon illustrates the impediments that can keep the "civic" virtue of a non-philosopher from becoming the "true" virtue of a Socrates. But it would be contrary to the spirit of the dialogues to say that they decisively demonstrate the superiority of Socratic virtue to other kinds of virtue. Socrates' conversations show how philosophy itself points to the limits of his knowledge and repeatedly compels him to examine how others experience and understand virtue. For one of the crucial lessons of Socrates' education in erotic matters is that he can vindicate his knowledge and his virtue only by remaining open to the possibility that non-Socratics and non-philosophers may have some intimation or divination or knowledge of virtue that he lacks.

## SOCRATIC EDUCATION IN LIBERAL DEMOCRACY

Even if we grant that Plato's dialogues demonstrate that Socrates is educated to virtue, we are still left wondering what bearing this has on non-philosophers like ourselves. Is a Socratic education an essentially private good for a few fortunate thinkers? Or can Socratic education set the tone for society as a whole? If so, how would the teaching of Socratic education in our universities benefit those who live and work outside the academy? To begin to answer these questions, it is important to recall how profoundly philosophy has shaped modernity and postmodernity. Liberalism's moral and political categories derive from Enlightenment philosophers such as Hobbes, Spinoza, Locke, Montesquieu, Hume, and Kant. The most powerful criticisms of liberalism originated with thinkers such as Rousseau, Marx, Nietzsche, and Heidegger. Even those postmodernists who argue that philosophy should not play a role do so on the basis of philosophic arguments. The philosophical origin of our political and moral vocabularies may expose them to the influence of Socratic rationalism. In fact, Socratic education has flourished occasionally in what seem even more unlikely settings, such as in Medieval Islam, Judaism, and Christianity. Yet there are great obstacles preventing Socratic education from decisively influencing our politics and culture. Because we lack a Plato or an Al-Farabi to present it to us afresh, because its themes run counter to democratic and liberal tastes, and because it requires years of painstaking study, it is not difficult to see why some of its most sympathetic supporters hesitate to claim that it can correct our politics and culture.[2] But leaving those obstacles aside for a moment, in the best case, were Socratic education to acquire the sort of currency achieved by existentialism or postmodernism, what difference would it make in society as a whole? Were it to help set the tone of liberal democracy, what tone would it set? How would it touch the lives of those who do not study philosophy and who do not read erudite political and legal journals? While I do not claim to have decisive answers to these questions, I am willing to offer possible benefits of Socratic education to society as a whole, if only to spark a more concrete discussion of its potential uses to liberal democracy. Yet I want to stress from the outset that I mean only to suggest some possible consequences were Socratic education to gain discernible influence in our culture. I do not expect this book alone to bring about such results.

Socratic education might serve a useful function by helping to transform heated, but generally limited, "academic" disputes into subjects of a broader public debate about virtue. It might, for example, have an especially helpful influence on the study, writing, and reading of literature. There is nothing new in recommending classical education to complement our thinking. Tocqueville argues that the writings of the ancient Greeks and Romans offer the single best corrective to democratic moral leanings and literary tastes. For classical literature counters the tendency of democratic thinkers to focus more on the useful than the noble; to pay attention to mass movements and the sweep of history rather than to the influence of individual actors; to prefer the sensational to the charming; and to invent exaggerated, artificial, abstract characters rather than to depict the full range of actual human types (Tocqueville 1969, 472–474, 487, 488–489, 525). Tocqueville argues that only by cultivating a taste for classical literature at some universities can an element of democratic society be reminded of the full range of beautiful and noble things. Perhaps studying the dialogues of Plato and Xenophon, as well as the poems, dramas, histories, and treatises encountered in Socratic education, would promote the desired classical counter-culture.

But in the eyes of many contemporary students of literature, to promote Socratic education would be less a complement to our limits than a concession to our biases. Some would object that philosophy is by its nature incapable of appreciating what is beautiful and true in dramas and novels and poetry. By introducing grand theories and "metanarratives" to our literature, philosophy is blinded to the unique, historical truths contained in a particular, "local" work of art (Elshtain 1995, 196–197; Havel 1991, 328–350). Others would grant Tocqueville's point that literary taste and sensibility is always shaped by the dominant political class. But, unlike Tocqueville, they would identify that class not as the majority of ordinary citizens but as the predominantly European, male, propertied class that steers our society. According to this view, our literature's sensationalism, its depictions of an abstract "everyman," and its claims about the order or purpose of history do not merely deprive us of examples of aristocratic art and noble individuals but, more importantly, conceal the existing marginalization of non-Europeans, women, the poor, and various minorities. In this context, Tocqueville's proposed remedy would not fully expose the political character of our literature. To contrast liberal and classical literature would only obscure the extent to which both are shaped by Eurocentrism, patriarchy, and oligarchy. Plato, of course, would be particularly inappropriate in that he is the father of the metanarrative that deprives particulars of the attention they are due. Rather than turn back to thinkers such as Plato, many writers and critics call for exposing the essentially political character of all literature and encourage those who have suffered exclusion to speak out in their own, distinct vocabularies. Thus, our "literary scene" seems divisible into at least two camps. On the one hand, we find a seemingly apolitical, often frivolous, sometimes coarse mass literature that is believed by many critics to exclude a host of political voices from expressing themselves. On the other, we find a less widely popular "multicultural" literature that professes to speak in many distinct and intensely political vocabularies.

Socratic education might help bridge the gap between these literatures and even raise the level of political culture. Far from contesting the claim that literature is deeply political, Socratics would begin by inquiring about what makes it political. Do we recognize it as political because it always reflects entrenched and therefore conflicting cultural and sexual and economic class interests? Or is it political to the extent that it says something about the fundamental issues that arise most vividly in heated political debates, such as, What is justice? What is sacred? What is admirable? What is good? Socratics would argue that we find "multicultural" literature political in this latter sense because it offers us moving insights—or because it makes provocative claims—about what merits our sympathy, our respect, and our blame. Socratics would ask what authors can see from their particular cultural or sexual or economic vantage points that eludes the "mainstream" of democratic society. They would ask what light they can shed on our history, on our failings as well as on our successes. But Socratics would also be alert to the possibility that what is most significant in "multicultural" literature are insights that defy translation into other, more universal vocabularies. Perhaps what is most important can only be hinted at or glimpsed in particular, ineffable, historical things and thus can be captured, to the extent it can be captured, only by literature rather than by philosophy. A careful, dramatic reading of dialogues such as the *Symposium* and *Republic* shows that Plato does not, as is often assumed, simply dismiss poetry as rhetoric or as a tertiary imitation of reality. Even in criticizing how poets give their readers a moral education, Plato's Socrates concedes that "sensible men" can learn about virtue and vice from reading their poems (*Republic* 396c–e, 606b, 607b–e). Socrates calls poetry the rival of philosophy because, among other things, he is open to the possibility that only poetry captures important particular, changing, mysterious things that reason fails to apprehend. Modern Socratics would look to "multicultural" literature for signs that it sees just things, sacred things, noble and good things to which philosophy is blind.

By reading "multicultural" authors with an eye to what they imply about justice and the rest of virtue, the Socratics would try to articulate their political claims. In the course of elucidating these claims, they would hope to provoke the writers of this literature not merely to "express" their insights but to engage directly in the political activity of persuading and educating their fellow citizens about virtue and vice. In the best case, this would induce writers to compete with one another to guide the reading public. In order to present their obscure or difficult insights in the fullest and most compelling way possible, writers might inquire more deeply into the experiences and thinking that shaped their own cultures. They might examine the sacred texts and writings of great minds that have enriched traditions such as Buddhism, Confucianism, Hinduism, Islam, Judaism, and Taoism. In order to defend liberal democracy, some might reflect on its moral foundations and vindicate it through dramas or novels or poetry, following the example of a Shelly or a Whitman. Still others might seek out forgotten insights from the West's pre-liberal poets, philosophers, and theologians. As these various authors respond to one another, they might reconstitute something of the great debates among civilizations and among thinkers that have arisen from time to time. If the writing is skillful and raises the most fundamental political issues, it may engage a wide range of readers. By making a significant part of the nation more literate about the controversies surrounding virtue, it could serve as a springboard for a more informed and passionate public deliberation about civic virtue.

Socratic education might elevate public discussion not only about the arts but also about the sciences. Science now seems as problematic as at any time since the beginning of modernity. The technology that was thought to harness energy to cure disease and save labor is now widely seen to have unleashed terrible powers that destroy whole species and ravage the earth. The discoveries that seemed to dispel onerous superstitions and cruel prejudices now seems to have led us to regard the earth as an object for exploitation rather than of wonder. Having lost its reverence for nature, humanity seems bereft of a home. The modern natural science on which technology depends has fallen under such suspicion that some wonder whether it, like literature, is a useful myth perpetrated by the dominant groups in liberal society. Some even propose developing non-Western and female forms of science to counter those that prevail in the modern West.

Accustomed to the reproaches of many religious fundamentalists, the scientific community has reacted to this new criticism with bewilderment and indignation. After reminding us of the undeniable evils alleviated by technology, scientists emphasize the distinction between technology and science itself. They note how scientists devote themselves to impractical subjects such as number theory out of a desire to know for its own sake. They point with pride to how theories such as quantum mechanics and the special theory of relativity account for an impressive array of phenomena. Reminding us of atrocities committed in the name of "Aryan" and "Marxist" science, proponents of science warn of accepting the subordination of science to ideology.

In addressing these disputes, Socratics might acknowledge the impressive evidence of modern science's ability to measure and account for phenomena. But Socratics would note how modern natural science declines to consider whether nature has ends or purposes and relies on an abstract, mathematical account of phenomena without pausing to wonder if this is an adequate way of measuring and accounting for them. Most importantly, they would note that science takes for granted the legitimacy of its own enterprise. According to Plato's Socrates, when he was a young man he was deeply attracted to the natural philosophy of thinkers such as Anaxagoras (*Phaedo* 96ff.). But Plato's *Phaedo* and *Symposium* recount how Socrates came to question the decisiveness of scientific explanations and to recognize that his own, youthful devotion to philosophy rests on assumptions about justice, nobility, and piety that need to be examined on their own pre-philosophic or non-philosophic terms. According to the Socratic view, the most massive problem of modern science is not that it is insufficiently theoretical but that it fails to pay enough attention to the questionable needs, beliefs, and expectations that animate it. Thus, a Socratic would ask modern scientists to vindicate their pursuits by learning to listen to and address those who question its validity on non-scientific, even pre-scientific, grounds. Were scientists led to examine themselves on non-scientific grounds, perhaps they would see the wonder of their own souls and the wonder of the nature of which they are a part. Perhaps they would find a way to accommodate technology to our deeper spiritual or moral concerns. Simply by acknowledging the religious, environmental, and existentialist concerns of those who fear that science degrades rather than ennobles humankind, scientists may turn a heated and mutual animosity among opponents and supporters of science into a serious inquiry into the place of reason in our lives. By at once focusing and broadening debate about the legitimacy of the arts and literature, Socratic education might help citizens outside the academy reflect on several concrete, alternative accounts of virtue.

Having helped to spark such reflections, Socratic education might shed additional light on the roots, the uses, and limits of civic virtue in particular. The great difficulty with this suggestion, of course, is that Plato's Socrates is famous for recommending one of the most illiberal civic educations ever imagined in the *Republic*. He argues in that dialogue that such an education is the best means of cultivating an erotic love of virtue among the citizenry (*Republic* 403a; cf. *Laws* 643d–e, 650b). Through the drama of dialogue, we see with our own eyes how Glaucon's erotic longing for noble virtue leads him to love justice, the city, and law. But in this dialogue Socrates also argues that civic virtue is distinct from, less noble than, and in some respects even less genuine than the virtue of the philosopher. In fact, Plato's dramatic presentation of Glaucon shows us how and why his particularly "civic" virtue falls short of Socrates' true independence of mind and virtue of soul. Thus, the *Republic* is not simply an endorsement of an illiberal civic education but also a profound reflection on the inevitable limits of civic education, even in the best case. By studying works such as the *Republic*, keeping before our eyes both its praise of and reservations about civic virtue, we might better judge the potential uses and limits of our civic virtues. More generally, by helping to stir the most important debates about liberalism itself, Socratic education might help us see anew its strengths and uses. It might show us that liberal democracy is not an obstacle to moral and intellectual seriousness but a solid and valuable setting for thinking about, arguing about, and pursuing virtue.

## PLAN OF THE BOOK

The first chapter examines Richard Rorty's claim that liberalism will flourish without relying on any traditional philosophic foundations. After recounting Nietzsche's withering attack on Socratism and Platonism as progenitors of modern democratic resentment and nihilism, I discuss Rorty's claim that we can practice our liberal "Socratic virtues" without relying on "Platonic" philosophic support. I argue that Rorty wants to jettison philosophy from our conversation because he fears that philosophy—especially in the form of Nietzsche's and Heidegger's insights into the self and truth—poses a grave danger to liberal morality and politics. But I argue that these philosophic challenges are so serious and tangible that it behooves us to muster a philosophic defense of the Socratic virtues. The second chapter examines the objection that Platonic political philosophy ultimately fails to support the Socratic virtues and celebrates in their stead non-Socratic, "Platonic" virtues. I argue, however, that this may exaggerate the differences and tensions between Socratic and Platonic political philosophy. I argue that there are sufficient signs even in what are called "Platonic" rather than "Socratic" dialogues that Plato continues to vindicate the dialectical political philosophy of Socrates.

The next chapters explicate Socrates' claim to know the eros for noble virtue. Following Plato's indication that Socratic philosophy emerged as a response to powerful criticisms of philosophic knowledge and virtue, the third chapter examines the poet Aristophanes' powerful criticism of Socratic philosophy in Plato's *Symposium* and in Aristophanes' *Clouds*. Following this is Socrates' own dramatic and dialectical account of his education in erotic matters in the *Symposium*. The key discovery is that his own love of philosophy may not be as noble as he believed; that it rests on previously unexamined opinions about nobility, justice, and piety; and that he must examine these matters to confirm his belief that philosophy is genuinely noble and good.

The next two chapters examine the challenges to Socratic wisdom that are represented by Alcibiades. Based on Plato's presentation of Alcibiades and Socrates in the *Alcibiades Major* and *Symposium*, the fifth and sixth chapters argue that Socrates ultimately shows that the soul is moved by an erotic desire to know that we are "noble and good" or "perfect gentlemen" and that only philosophy gratifies that desire. The seventh chapter explains how Socrates demonstrates that his way of life is most virtuous by examining the distinction between philosophic and civic virtue. Based on Plato's presentation in the *Republic*, it explores the origins, uses, and limits of civic virtue. In particular, it explains how Socrates affirms through conversing with Glaucon that the virtue of the philosopher is more genuine and nobler than that of the non-philosopher. The conclusion discusses how Plato's account of Socrates' education to virtue constitutes a response to great critics of Socratic philosophy such as Aristophanes and Nietzsche and how the modern study of Socratic education could elevate the political culture of liberal democracy.

# CHAPTER 2

# *Platonism and Liberalism*

Even as leading political thinkers emphasize the importance of tolerance, respect for rule of law, and other liberal virtues, few express much confidence that the philosophic grounding that shaped and guided liberalism since its inception is adequate to inform and resolve many political and social problems we now confront. In fact, many theorists voice suspicions that liberalism's foundational account of human nature and of the sanctity of individual rights is largely responsible for the social coarseness and fragmentation that characterizes modern liberalism. Typically, it is said that liberal philosophers such as Hobbes and Locke rely too heavily on modern natural science in their depiction of the human situation. By conceiving of us only as bodily, solitary, and calculating beings, they obscure our spiritual, social, and historical character. Similarly, it is claimed that Kant's attempt to rescue liberalism from its materialist and reductionist foundations merely exacerbates the problem, for by portraying the self as radically autonomous and subject to universal laws, Kant leads us to respect only what is homogeneous, abstract, and ultimately disconnected and to neglect precisely those distinct, incommensurable qualities which make us capable of becoming interdependent and valuable to one another in a community. While some theorists may be accused of criticizing liberal political philosophy without having fully confronted the subtlety or probity of its founders' thought, there is an ever-widening consensus among scholars of all stripes and calibers that we need to reconsider the theoretical foundations of liberal democracy. As confidence in liberalism's theoretical foundations continues to wane, many have come to question the very existence of substantive rational grounds for making political and moral judgments. Leading theorists claim that we are witnessing the unraveling not merely of liberal political rationalism but of what Heidegger called the "onto-theological" tradition of Western thought. But the practical, political ramifications of this purported event are uncertain and the subject of intense debate. Nietzsche and Heidegger, the philosophers who offer the most original and influential critiques of the rationalist tradition, claim that their insights into the historical character of self and of truth call for a politics that is neither liberal nor democratic. Yet many contemporary thinkers insist that it is possible to accept the core of Nietzsche's and Heidegger's diagnosis of the tradition without having to embrace their prognoses and prescriptions. Among the most prominent of these postmodern thinkers is Richard Rorty, who has stirred much controversy and won a considerable following among political, legal, and philosophic scholars by arguing that liberal democracy would become even more confident, public spirited, and diverse were it suffused in "irony" and "pragmatism" rather than grounded on philosophic foundations. The purpose of this chapter is to examine whether Rorty provides a convincing response to Nietzsche's original claim that his insights into the historical character of the self call for overturning liberal democratic morality and politics.

According to Nietzsche, liberal democracy has relied on rationalism and on rationalism's specific accounts of the self and of truth. Nietzsche traces the origin of the rationalist tradition back to Socrates, whom he calls the "turning point and vortex of so-called world history." Prior to Socrates' decisive influence, men who were "productive" derived their judgments and commitments from their instincts, from the sensual, contradictory, and unfathomable drives of the unconscious. Reason came to such men only to criticize or make sense of what their instincts created. Socrates, however, was a "monster" or freak of nature. Because his "instinct-negating" reason was "over-grown" and spoke to him prior to his instincts, he did not learn through the instincts how life itself is a chaos of creativity and destruction. While others saw in Greek tragic poetry a consoling expression of and reconciliation with the suffering and mystery at the core of life, Socrates saw only a regrettable confusion. Socrates had an unshakable faith that thought can penetrate and even correct "the deepest abysses of being." Despite the extraordinary magnitude of Socrates' hopefulness, his outlook was merely that of a vulgar utilitarian. He devoted himself to knowledge because he believed it would make him both happy and virtuous, without any need for sacrifice or self-overcoming. But even Socrates eventually gazed into "what defies illumination" and realized that he knew nothing (*Birth of Tragedy* 13–15). He saw that reason is not a cure for the instincts but merely a negating form of instinct that imposes its tyrannical order on the others. Yet being vulgar and spiteful, he continued to use dialectical reason to humble his noble victims. The aristocrats not only were susceptible to Socratic domination but welcomed it. In the course of history, says Nietzsche, every aristocratic class necessarily degenerates with the result that the soul of the typical aristocrat becomes a chaos of weakened but warring drives. Wracked by internal disorders, the upper class embraced the tyranny of Socratic reason as a remedy for their affliction (*Beyond Good and Evil* 190, 202, 208, 212; *Twilight of the Idols* "Problem of Socrates").

Socrates wielded an enormous influence among his contemporaries; but the Socratic revolution took on its world-historical significance through Plato's dialogues. Nietzsche says that even though Plato was enthralled by Socratism, he was "too noble" to accept it as such. In one sense, this seems to mean that Plato was too noble to believe that reason aims at one's own happiness rather than at what is good in itself. Yet in a deeper sense, it means that Plato's nobility led him to use Socratism as a means for his own creative self-transformation. Plato's psyche became the site of a fierce struggle between Socratic rationalism and Plato's aristocratic instincts. Exercising the greatest strength ever possessed by a philosopher, Plato appropriated Socrates' judgments and imposed on them his own. By creating a distinctly new understanding of the soul and the good, Plato was able to "overcome" both Socrates and himself. He was the first to conceive of a fixed, autonomous mind or spirit that is moved by a pure desire to rise above the deceptions of the senses and to know the one thing that is permanently and knowably good. Contrary to Socrates' explicit teaching, the instincts can join with reason in disregarding everything particular, changing, and incommensurable and in pursuing "one goal, the good, God." Together, instinct and reason lift Plato above the realm of appearances to a "true world" in which a permanent reality becomes fully intelligible. Having ascended to that world, says Plato, one is able to know and share in perfect goodness (*Beyond Good and Evil* "Preface," 14, 191; *Twilight of the Idols* "How the True World at Last Became a Myth"; *Will to Power* 572).

According to Nietzsche, Platonism achieved its greatest influence through Christianity. The weak and resentful masses eagerly accepted the Christian concept of the free will that allows them to blame the strong for choosing to be strong and to praise themselves for choosing to be meek. Moreover, they seized on Christianity's promise that after death they would ascend to a "true world" in which they could revenge themselves against the strong and proud. Yet these were not the sole converts to Christianity. The intellectual atmosphere of Imperial Rome was shaped by long-running disputes among "skeptical" and "free-spirited" philosophical schools. Out of this irreligious culture emerged unbelieving philosophers who saw in Christianity the opportunity to transform or overcome themselves. They accepted the Christian demand that they sacrifice everything they loved, their freedom, pride, and confidence, and imposed on it the further requirement that they be excruciatingly truthful before the transcendent God. They questioned and sacrificed everything they loved until they finally examined God himself and found it impossible to believe in his providence. God was killed not by skepticism but by Christian probity (*Beyond Good and Evil* 46, 53–55; *Genealogy of Morals* 3:24; *Will to Power* 1, 17; Heidegger 1979, 160).

While this Christian probity gradually revealed the demise of God, the democratism at the heart of Christian morality continued its assault on the aristocracy. By seducing aristocrats into directing their will to power against itself, Christianity gradually weakened them and leveled the classes. With the eventual disappearance of the "highest types," the "lower species" of mankind, the "mass," the "herd," "society" has unlearned its modesty and inflated its needs into "cosmic and metaphysical values." In staking its moral claims, it "monopolizes" virtue by demanding that everyone serve it unconditionally. It elevates public spirit, benevolence, consideration, industriousness, moderation, modesty, indulgence, and, above all, compassion for the weak, for these are the qualities that protect, comfort, and flatter them. Those who are severe toward themselves and toward others, who have a sense of distance and rank, who feel noble and strong, are now accounted evil, for they threaten the peace and belie the dignity of the "good" man. Confronted by an undisputed morality of pity, the healthy and strong are persuaded that they are akin to and responsible for the sickly; they labor fruitlessly to succor them until they, too, are ultimately infected by their sickness (*Beyond Good and Evil* 62, 201, 203, 260; *Genealogy of Morals* 1:7–8, 3:14; *Will to Power* 27, 30, 209, 253, 339, 373, 464, 765, 1017).

Much as earlier philosophers supported Christianity, modern philosophers offer democratic morality its rational foundations. But unlike their predecessors, modern philosophers regard the "true world" of "being-in-itself" as unknowable and ultimately as unimportant. Turning their gaze from the realm of metaphysics, they focus instead on the "apparent" world. But in observing that world, they prove to be selective: They regard as "real" only what is universal, knowable, and manipulable and dismiss as accidental all that is exceptional or fleeting or incommensurable. On the basis of this scientific outlook, only the homogeneous herd's enduring desires for peace, material prosperity, and dignity seem genuine and worthwhile. Nature herself seems to live under a democratic "rule of law" and to be readily manipulable in the service of the majority's demands (*Beyond Good and Evil* 14, 22, 204; *Genealogy of Morals* 2:12, 3:9; *Will to Power* 51). By taking on this vulgar, practical, Socratic character, modern rationalism helps to bring about a world without suffering and conflict, without contempt or inequality. But should it ever eliminate all hardship, longing, opposition, struggle, and rank, it would do away with the very preconditions for self-overcoming and creativity. Thus, modern science is the fullest expression of the leveling, egalitarian utilitarianism that points us toward the herd of "last men"; and the forerunners of the last men, though not the last men themselves, need faith in the truth of science (*Beyond Good and Evil* 22, 203, 212, 225; *Twilight of the Idols* "Expeditions of an Untimely Man" 39).

According to Nietzsche, however, fissures in democracy's epistemological foundations have come to sight. For it is beginning to occur to a "few minds" that physics, along with metaphysics, is merely an interpretation of the world. By positing the existence of atoms and simply by relying on the selective testimony of the "common man's" senses, physicists assume a natural distinction between "real" and "apparent" phenomena and presuppose necessary relations between cause and effect, just as traditional metaphysics assumed a "true world" of "beings-in-themselves." As more discern how our understanding of the "external" world depends on our "inner" world, new psychologists will come forward to scrutinize the "subject." Following Nietzsche, they will ask whether the modern concept of the "subject" who wills and thinks has merely been inferred from the experience of willing and thinking (*Beyond Good and Evil* 12, 16, 17, 19). Perhaps only a prejudice in favor of reason or a prejudice in favor of our grammar leads us to believe that there is a unified substance, an "ego," that stands back and causes what is willed and thought (*Beyond Good and Evil* 17; *Genealogy of Morals* 1:17, 3:12; *Twilight of the Idols* "'Reason' in Philosophy" 5). On the basis of such insights into perspectivism and with an historical sense, intrepid psychologists, philologists, and philosophers will learn to doubt the existence of a fixed, autonomous subject who longs to know and attain one transcendent good. Instead, they will come to see the "self" as a bundle of shifting, competing, unconscious drives. They will perceive that when one of these drives masters the others, it christens itself the "subject" or the "soul" and posits as "true" and "good" whatever sustains its dominance. But having been educated by Platonism and Christianity to esteem only what is permanent and universal, many of these thinkers will judge man false. Unable to revere ideals that man unconsciously created for himself, many will become pessimistic and gloomy (*Genealogy of Morals* 1:12; *Will to Power* 12, 18, 483, 552; Heidegger 1982, 24–35; Pangle 1983, 65).

A few, however, will respond to the insight that science and democracy are products of historical creativity or will to power by recognizing an opportunity for a new aristocratic radicalism, fueled partly by the recognition that science and democracy are expressions of what is despicable in man. Accepting that the self and its "truths" are historical and shifting, they will strive to replace traditional ideals with ones that can inspire reverence for mankind. Some challenge the feasibility of Nietzsche's new aristocracy on the grounds that it would be vulnerable to renewed democratic resentment and revenge (Connolly 1988, 159–160; Ansell-Pearson 1994, 154–155). But Nietzsche indicates that philosophers of the future will beware of ideals that turn the will to power against itself and infect them with compassionate sickness. By giving birth to ideals that celebrate sensuality, appearance, change, longing, suffering, mortality, and conflict, philosophers of the future will become ever stronger than and more distant from the herd—and thus less vulnerable to the eviscerating morality of pity (*Genealogy of Morals* 3:26; *Twilight of the Idols* "Expeditions of an Untimely Man" 38).

Nietzsche professes to lack sufficient vigor to create the new goals that would restore mankind's vitality and self-respect. His task is to help bring about the younger, stronger "philosophers of the future." According to Nietzsche, philosophers are fundamentally concerned with changing how others think and live: The philosopher is by nature a commander and legislator (*Beyond Good and Evil* 211; *Genealogy of Morals* 1:17, 2:24–25, 3:14, 28). Scholars disagree about whether Nietzsche means to recommend actual political reforms. Kaufmann and others have properly challenged the assumption that Nietzsche's teachings had a *solely* political (and especially fascist) purpose and highlighted the unmistakable importance of solitude and self-transformation to the Nietzschean philosopher (Kaufmann 1968; Thiele 1990). Nonetheless, Nietzsche frequently encourages his readers to conclude that actual illiberal and undemocratic political reforms are needed to produce philosophers of the future. Perhaps the clearest statement to this effect is the first aphorism of the chapter "What is Noble" in *Beyond Good and Evil*:

> Every enhancement of the type "man" has so far been the work of an aristocratic society—and it will be so again and again—a society that believes in the long ladder of an order of rank and differences in value between man and man, and that needs slavery in some sense or another. Without that *pathos of distance* which grows out of the ingrained difference between strata—when the ruling caste constantly looks afar and looks down on subjects and instruments and just as constantly practices obedience and command, keeping down and keeping at a distance—that other, more mysterious pathos could not have grown up

> either—the craving for an ever new widening of distances within the soul itself, the development of ever higher, rarer, more remote, further stretching, more comprehensive states—in brief, simply the enhancement of the type "man," the continual "self-overcoming of man," to use a moral formula in a supermoral sense. (257)

According to Heidegger, Nietzsche's call for "grand politics" (*die Grosse Politik*) is not a simple endorsement of "the exploitative politics of imperialism"; that is, Nietzsche does not mean merely to recommend that strong countries conquer weaker ones. More importantly, Nietzsche means that Europe must be united politically for the express purpose of establishing new goals or ideals in a "grand style" (Heidegger 1979 [1961], 158–159; Nietzsche *Beyond Good and Evil* 208; *Will to Power* 978). Nietzsche is especially critical of liberal institutions that permit us to become lax and that emphasize what we have in common rather than what elevates a few above the rest; for these institutions merely strengthen democratic morality and inhibit the longings, internal tensions and inner discipline needed to create new values (*Twilight of the Idols* "Expeditions of an Untimely Man" 38). Insofar as Nietzsche believes that political reforms can overcome the obstacles to greatness presented by democratic morality and liberal institutions, he may mean precisely what he says in claiming that the spiritual longings that created the Platonic tradition can only be turned away from "nihilism" and renew themselves through great wars and planetary aristocracies (*Genealogy of Morals* 2:11; *Beyond Good and Evil* 203, 208; *Will to Power* 960, 982; Ansell-Pearson 1994; Detwiler 1990; Löwith 1964, 262).

According to Rorty, Nietzsche's analysis of the collapse of transcendent values is now widely accepted. There is broad agreement that Plato was wrong to think of moral philosophy as "discovering the essence of goodness" (Rorty 1982, 163; 1989, xiii). The philosophic tradition is viewed as merely a "literary genre" of failed attempts to define "good" and "truth" (1982, xiv). Philosophers such as Heidegger and Gadamer have exploded the traditional account of human nature by giving us "ways of seeing human beings as historical all the way through," while others such as Davidson and Quine have blurred distinctions between "permanent truths of reason and temporary truths of fact." Similarly, psychoanalysis has "blurred the distinction between conscience and the emotions of love, hate, and fear, and thus the distinction between morality and prudence." These developments erase "the picture of the self common to Greek metaphysics, Christian theology, and Enlightenment rationalism: the picture of an ahistorical natural center, the locus of human dignity, surrounded by an adventitious and inessential periphery" (1989, 33; 1991, 176; 1991a, 143–163).

Having been liberated from such pictures, we are left wondering who we are and how are we to act, individually and collectively. According to Rorty, we can and should understand the self to be a network of "beliefs, desires, and emotions with nothing behind it," a network that constantly reweaves itself in a "hit or miss way" to "meet the pressures of the environment" (1991, 192–193, 199). We should believe that there is neither a pure will to know the truth nor any unchanging truth about human beings to be known. Lacking a "God's eye view" of our selves and our situation, societies posit various criteria, values, virtues, to pursue various contingent objects at various times (1982, 13; 1989, 201–202). These criteria are as "plentiful as blackberries" and impossible to rank or validate by any transcultural or transhistorical standard (xli–xlii; 168–169). Those who recognize that the self is a shifting, subjective network and that our moral horizons are at bottom contingent but useful vocabularies are what Rorty calls "pragmatists," for these are people who take their bearings from what "works" rather than from purportedly objective standards of goodness and truth (xvii; 1991, 33). They can be at the same time "ironists" who have "radical and continuing doubts" about their vocabularies, who realize that no vocabulary carries with it arguments to support it, and who see that every conceivable vocabulary is equally distant from "reality" (1989, 73). According to this understanding, even Nietzsche and Heidegger qualify as both pragmatists and ironists (1989, 83; 1991a, 2–5).

Contrary to the assumption that adopting Nietzschean and Heideggerian notions about truth and the self will promote antiliberal and antidemocratic politics, Rorty claims that there is no essential connection between philosophy and politics (1989, 111). In the past, it was assumed that moral and political commitment depends upon belief in the veracity of theological or metaphysical dogmas; but we can derive our commitments, including the commitment to liberal democracy, simply from our community (1982, xviii; 1991, 33). We can adopt a "'merely' ethical foundation for our sense of community"—or, even better, we can "think of our sense of community as having no foundation except shared hope and the trust created by such sharing" (1991, 33). Following Schumpeter, Rorty argues that to be civilized means to stand unflinchingly and courageously by the convictions (or "vocabulary") of our community in full awareness that they are only "relatively" valid or contingent (1989, 46–47). Contrary to Nietzsche, we can dedicate ourselves to our morality without having to avert our eyes from the collapse of transcendent values. Liberalism can take its bearings from the existing, contingent social solidarity that happens to be liberal and democratic. We are members of a liberal community to the extent that each of us, whether on left or right, shares a commitment to the "Socratic virtues," which Rorty identifies as the willingness to talk, to listen, and to weigh the consequences of our actions upon others (1982, 172; 1989, 60; 1991, 29, 191). We are "heirs of Socrates" who wish to "link" our days "dialectically each to each" (1991, 29). Far from requiring us to relinquish the Socratic virtues that are the very heart of our civic virtues, the failures of Platonism permit us to see that those qualities

> are simply *moral* virtues. They cannot be inculcated nor fortified by theoretical research into essence . . . We are not conversing because we have a goal, but because Socratic conversation is an activity with its *own* end. (1982, 170)

Socratic conversation is moral simply because we engage in it without rational grounding and without some further purpose.

Why will we continue to engage in specifically Socratic conversation rather than in some other activity? In part, because we have no choice, because our culture and history give us no option but to work from the starting points they provide (1982, 173–174; 1991, 195). Just like any other culture, we acquire our values from ethnocentrism or "cultural bias" (1991, 13–15, 28–29, 176, 188, 203, 207). Socialization goes "all the way down" (1989, xiii). To begin discussion from the beliefs and desires that we hold dearest, from our cultural starting point, is not arbitrariness but "sincerity" (1991, 195). This is not to say that Rorty endorses bigotry or abandons himself to dogmatism, for he encourages us to overcome mere "acculturation" by fostering and exploring internal social "splits," tensions, and differences that widen the purview of the community (1991, 13–14). Moreover, he suggests that a pragmatic commitment to liberalism will make our society all the more diverse. Liberalism can be "redescribed" as the hope that culture can be "poeticized" rather than as the Enlightenment hope that it can be "rationalized" or "scientized": "We need to substitute the hope that the chances for fulfillment of idiosyncratic fantasies will be equalized for the hope that everyone will replace 'passion' or fantasy with 'reason'" (1989, 53). Were liberal culture to build its "rhetoric" around the thought that vocabularies are "human creations, tools for the creation of such other human artifacts as poems, utopian societies, scientific theories, and future generations," it could become "poeticized." Based on the "appreciation" that all our "touchstones" are "human artifacts," the poetic liberal society's goal would become "the creation of ever more various and multicolored artifacts" (1989, 53–54).

Rorty is, however, adamant that no community can extend its range of participants and views infinitely. There are limits beyond which we need not and cannot go. We need not be so liberal that we entertain nonliberal and antidemocratic options. We must not become so Socratic that we permit ourselves to question and justify the value of the Socratic virtues before an allegedly objective, external authority. Pragmatists "must insist that the fact that nothing is immune from criticism does not mean that we have a duty to justify everything." Western liberal intellectuals "should accept the fact that we have to start from where we are" and simply cannot take seriously many views or use them as rules for action. For us, they are not "live options." Rorty does not deny that some will find nonliberal and antidemocratic options to be "live." Some "have always hoped to become a New Being" and "have hoped to be converted rather than persuaded" (1991, 28–29). But we do not need to include such people in our Socratic conversations. We regard thinkers such as Nietzsche or Loyola as "mad" or "crazy" because our upbringing and historical situation prevent us from imagining them fitting into liberal society and from taking them seriously (1991, 187–188). The long felt Western need to speak to everyone and to justify oneself to external, objective standards reflects what Nietzsche identified as an ancient need for "metaphysical comfort," a desire for solace that stems from our fear of society's death, from the presumably naive and cowardly hope that even if our society dies, its core values will not perish and can be reembodied in some future state (1982, 166; 1991, 32).

Rorty's account of an ideal society has provoked some to question whether its members are likely to stand unflinchingly on behalf of values which they know to be conventions devised for contingent social ends (Guignon and Hiley 1990, 344, 361; Rorty 1982, xli).[1] Rorty claims that recognizing that we have unknowingly created our traditions and virtues will only make us respect them more. We will be committed to them precisely because we shall see that they are the product of our particular collective action:

> our identification with our community—society, political traditions, intellectual heritage—is heightened when we see that this community is *ours* rather than *nature's*, shaped rather than found, one among many which men have made. (1982, 166)

While Rorty argues in these and other passages that "our loyalty to other human beings clinging together in the dark" rather than any "hope of getting things right" will sustain our sense of community (1982, 166; 1989, 59), he also acknowledges that loyalty to our community and its vocabulary will not be unconditional. Mere comradeship or pride in our collective workmanship cannot keep society together. Like earlier generations of liberals, ironist liberals will remain committed to their community only if they have reasons to believe that it will realize their hopes that "life will eventually be freer, less cruel, more leisured, richer in goods and experiences, not just for our descendants but for everybody's descendants" (1989, 85–86). According to Rorty, liberal societies have never been bound together by common philosophical beliefs but by "common vocabularies and common hopes" that are sustained in "modern, literate, secular societies" by the existence of "reasonably concrete, optimistic, and plausible *political* scenarios, as opposed to scenarios about redemption beyond the grave." He claims that it has been difficult to sustain such hope in the last half of this century because "contingent" developments have prevented us from telling ourselves a plausibly hopeful story about the future (86). But Rorty does not explain why we should be confident that the future will be freer, kinder, more leisured and more prosperous. Nor does he explain why we should expect fewer threats from fascist, communist, and other radical adversaries of liberal democracy. In fact, it seems difficult to predict how ironic and pragmatic liberals will respond to the sort of situations that confronted previous generations, who understood their commitment to the community to be supported by divine, natural, and historical forces. In order to make a concrete and plausible case that liberalism will survive without its philosophic foundations, Rorty needs to explain why ironic and pragmatic citizens can be expected to identify with and sacrifice for a society whose problems and vocabularies will vary significantly over time.

Rorty seems to address this challenge by explaining that those who understand their language, conscience, morality, and highest hopes to be "contingent products" will readily adopt a "self identity" that suits them for citizenship in an "ideally liberal state" (61). This group of ideal citizens would especially include intellectuals, aesthetes, poets, and revolutionary scientists who prize liberalism's commitment to a sanctified private sphere in which they can maximize their opportunity to create their own vocabularies and identities in pursuit of "private perfection," "self-creation" and "private spiritual liberation" (65 ff.). Rorty describes the "social glue" binding these intellectuals to society as consisting

> in little more than a consensus that the point of social organization is to let everybody have a chance at self-creation to the best of his or her abilities, and that that goal requires, besides peace and wealth, the standard "bourgeois freedoms." (84)

This glue would be a conviction based on "nothing more profound" than the "historical facts" that imply that the protection of "something like the institutions of bourgeois liberal society" makes it more likely that we will work out our "private salvations," create our private self-images, reweave our "webs of belief and desire" in light of "whatever new people and books" we happen to encounter (84–85).

Rorty anticipates the challenge that it will be extraordinarily difficult, if not impossible, to lead a life of idiosyncratic, sublime creativity while acting and speaking in public as a liberal (88). He replies that the ironists' sense of solidarity will make it easy for them to imagine what it means for others to suffer and thus to imagine how what threatens others threatens themselves (xv–xvi, 91–92, 192). In the tradition of Hobbes and Locke, these ironic liberals will be drawn to political society, not because they seek some common good, but because they flee a common evil. The evil is cruelty or, more precisely, the cruel humiliation of being "redescribed" in a manner that makes what is most important to one look "futile, obsolete, and powerless" (65, 89). The liberal ironist "thinks that recognition of a common susceptibility to humiliation is the *only* social bond that is needed" and feels a sense of human solidarity based "on a sense of common danger, not on a common possession or shared power" (1989, 91; 1993, 148). In private, liberal ironists may redescribe others in any manner they wish; but in public, they will be liberals who assiduously avoid using final vocabularies that might degrade others (1989, 91). Here, Rorty is far from claiming that socialization or moral commitment to the community will, by itself, sustain liberal social hope in an ironic age. His ironists will speak in a liberal vocabulary and practice the Socratic virtues because these are the most practical means for safeguarding their private pursuits and fragile reputations. Because Rorty rests liberalism on this pragmatic, prudent fear of a common evil, his ideal liberal democracy seems to avoid rather than to enrich political dialogue or political life. The desire for "dialectical linkages" that make us Socratics will be satisfied in the shared agreement not to redescribe one another in humiliating ways. The agreement of a need for this safeguard would neither demand nor inspire political participation. Indeed, every reader of Hobbes will recall that one can at least conceive of a society that is dedicated to guarding individual rights but makes no place for democratic forms or public deliberation. Contrary to his assurances that ironic liberals will love the Socratic virtues as ends in themselves and care for their community as something they have created together, he implies that they will view these things as practical means to private vocabulary building and self-creation.

This account of why ironists will publicly support liberalism raises several questions. Primarily, it is not clear why Rorty expects ironists and pragmatists to fear humiliating redescriptions more than anything else. After all, in an ironic culture all descriptions are believed to be contingent and perspectival, without any necessary or even intelligible relation to "reality." Neither is it clear why their concern with redescriptions will consist solely in a fear of degradation rather than in a desire to be praised as they wish. Why should their imaginative sympathy be confined to envisioning others' pain? Why could it not be in the service of a positive love of others and a desire to enrich their vocabulary through one's own? Furthermore, it is not clear why, having abandoned traditional rationalism in favor of poetry, passion, and fantasy, ironists will continue to use "instrumental rationality" to secure their security from insult. And even if ironic individuals were to care only about avoiding humiliating redescriptions, it is unclear why they would be willing to risk their lives to protect liberalism against its violent adversaries, especially since they will have abandoned all hope for "post-mortem rewards" (Rorty 1989, 85). In order to supply the concrete and plausible evidence needed to sustain our social hope, we need to inquire further into Rorty's account of the ironic liberal self.

Rorty argues that we do not need any account of the self to be liberal democrats. He says that if one *wants* a model of the self, then an account of the self as a "centerless web" will suffice; but for purposes of liberal social theory and of moral and political deliberation and conversation, one can dispense with all models and rely on common sense and social science, which are "areas of discourse in which the term 'the self' rarely occurs." Those whose vocation is philosophy will want a model of the self; if they are liberal democrats like Rorty, they will "commend" a model that is decentered and contingent (Rorty 1991, 192–193, 199). If they are instead like Nietzsche, they will need a more complex model of the self in order to weave together their conceptions of nature or history; but regardless of their picture of the self,

> such persons may, for pragmatic rather than moral reasons, be loyal citizens of a liberal democratic society. They may despise most of their fellow citizens, but be prepared to grant that the prevalence of such despicable character types is a lesser evil than the loss of political freedom. (192)

After concluding that we are free to "rig up" models of the self to suit our politics, religion, and (or) private sense of the meaning of life, Rorty anticipates an objection that his claim that there is no objective truth about the self is itself an assertion of an objective truth. There seem to be "matters of fact" concerning the self. But instead of explicating those facts, Rorty abruptly announces that questions about them can be safely "thrown away" (192). Rorty pauses, however, to apologize for his "light-mindedness" in this matter (1991, 193; 1991a, 145). To offset the "air" of light-minded aestheticism that he admits he adopts toward "traditional philosophical questions," he claims that he does so with a "moral purpose."

> Like the rise of large market economies, the increase in literacy, the proliferation of artistic genres, and the insouciant pluralism of contemporary culture, such philosophical superficiality and light-mindedness helps along the disenchantment of the world. It helps make the world's inhabitants more pragmatic, more tolerant, more liberal, more receptive to the appeal of instrumental rationality. (1991, 193)

Rorty discourages us from inquiring seriously into the self as a practical means for realizing his moral aims. These aims are best served by allowing the prevailing cultural climate to rest undisturbed. This suggests that ironists will not be liberal simply because liberalism secures their private projects of self creation. More fundamentally, they will be liberals because the spiritual flatness of liberal culture will keep them sufficiently fearful of degradation, compassionate, and calculating to prevent their creative projects from straying beyond the bounds of bourgeois sensibility. Despite making an alluring promise that an ironic society will be more poetic, passionate, and diverse, Rorty quietly assures us that it will be as pervasively pragmatic, cautious, and monotonous a society as traditional liberalism. Thus it appears that Rorty accepts much of Nietzsche's analysis of what sustains our commitment to liberal democracy: our morality prevents us from longing to transform ourselves and from possessing the psychic wherewithal to do so.

Nonetheless, Nietzsche claims that even in modern democracy a few, rare individuals are emerging who will long to give birth to new values and who will be capable of leadership. How will liberalism defend itself against those who reject its light-mindedness and disenchantment and who resolve to overcome both liberalism and themselves? Perhaps Rorty would argue that liberalism is safe because the self is so plastic that everyone will grow up with a fundamental sense of vulnerability to degrading words and with practical rationality. But this answer is not Rorty's last word, for he readily concedes that every self is neither equally susceptible to socialization nor identically constructed: Even in the ideal liberal society, there will be future Nietzsches and Heideggers, people who seek a "New Being" and "conversion rather than persuasion" and who are more complex than ordinary liberals (1991, 28–29, 192). The key question is whether there is any concrete and plausible reason to believe that future Nietzsches and Heideggers will be more willing to support—or be any less able to threaten—liberal democracy.

Rorty's explanation of why future Nietzsches will accept liberalism appears in scattered references and a few thematic discussions of why the original Nietzsche's political thinking is contingent to his philosophic discoveries. According to Rorty, Nietzsche reacted to his own discovery that it is impossible to achieve the rational certainty sought by Plato with a mixture of despair, intoxication, and resentment (1982, 46; 1991, 33). Future Nietzsches will presumably be more familiar and at ease with the historical character of the self and of truth. Most importantly, Nietzsche's peculiar and extreme reactions seem to have prevented him from recognizing the consistent moral and political implications of his thought. According to Rorty, there is nothing more "powerful" or "important" for Nietzsche than self-redescription (1989, 99). Like Hegel and Heidegger, Nietzsche believes that things "large enough to have a destiny"—such as history or Western man or metaphysics—have become exhausted and that all things can be made new. He wants this "larger newness" to provide him with autonomy, with the sublime and ineffable, and with "something incommensurable with the past" (101). Nietzsche in particular wants to be the "last philosopher" and to be safe from being redescribed by others. To seek the sublime requires not only creating the "taste" by which one judges oneself but also finding a way to preclude being judged by others according to any other taste. According to Rorty, as long as Nietzsche is "relativizing and historicizing his predecessors," he is

> faithful to his own conviction that the self is not substance, and that we should drop the whole idea of "substance"—of something that cannot be perspectivalized because it has a real essence, a privileged perspective on itself. (106)

But when he imagines a superman who will not be merely a "bundle of idiosyncratic reactions to past stimuli" but "will be *pure* self-creation, pure spontaneity," Nietzsche forgets about his perspectivalism. When he explains "how to be wonderful and different and unlike anything that has ever existed," he talks about selves "as if they were reservoirs of something called 'will to power' " (Rorty 1989, 106) and thus commits the error that leads him to act as if he were moved by will to power, attempting to shape others through philosophy and politics. Had Nietzsche been consistent, he would have seen that his "truth" is simply one more perspective among others and would have doubted that he was moved by will to power and tempered his desire to recast the West.

Rorty makes a comparable critique of similarly nonliberal selves in his 1993 autobiographical "Trotsky and the Wild Orchids." He calls the "single-mindedness" of a Sartre or Savonarola in condemning the works of others for being "irrelevant" to the "only thing that matters," a

> quest for purity of heart—the attempt to will one thing—gone rancid. It is the attempt to see yourself as an incarnation of something larger than yourself (the Movement, Reason, the Good, the Holy) rather than accepting your finitude. The latter means, among other things, accepting what matters most to you may well be something that may never matter much to most people." (1993, 147–148)

Were creative philosophers, poets, and prophets to accept that what matters to them individually may have no meaning for others, they will temper their attachment to their idiosyncratic favorite, for their "Wordsworthian moments," lover, family, pet, favorite lines of verse, or "quaint religious faith" (148). Nor should they believe that there is anything

> sacred about universality which makes the shared automatically better than the unshared. There is no automatic privilege of what you can get everybody to agree to (the universal) over what you cannot (the idiosyncratic). (148)

The very fact that we have moral obligations to others does not in itself entail that what we share with others is more important than anything else (148). Thus, had Nietzsche been true to his perspectivalism or accepted his finitude or had not been impressed by his ability to alter what others think, he would not have believed he was moved by will to power and would not have attempted to overturn democratic values.[2] Accustomed to the absence of transcendent truths, never tempted to distinguish themselves idiosyncratically, and never awed by what is universal or shared, Nietzsche's successors will contentedly recreate themselves in private and accept their liberal obligations in public.

Yet there are lingering difficulties with Rorty's contention that liberalism will not be threatened by "future Nietzsches." Primarily, even if a philosopher's "truth" is inevitably colored by his own subjective purposes, it is still possible that some perspectives are less distorting than others. Nietzsche's perspective could be the one that is most in keeping with the actual character of nature or life (*Beyond Good and Evil* 1, 2, 9, 259; *Will to Power* 853). Nietzsche says that

> These are beautiful, glittering, jingling, festive words: honesty, love of truth, love of wisdom, sacrifice for knowledge, heroism of the truthful—they have something that swells one's pride. But we hermits and marmots have long convinced ourselves in the full secrecy of the hermit's conscience that this worthy verbal pomp, too, belongs to the old, mendacious pomp, junk and gold dust of unconscious human vanity, and under such flattering colors and make up as well, the basic text of *homo natura* must again be recognized. To translate man back into nature; to become master over the many vain and overly enthusiastic interpretations and connotations that have so far been scrawled and

> painted over that eternal basic text of *homo natura*; to see that man henceforth stands before man as even today, hardened in the discipline of science, he stands before the *rest* of nature with intrepid Oedipus eyes and sealed Odyssean ears, deaf to the siren songs of the old metaphysical bird catchers who have been piping to him all too long "You are more, you are different, you have a different origin . . ." (*Beyond Good and Evil* 230)

Thus, Nietzsche's description of human nature is not necessarily one more description. While he does not expect to be the last philosopher, he may be the first to acknowledge the "truth" that something in every philosopher's "truth" is *in part* the philosopher's own creation.

If, moreover, future Nietzsches come forward, it is not clear why they will be obliged to disregard any political and moral implications of their perspectives simply because they are "mere" perspectives. After all, Nietzsche is fully aware of what is problematic in saying that the doctrine of will to power is *the* truth—and yet be willing to act on that doctrine insofar as it is *his* truth. Truth left unvarnished may be "contrary to life" and of dubious value (*Beyond Good and Evil* "Preface," 1–9). The perspectives that come to or come over Nietzsche "work" for him. As Nietzsche indicates in subtitling *Thus Spoke Zarathustra* "a book for everyone and for no one," he regards the most important truths to be in some sense intrinsically personal and idiosyncratic. Thus, it seems utterly arbitrary for Rorty to insist that a future Nietzsche *must* be subject to internal intellectual and (or) moral constraints that would prevent him from unleashing whatever political projects he might envision. If there is no "metaphysical" standard for measuring wills or judgments, then there are none for criticizing Nietzsche's. The heart of Rorty's criticism of those who would draw Heidegger into an argument expecting him to submit to the rational standards that he calls into question would seem to apply to Rorty's criticism of Nietzsche:

> There is no standard by which one can measure him without begging the question against him. His remarks about the tradition and his remarks about the limitations the tradition has imposed on the vocabulary and imagination of his contemporaries, are beautifully designed to make one feel foolish when one tries to find a bit of common ground on which to start argument. (Rorty 1982, 39)

In order to *refute* Nietzsche's claim to have glimpsed the frightening, unbearable truth of nature, Rorty would somehow have to prove that we cannot know even an aspect of nature, of life, of Being. Indeed, in some passages Rorty claims to know that we cannot know anything because of the blinding influence of history and language (1989, 48). The greatest historicists such as Heidegger offer nothing useful but critiques of the tradition. Their positive political and moral prescriptions remain mired in "Platonism" and "metaphysics":

> The politics which one can imagine stemming from Heidegger's notion of technology's relation to man are more awful than the apparatus of technology itself, and for neither Dewey nor Heidegger is there a way to separate that sort of relation to politics from "philosophical truth." Heidegger's attachment to the notion of "philosophy"—the pathetic notion that even after metaphysics goes, something called "Thought" might remain—is simply the sign of Heidegger's own fatal attachment to the tradition, the last infirmity of the greatest German professors. It amounts to saying that even though everybody who has previously counted as a paradigm of philosophy—Plato, Thomas, Descartes, Nietzsche—turned out to be a step on a path toward chaos, we must still try to be philosophers . . . If he were true to his own dictum that we should "cease all overcoming, and leave metaphysics to itself," he would have nothing to say, nowhere to point. (1982, 52)

Yet elsewhere Rorty acknowledges that his own discussion of the historical and nominalist character of the self implies that there are important "facts of the matter"—that is, facts about the self—that might be known (1991, 193). Rorty does not draw our attention to these facts because, as he says, philosophy and politics are contingent (1989, 111) and the facts can be safely thrown away (1991, 192). But Rorty's claim that philosophy and politics are simply contingent is inconsistent with Rorty's willingness to argue that Nietzsche *should* have recognized that his historicist account of the self and of its truths implies that he should accept liberalism. Moreover, it is also inconsistent with his strategy of encouraging light-mindedness about the self. For if inquiries into the self yielded either no knowledge at all or else knowledge with no political implications, such inquiries would not threaten liberalism. But

Rorty fears that studying the self will undermine our faith in liberal democracy and urges us to throw away the facts about the self. In his autobiographical "Trotsky and the Wild Orchids," Rorty remarks that he has learned that it is a mistake to try to hold "reality and justice in a single vision." He claims to have learned not that it is impossible to know reality but that reality is incompatible with his liberal democratic morality (1993, 147–148). He believes nonetheless that even though Nietzsche and Heidegger lack a "God's eye view," they have nonetheless understood something intelligible and lasting about the self or nature or Being. He believes that even though they have shown that the philosophical tradition leads *toward* chaos, they still manage to reveal enough order in that chaos to allow us to distinguish between the human and the non-human, between darkness and lightness, between technology and revelation. Moreover, Rorty believes not only that they have understood some facts about the self but also that they have drawn consistent political and moral conclusions from those facts. But he recoils in moral revulsion from such awful conclusions, calling for a boycott of serious public dialogue about the self. Rorty sometimes slips into what seem to be contradictions about why Nietzsche should have resisted politicizing the values he created or about why philosophy is impossible not because he is deeply confused or light-minded but because he is heart-broken at the thought that philosophy threatens liberal democracy. He uses a range of sometimes brilliant arguments to persuade us that there is nothing very valuable or dangerous in the thinking of those who seriously inquire into the nature of the self or of truth—even as he warns us against proceeding down that path. He even seems to blur intentionally essential differences between philosophers such as Heidegger and pragmatists such as Dewey in order to prevent readers from following Heidegger too faithfully (e.g., 1982, 86–87). While Rorty faults others for insisting that "Philosophy" is possible only because they want it to support their personal moral convictions and political programs, he apparently insists that self-knowledge is utterly impossible because he believes it conflicts with a morality and politics that he cannot help but support. In saying that "the facts" can be "safely thrown away," Rorty means that *only* if we throw them away might liberal democracy be saved.

Yet, one is bound to wonder, what possible threat could the thinking of a Nietzsche pose to our politics? And is not Rorty himself convinced that it is ludicrous to think that any society has ever been bound together by philosophy (1989, 86)? But even if no society has ever shared a common grasp of any philosophic teaching, societies have been shaped by philosophers, as Rorty acknowledges when he says that the Western democracies were created by "the hopes of the Enlightenment" (1991, 34). To this day, differences between the right in Germany and America can be traced to the different philosophical traditions in which they have been educated (1988, 574). Perhaps, however, contemporary politics is no longer susceptible to philosophic influence. According to the "Deweyan" view, says Rorty, intellectual disputes about the philosophic foundations of the Weimar Republic or about the grounding of truth or about the historical character of rights have no impact on our elections or on our willingness to resist "fascist takeovers" (32). But in making such statements from an explicitly *pragmatic* way of seeing, Rorty compels one to wonder if he believes that such controversies are necessarily irrelevant or whether he thinks that seeing them as irrelevant is "useful" or politically salutary (1982, xiv, xxv; 1991, 33). In fact, Rorty's very attempt to use philosophic arguments to persuade us not to bring philosophy to bear on politics reflects his own abiding faith in the power of argument to affect politics.

In order to understand how philosophy might imperil liberal democracy, it is useful to review Rorty's account of our morality's "foundations." According to Rorty, liberals should concede to critics that liberalism produces "bland, calculating, petty and unheroic" people, but they should add that this may be the price of political freedom (Rorty 1991, 190–191). Why should this be the inevitable cost of freedom? What prevents us from infusing our political culture with a sense of greater purpose? With an heroic longing for something grander than ourselves? Rorty suggests a troubling answer when he remarks that he promotes "philosophical superficiality and light-mindedness" because such things make us disenchanted, pragmatic, tolerant, and liberal (193). He thinks we need this frivolity along with narrow selfishness because it is precisely these qualities that make us indifferent to how others live, fearful, practical-minded, and thus supportive of liberalism for our own protection. The core of toleration, it seems, is the lack of passion, including the lack of love (Nietzsche *Beyond Good and Evil* 104; Bernstein 1987, 544). The implication is that were an exhilarating philosopher or prophet or ideologue to inspire us with a sense of seriousness, with a longing for something beyond ourselves, some of us might try to "save" or subjugate others without much concern for their privacy or pain. But why would Rorty regard philosophy, rather than religion or mere ideology, as an especially powerful threat? Rorty has remarked that he thinks Nietzsche, Derrida, and Foucault are, broadly speaking, "right" and that they cannot be used "for the purposes for which the left would like to use them" (Rorty 1987, 572). Rorty sheds some light on his agreement with Nietzsche in *Contingency, Irony, and Solidarity*, where he says that Nietzsche seems correct that at the bottom of every "final vocabulary" looms a desire to increase our power, a desire to "get what we want" (1989, 115). He suggests, in other words, that we are moved by a fundamental will to power that is, at bottom, less a desire for "subjectivity" or "self-knowledge" or "difference" than a will to make one's own judgments and master other wills. His fear that Nietzsche is correct about the tension between will to power on the one hand and pluralism and equality on the other may have helped persuade him that one cannot hold reality and justice in a single vision. In light of such concerns, he wants to relegate philosophy to the perusal of apolitical, ironic aesthetes, lest genuinely Nietzschean insights into the self and truth persuade enough of us to pursue "what we want" on a grand scale and without regard for the security, comfort, and dignity of liberal democrats.

Because of the risks and uncertainties of relying on philosophy for political guidance, it might seem that liberal democrats have nothing to lose in declining to inquire into the self. But to accept Rorty's melancholy belief that genuine self-knowledge threatens liberalism would not only reflect a disturbing lack of confidence in liberalism but also invite its adversaries to assail it on just this point. Can we be assured—do we want to be assured—that we would shrug off all radical critiques that appeal to standards beyond our particular moral horizon or to a spirit of seriousness? Without any substantive rational grounds to support it, liberalism might simply give way if and when future "Nietzsches" or "Loyolas" or "Trotskys" come forward with rekindled moral, religious, and political passions. It seems that by forswearing "Philosophy" and embracing irony and pragmatism Rorty would permit the reemergence of these "instincts" and desires, but for the first time in a millennium without the respect for rationalism that has moderated them in the West. One fears that Williams will be proven correct by history that Rorty has a "shallow way of thinking about what happens to a society when rational civility collapses" (Williams 1990, 35).

Those who are troubled by liberalism's vulnerability and by the uncertainty of historicist and nominalist philosophy's efforts to reconstitute and justify it may wish that they could support it with invincible rational foundations. Yet any desire we may feel for such defenses does not mean that we have the means to supply them. In order to understand the enormity of such an enterprise, it is useful to consider more closely why Rorty finds it necessary to abandon "Platonism" or "Philosophy" in the first place. Rorty says that he agrees with Donald Davidson that the "rational self-criticism and reform" that was once considered the "essence of rationality and the source of freedom" is, at bottom, merely "irrational." Rorty concedes that he and Davidson would be wrong "if self-criticism and self-improvement always take place within a framework of nontrivial highest-possible order desires, those of the *true* self, the desires which are central to our humanity." But the only candidates for such highest-level desires are so abstract and empty as to have no mediating powers. They are "I wish to be good," "I wish to be rational," and "I wish to know the truth" (Rorty 1989, 49). To reestablish Philosophy's authority as a foundation for liberalism, one would have to show that such philosophical teachings about goodness, rationality, and truthfulness are not platitudes whose meaning shifts through time and from person to person. One would have to offer some sort of evidence that such statements have one concrete meaning and vindicate one specific way of life. And one would have to establish that one can lead this way of life as a responsible liberal democrat. In undertaking this task, one would have to confront the problem that serious and well meaning thinkers find liberalism spiritually barren. Liberal political and moral thinking seems blind to what is noble, what is sacred, and what is valuable about the particular. Rather than assume that liberalism's original foundations have been decisively refuted, one might ask if the thinking of the liberal philosophers has been deeply misunderstood or misapplied. After all, our doubts about the reliability of the philosophic tradition allow us to question the conventional understanding of the philosophers themselves. Perhaps a fresh examination of Locke, Montesquieu, Hume, and Kant would reveal forgotten possibilities and justifications. But distrust of Enlightenment rationalism is deep and difficult to shake off. Moreover, liberalism's failure to sustain its original hope and legitimacy suggests that its philosophers at least partly misunderstood what we need and seek and respect. Many claim that grave social and political problems such as the breakdown of civility, the family, and the schools can be resolved only by developing virtues that do not follow naturally from liberalism. It is partly because liberalism has lost much of its power to inspire that Rorty and others attempt to ennoble our liberal virtues by identifying them with the premodern virtues of Socrates. But the mere resemblance of Socratic open-mindedness, curiosity, and courage to some of the qualities of a good liberal does not, in itself, offer the rational grounding needed to support and strengthen liberalism. Perhaps we could find some of that grounding by showing that Plato's original vindication of the Socratic life offers tangible evidence that his virtues *are* virtues, that his non-dogmatic, respectful, and deliberative way of life meets abiding human needs and excites genuine admiration. But to accomplish this one would have to show that Plato's teachings about goodness, rationality, and truthfulness vindicate the Socratic life of dialectical inquiry above all others. One would have to understand Plato's doctrine of the ideas and his teaching about the "true world" not as alternatives to Socratic philosophy but as elements in dramas that ultimately vindicate Socratic dialectics. One would have to demonstrate that far from being blind to what is noble or sacred or particular, Socrates is able to clarify and deepen how we understand these things; one would have to show not only that Socrates' virtues are compatible with those of a liberal democrat, but also that they can broaden and lend dignity to liberalism's moral horizon. Perhaps Plato's dramas provide us a long neglected vindication of Socrates' way of life. But even if those dramas offer us a persuasive praise and justification of Socratic rationalism, there is reason to wonder whether reviving Socratic virtues would be adequate to remedy the ills that now beset liberalism. For what may prove most necessary to resolve contemporary problems may be qualities such as reverence or awe, qualities that we are not likely to associate with Socratic rationalism. Plato's most valuable contribution to contemporary liberal democracy may come in showing us how Socrates' virtues enable us to experience and understand the fullest range of human excellence and greatness.

# CHAPTER 3

# *The Problematic Foundations of Socratic Virtue*

The task of recovering Plato's vindication of Socratic philosophizing is enormously complicated by the fact that many scholars agree with Nietzsche that Plato fundamentally transforms the historical Socrates, imposing his own "Platonic" conception of philosophy and of virtue on the figure of his teacher. Unlike Nietzsche, however, most scholars attribute to Socrates public-spirited and pious motives for engaging in dialectics. Many believe that the historical Socrates turns to dialogue because he is alarmed at the success of the Sophists, physicists, "realists," and "relativists" in ancient Greece. According to this view, Socrates counterattacks the Sophists' assault on morality by engaging in *elenchos*, a refutational form of conversation at which he excels (Klosko 1986, 3ff.; MacIntyre 1984, 69–70). By conversing with his opponents, Socrates is able to expose contradictions in their arguments and ways of life, reducing them to anger or consternation. In addition to engaging in this "negative" use of *elenchos*, Socrates also employs it to waken his fellow citizens to their moral shallowness and complacency (Klosko 1986, 36ff.). He is sometimes said to go further, employing this procedure to test and even to promulgate his own theories about the soul and its virtues (Irwin 1977, 37ff.). When Socrates trains his dialogical guns on his own account of the soul and its virtues, he finds it consistent and better able to withstand the *elenchos* than is that of others (Irwin 1977, 40). But scholars also claim that this Socratic method begs decisive questions. Through the process of refutation, Socrates can do no more than to think through the premises from which he and his interlocutors begin. In winning an argument, all he knows for certain is that he is a "better debater" (Vlastos 1985, 19). Insofar as Socrates takes consistency to be *the* standard of truth, he has not overcome the possibility that one could be consistently crazy (Irwin 1977, 41). Moreover, Socrates cannot refute those whose standards differ from his and yet manage to be equally consistent (MacIntyre 1984, 72–73). It is in light of his own awareness of these shortcomings that Socrates declares that he "knows he knows nothing." Recognizing that his conclusions always depend on hypotheses that cannot be demonstrated, he disavows "moral knowledge" in the strictest sense and regards his human wisdom as nothing more than "justified true belief" (Vlastos 1985, 6–11 passim; 1991, 32). Both the conclusions that he draws from dialogue and his confidence in the authority of dialogue itself rely on "conviction" rather than on knowledge (Irwin 1977, 40).

In order to grasp the full implications of this account of Socrates' disavowal of knowledge for Socrates' claims about the philosophic life, it is useful to review precisely what he claims to "know" or "believe" in the "Socratic" *Apology*. The Socrates of the *Apology* does not *merely* profess his ignorance, nor does he *merely* turn to dialogue to demonstrate that others are also ignorant about the "greatest things." In fact, he uses dialectics to further his "human wisdom." When describing his reaction to the Delphic Oracle's claim that no one is wiser than he, Socrates says that he was amazed because he was already aware that he was not wise and that it is not lawful for the god to lie (*Apology* 21b). While he knows of the god through the law, he knows of his ignorance through his own discovery.

Socrates says that he determined to refute the oracle and set about finding someone wiser than he. But upon examining the politicians, poets, and craftsmen whom the city regards as wise, he discovered that none of them knew what is "noble and good," that none of them could give a coherent account of what it means to be a "perfect gentleman" or moral man. After reaching this conclusion, he went off *by himself* and reasoned that the Oracle is after all correct that he is wisest since he alone knows that he does not know what is "noble and good" while the others do not know either but believe that they do (*Apology* 21d, 22d–e; *Euthyphro* 16d; *Meno* 71b; *Symposium* 175e, 216d, 219a). The question is how Socrates knows that their failure to answer his dialectical questions reflects their ignorance about the greatest things.

Perhaps one can say that he drew this reasonable inference from the Oracle's announcement that he is wisest and from its command that he examine others—except that the Oracle never said that he was wisest and never commanded him to do anything. According to Socrates' first account of the Oracle, all it said was that no one is wiser than he. It never claimed that he is wiser than anyone else and never ordered or advised him to take any action. It was through his own investigations and reflections that Socrates came to believe that he is wiser than others. And it is on his own that he quietly, even surreptitiously, attributes these insights to the Oracle (*Apology* cf. 21a and 23b). Socrates apparently corrects the Oracle in light of his own thinking and discoveries.[1] Furthermore, near the end of his first speech, Socrates claims to know many of the greatest things, such as that injustice is worse than justice, that there is a soul, and that its virtues are more important than wealth or life. In fact, Socrates even claims to know that he makes his hearers better by speaking to them (*Apology* 29a–30c). Moreover, near the end of his final speech, after he has been convicted, Socrates affirms that he would never cease examining himself and others, not only because he follows the god's command, but also because of his own belief that examining himself and others is the greatest good for a human being (*Apology* 38a).

If Vlastos and other classical scholars are correct, then Socrates' reliance on his own thinking to guide his actions and to re-interpret the meaning of the Oracle rests on the strength of his "justified true beliefs." But these "true beliefs" are "justified" only insofar as he can safely assume that dialectics and his interpretation of the results of dialectics are legitimate standards for justifying beliefs. It seems that all of Socrates' claims about his human wisdom and about the need to philosophize to live well rest on convictions and even assumptions. To defend Socrates' reliance on *elenchos* despite its uncertain foundations, Vlastos adduces an example from ordinary life: He notes that despite his recollection that he locked his door when he left home in the morning, he does not know with absolute certainty that he did so. To make sure that the door is locked, he could frantically telephone his neighbors or rush home. He says that if he had left a valuable Picasso in his living room, such precautions would be "reasonable"; but since "nothing much is in jeopardy," he can be "well content" to trust his recollection that he locked the door (Vlastos 1985, 13–14). He writes:

> If I were not content to live with such deflation of the demands for certainty I would, quite literally, go mad: I would join the compulsive handwasher, who will not accept the fact that he has scrubbed his hands with hisofex just ten minutes ago as a good reason for believing that they are now free from deleterious germs. The willingness to live with fallible knowledge is built into the human condition. Only a god could do without it. Only a crazy man would want to. (4)

Vlastos contrasts this fallible knowledge to the certain, "infallible" kind that Socrates says exists at the top of the "divided line" in the *Republic* and that Aristotle describes in the *Metaphysics* and in the *Prior* and *Posterior Analytics* (15–17).[2] In examples such as the one adduced by Vlastos, it may make sense for Socrates to trust in "justified true beliefs." But there seems to be far more at stake than a valuable work of art in Socrates' devotion to dialectical political philosophy. His inquiries convince his accusers that he is unjust and impious. Socrates claims that the charges against him arise merely from his accusers' envy. Wishing to discredit him in any way possible, they repeat some ancient slanders that he was once a natural philosopher who commits injustice and impiety by investigating the heavens and the things beneath the earth (*Apology* 18b–c, 19b–c, 23; cf. Aristophanes *Clouds* 171–173, 188 passim). But could he not be suspected of impiety by those who honestly believe that it is wrong for human beings to use reason to inquire into matters that the gods forbid us from knowing (*Laws* 821a; Hesiod *Works and Days* 54–55; cf. *Genesis* 3:3–8)? To the extent that some think that philosophic inquiry as a whole is unjust and impious, Socrates seems to be taking enormous risks by trusting in the legitimacy of his dialectics. Vlastos claims that Socrates sees no difficulty in being both a rationalist and pious because his own moral convictions make him certain that the gods must also be rationalists (Vlastos 1991, 164, 171–172). But is this "certainty" justified? How does Socrates know that the gods he honors are rationalists or even well disposed to rationalists?

Classical scholars regard Plato, on the other hand, as a philosopher who shares Socrates' goals but is deeply dissatisfied with Socrates' failure to find solid grounds for his arguments. According to this view, Plato supplies foundations for Socrates' enterprise by transforming it into a new, "Platonic" form of philosophy. In the course of his "development," Plato introduces a "new" Socrates whose knowledge of the ideas provides him certain knowledge of the virtues. The Platonic philosopher's "knowledge of and communion with the divine makes him like the divine and so begets a perfect virtue." He acquires a "perfect order of the soul" in comparison to which the virtue of the mass of mankind is "a poor imitation" (Klosko 1986, 99). Moreover, he possesses "a kind of wisdom that obviates the need for Socratic dialectics and legitimates the authoritarian politics of the *Republic*." The Socratic wisdom that consists in "recognizing one's own ignorance" and that leads to "unending dialogue" is said to be "at odds with Plato's suggestion in the *Republic* that there exists an absolute truth to which one may not only aspire but indeed attain" (Roberts 1994, 72).

It is now almost universally accepted that Plato's ardent love of the ideas blinds him to his own motivations and distorts his knowledge of human nature. Vlastos claims that Plato's philosophic eros is manifestly too "ideocentric," too captivated by "abstractions of universal significance" and entities such as the "Idea of beauty in its sublime transcendence." Because of his excessive love of the ideal, Plato neither loves nor recognizes what is valuable in the particular, unique, "whole person." Consequently, he is unaware that one must love the beloved as a whole person, respecting his or her unique integrity and subjective preferences, to sustain mutual love and concern. When "translated" to politics, Plato's failure to love whole persons blinds him to the requisites of genuine political community, as we see in the *Republic*, where ideal political reforms meant to foster "civic love" instead obliterate civil liberty (Vlastos 1981, 31–32; also Klosko 1986, 152–153).

Martha Nussbaum, however, raises a powerful objection to Vlastos by observing that Plato's *Symposium* contains not only Aristophanes' description of eros for a whole person but also the moving, dramatic presentation of Alcibiades' "personal" eros for

Socrates. Plato is not blind to the power and importance of such a love, but he self-consciously rejects it as antithetical to the "rational self-sufficiency" that is the goal of philosophy. Plato's Socrates dedicates himself to philosophy not only because he enjoys the stability and purity of the contemplative life but also because philosophy provides him with the "detached," "extrahuman," "pure," and "passionless" viewpoint that is crucial for genuine understanding. But to ascend to this stable, pure, and truthful existence, he must distance himself from all disruptive contingencies, from all physical pains and pleasures, from all emotions and external attachments and become ascetic, unchanging, cold, hard, stonelike (Nussbaum 1986, 91–92, 132–133, 154–157, 173, 183). While dispassionately contemplating the forms may provide the philosopher with self-sufficiency and insight, these things are attained at the cost of another kind of knowledge. Operating apart from the senses, Socratic philosophy discovers only universal truths and issues only universal rules that differ from Alcibiades' insights, which are born of a "supple interaction of sense, emotion, and intellect" that "yields particular truths and judgments that are prior to any rule to guide." Nussbaum argues that, for practical purposes, the loving, emotional, Alcibiadean knowledge of particulars is more nuanced, richer, more complex, more helpful, and more "deeply true" than Socrates' abstract, merely "universal" knowledge and may even lead to a self-understanding that is "fundamental to the flourishing of practical wisdom in other areas of life as well." By presenting these two kinds of rationality as incommensurate and incompatible, Plato teaches that there is no one, truly comprehensive, rational perspective from which to give practical political guidance. Forced to choose between the two ways of life and knowledge, the Platonic philosopher ascends to the orderly, rarefied world of contemplative self-sufficiency ultimately in the awareness of philosophy's "tragic" limitations (186, 190–191, 230–231, 312).[3]

Yet there are aspects of Platonic philosophy for which Nussbaum has difficulty accounting. Acknowledging that a "prominent part of the philosophical tradition" holds that the "pursuit of self-sufficiency requires us to cultivate a solitary life, one that neither relies on nor ascribes value" to "fragile" things such as "friendship, love and politics," she offers no explanation for why Socrates fails to jettison the political and social "components" of his life along with the erotic in pursuit of such independence (344, 197). In addition to calling the contemplative life solitary, Nussbaum says that it depends on a faculty that can be exercised regardless of political circumstances and whose "most highly valued aspect" is mathematical and scientific reasoning (147, 159, 184, 238). She even concedes that the philosopher would find political attachment an entanglement at the opposite end of "the self-sufficiency spectrum" from contemplation and would regard public life as a "wrenching descent" from the "lonely height of contemplation" (343, 70, 159). Yet in every dialogue, Socrates assiduously examines the "human things," scrutinizing justice and noble virtue, bringing to light precisely those concerns that move one to care about others rather than about one's own well-being. Does he inquire into these matters because he is moved by concerns for the well-being of others that are at odds with his aspiration to rational self-sufficiency? Or is it because his desire for rational self-sufficiency is a form of "will to power" that seeks to use the "controlling power of reason" to master all contingency, including politics (3, 99, 159, 161, 196, 260)? Or is there a "strictly philosophical" need that leads him to scrutinize particular human beings and to explore political questions? Nussbaum does not resolve whether the Nietzschean or the Platonic interpretation of Socrates is more accurate.

A further problem, not merely with Nussbaum's understanding, but with the widespread belief that the Platonic Socrates' love of the ideas blinds him to particulars, is that the dialogues show Socrates' extraordinarily ability to size up quickly each interlocutor and to ask exactly the right question that exposes the soul of everyone with whom he speaks. Socrates is, as Nietzsche himself suggests, a "genius of the heart" (Nietzsche *Beyond Good and Evil* 295). Conversing with children or adults, with ordinary citizens or rhetoricians, he is amazingly resourceful, "defeating all opponents," fascinating those who resist him, exposing those who wish to conceal their secrets, silencing those who want to derail the conversation, in short, constantly displaying a profound knowledge of the human heart in its particularity.

The additional claim that Plato makes a radical break from

Socratic political philosophy in the course of his writing is called into question by Plato's presentation of Socrates' early education. For if Plato's own philosophic education had been fundamentally transformed by a midlife discovery of the theory of the ideas, then would he not have portrayed his Socrates as having undergone a similar midlife transformation? One prominent explanation of Socrates' "evolution" in the Platonic corpus appears to be that Plato faithfully reports the historical Socrates' thinking in the "early" dialogues. But, according to this view, when Plato transcends Socratism through his discovery of the theory of the ideas, he cannot bring himself to attribute his new thinking to anyone but his mentor. Consequently, he places non-Socratic arguments in Socrates' mouth in the "middle" and "later" dialogues. Now, assuming this is what happened, would it not make more sense for Plato to claim that at some point Socrates himself learned about the ideas, thus providing his mentor with an excuse for the apparent inconsistencies between what he says in the "early" and "later" dialogues? By choosing not to do this, by claiming that Socrates knew of the ideas from the beginning of his enterprise as a political philosopher, Plato at least leaves open the possibility that those apparent inconsistencies are not due so much to changes in Plato's philosophic orientation as to differences in the subject matter of Socrates' conversations. Instead of portraying Socrates as having undergone a transfiguring change in the course of the dialogues, Plato consistently presents Socrates as having been exposed to or having known about the ideas as a very young man or at least from the outset of his inquiries into political philosophy (*Parmenides* 127c, 128e–130b; *Phaedo* 100b; *Symposium* 201d). In doing this, Plato suggests that Socrates was (or at least could have been) familiar with the theory of the ideas from the start and still went on to be a Socratic philosopher.

In raising these considerations, I am not claiming that there are no important differences between Socratic and Platonic political philosophy. Nor am I claiming that Plato's teaching about the ideas is mere rhetoric or propaedeutic. Nor am I alleging that Plato provides us with indisputable proof that the Socratic life is the best life for a human being. But I am questioning whether Socratic and Platonic political philosophy differ *as radically* as many claim. I do challenge the view that Plato believes his account of the ideas—or any other "Platonic" element of the dialogues—obviates the need for Socratic inquiry into political, moral, and religious questions. And I will argue that even so-called "Platonic" dialogues recommend and vindicate the Socratic life above all others.

One of the most revealing dialogues for understanding the origins, purposes, and character of Socratic political philosophy is Plato's *Symposium*. For this dialogue reports how the young Socrates acquired the only positive education that he ever claims to possess, his education in "erotic matters." These lessons are so important to Socrates that he repeatedly identifies his knowledge of eros with the whole of his knowledge (Plato *Symposium* 177d7–8, 212b5–6; *Theages* 128b1–4; *Lysis* 204b5–c2; *Charmides* 155d4–e2; *Phaedrus* 257; cf. Xenophon *Memorabilia* 2.6.28). Socrates' knowledge of erotic matters is significant in large part because it includes knowledge of how to cultivate and gratify his erotic desire to be "noble and good," "a perfect gentleman," a "moral man." According to Socrates, he became an expert in erotic matters by conversing with a foreign priestess named Diotima. Socrates says that Diotima taught him that the only way to fulfill this eros is to "be together" with the "beautiful itself" because only through communing with it can one "give birth" to true virtue (*Symposium* 210a, 210dff.; cf. *Phaedrus* 243–257; *Republic* 474d-475a, 485b–c, 490b, 499c, 501d, 521b). But if the sequence of events in the *Symposium* is to be taken seriously, it seems that after the young Socrates heard Diotima's quintessentially "Platonic" account of philosophy as an ascent up to the idea of the beautiful, he came away a *Socratic* political philosopher. The implication seems to be that it was by listening to and reflecting on Diotima's teaching that the young Socrates resolved to turn away from the apolitical natural philosophy of his youth (*Phaedo* 96ff.) and to launch the dialectical inquiry into political, moral, and religious questions that we see carried out in the dialogues. Some claim that the difference between Socrates and Diotima is meant to reflect the difference between Socrates and Plato (e.g., Bury 1932, 123–124; Cornford 1971, 125; Vlastos 1981, 21). But Socrates contradicts in advance those who claim that he never reaches the peak of knowledge of erotic matters and remains at a lower rank than the Platonic philosopher, for twice in the dialogue he repeats his claim that he has expert knowledge of erotic matters (*Symposium* 177d7–8, 212b5–6). Even though he allows that his knowledge is disputable (*Symposium* 175e, 216d, 219a; *Apology* 21d), he continues to claim to know erotic matters and never, in any dialogue, concedes that anyone knows more about eros than he.[4] In fact, Diotima herself describes the very nature of philosophic eros in a way that unmistakably resembles Socrates:

> He is always poor, and rather than being tender and beautiful, as the many believe, he is tough, dry, shoeless, and homeless, always lying on the ground without a blanket or bed, sleeping in doorways and along roads. By the nature of his mother, he always lives in need. By his father's, he plots to capture the beautiful and good, and is courageous, manly, and keen, a skilled hunter, always weaving devices, desiring prudence, inventive, philosophizing through all his life, a skilled magician, druggist and sophist.(*Symposium* 203c–d)

By reminding us in the *Symposium* that Socrates is always barefoot (except when he wants to make an especially good impression on sophisticated people), that he rests habitually in doorways, that he has extraordinary powers of endurance, that he weaves beautiful speeches, that he eschews going home (*Symposium* 174a, 174d, 175a, 175c–d, 215b–e, 219e–220d, 223d), Plato implies that Socrates exemplifies philosophic eros in its natural and purest condition.

To recover how Socrates learned to cultivate and gratify his erotic longing to be "noble and good," it is necessary to pay the strictest attention to what Socrates says about the way he presents Diotima's teaching. For Socrates says explicitly that he recounts only the beautiful parts of what she said about eros (*Symposium* 198d). In order to recover as much as possible of what she taught the young Socrates, one must think through the many questions and objections that Socrates raised when he first heard her lessons.

Before we can begin examining what Socrates knows about the love of noble virtue, it is important to consider that Plato presents Socrates' account of his knowledge in a series of speeches praising the god Eros. Among the five speeches that precede

Socrates' speech, one in particular stands out. Aristophanes' account of what we love and why we love is one of the most moving and popular passages in all of classical literature. But the significance of his speech goes well beyond what it tells us about eros, for Aristophanes is one of Socrates' most profound and influential critics. Plato's presentation of Aristophanes in the *Symposium* exposes us to one of the most serious challenges and alternatives to Socratic philosophy. By helping us to see more clearly what Aristophanes claims to know about eros, human nature, and the gods, Plato's presentation of Aristophanes in the *Symposium* allows us to recognize more precisely what Aristophanes thinks Socrates does not know in his presentation of Socrates in the *Clouds*. By giving us a taste of Aristophanic wisdom, Plato implies that it is only by first understanding what Aristophanes finds so questionable about the Socratic life that we can fully understand and be persuaded by Plato's defense of that life in the *Symposium* and other dialogues.

# CHAPTER 4

# *Plato's Aristophanes: The Poet's Challenge to Socrates' Human Wisdom*

In recounting the origins of Socratic political philosophy, Plato informs us that it emerged in response to powerful criticisms of philosophy. Socrates offers his most famous account of the philosophic life in his defense speech in the *Apology*. Socrates is forced to make that speech because he is formally accused of acting unjustly by introducing strange, daimonic things into the city and corrupting the young. He claims that these formal charges are neither the first nor the most damaging accusations against him. A whole generation has been prejudiced against him by an older, graver set of accusations. The only one of the older accusers whom Socrates identifies by name is the comic poet Aristophanes, whose *Clouds* ridiculed him as an atheistic natural philosopher and amoral teacher of tricky rhetoric (*Apology* 18b, 19b–c, 23e). The action of Aristophanes' comedy implies that Socrates eagerly corrupts students by teaching them that neither Zeus nor justice exists (*Clouds* 247, 367, 902ff.). Because Aristophanes' critique deeply tarnished his reputation, Socrates fears that he cannot respond to it persuasively in the short time provided him for his defense speech (*Apology* 18e–19a). Insofar as one purpose of Plato's dialogues as a whole is to present Socrates' full response, Aristophanes' assault on the Socratic life appears to initiate an important event in the ancient and ongoing quarrel between poetry and philosophy (*Republic* 607b).

Even though Socrates' explicit references to Aristophanes as one of his most influential accusers seems to call for a serious examination of the Aristophanic critique of Socrates, many scholars readily accept Socrates' claim that he never engaged in the natural philosophic investigations ridiculed in the *Clouds* and argue that Aristophanes never really knew who Socrates was or what he did. Dover (1980) and Solomos (1974) claim that Aristophanes' portrait of Socrates as an atheistic and amoral natural philosopher is simply a case of mistaken identity. Aristophanes, they say, did not know Socrates very well and confused him with the Sophists. But other thinkers point out that Aristophanes is very familiar with both idiosyncratic personal and philosophic traits of the Socrates whom we know from Plato (Nussbaum 1980, 71–76 passim; O'Regan 1997, 142 n. 13; Reckford 1987, 392; Strauss 1966, 8, 50–52, 313–314; West and West 1984, 30). Plato himself indicates that Socrates and Aristophanes knew each other well, for in the *Symposium*, not only does Alcibiades remark that he expects to find Socrates at Aristophanes' side, but also Aristodemus reports that the two conversed in a friendly manner (*Symposium* 213c, 223c). Having established their familiarity, Plato affirms the importance of understanding Aristophanes' critique of Socrates in the *Symposium*, where Plato explicitly contrasts their alternative claims to possess human and divine wisdom (cf. *Clouds* 522 and *Symposium* 177de, 212c, 223c). In fact, the repeated, subtle references to Aristophanes throughout the works of both Plato and Xenophon suggest that these Socratics want even their most sympathetic and careful readers to bear in mind Aristophanes' challenges to understand all that is at stake in Socrates' defense of philosophy (e.g., *Lovers* 134b; *Philebus* 48a–50a; *Phaedo* 70b–c; *Theages* 122a; cf. Xenophon *Oeconomicus* 11.18 with *Clouds* 35; *Symposium* 6.6.8).

Plato's severest modern critic, Nietzsche, further attests to the power of Aristophanes' critique of Socrates. He indicates that Aristophanes was gifted with a profound instinct about what was wrong with Socrates (*Birth of Tragedy* 13). Aristophanes apparently saw the "overgrowth" of rationalism in Socrates and its deep antipathy toward all that is healthy. According to Nietzsche, Aristophanes is the "transfiguring, complementary spirit for whose sake one *forgives* everything Hellenic for having existed, provided one has understood in its full profundity *all* that needs to be forgiven and transfigured here" (*Beyond Good and Evil* 28). Nietzsche admires him for undoing some of the philosophic and moral influence of Socrates and Plato by letting loose a mocking "derision of the world" (*Beyond Good and Evil* 223; Lampert 1986, 342). According to Nietzsche, Aristophanes ranks among the greatest human beings and creators, along with Caesar, Homer, Leonardo, and Goethe, for his "slackness, skepticism, 'immorality,' right to throw off a faith" and "freedom of the will" (*Will to Power* 380). Nietzsche is so impressed with Aristophanes that he takes an ancient rumor that a volume of his comedies was found beneath the pillow of Plato's deathbed to be a sign of Plato's subtlety and greatness, apparently on the grounds that Plato's attraction to the comic poet reflects that philosopher's secret suspicion that his whole philosophic project is a fabrication (*Beyond Good and Evil* 28; cf. 5, 6, 8). If one resists Nietzsche's claim that Plato privately doubted the foundations of his own philosophy, one can at least take this ancient story as further evidence that Plato took Aristophanes' challenge to Socratism seriously until the very moment of his death.

In order to make sense of Aristophanes' critique of Socrates, some have, naturally, focused solely on the *Clouds*. In order to approach Aristophanes' quarrel with Socrates from a new direction, this chapter begins by examining Plato's presentation of Aristophanes in the *Symposium*. It is my contention that Plato's portrayal of Aristophanes is meant not to ridicule the comic poet but to help acquaint us with the power of his challenge and alternative to Socratic philosophy. By helping us to see the core of Aristophanes' teaching about eros, human nature, and the gods, Plato's presentation of Aristophanes in the *Symposium* helps us to recognize what the poet's *Clouds* is claiming Socrates does *not* know about these matters. This chapter will explore Plato's account of the dispute between Aristophanes and Socrates primarily by examining how Plato presents Aristophanes and his claim to wisdom. It will then use that presentation to help bring out some of the most important themes of *Aristophanes'* criticisms of Socrates in his *Clouds*. Finally, the chapter will sketch the Aristophanic alternative to Socratic philosophy that emerges from *both* Plato's presentation of Aristophanes and Aristophanes' self-presentation. In this way, this chapter aims to familiarize us with the most serious doubts about Socratic philosophy and Socratic education so that we might be in the best possible position to accept or answer them.

## PLATO'S ARISTOPHANES

Aristophanes appears as a character in only one Platonic dialogue, the *Symposium*. According to that dialogue, the disagreement between Aristophanes and Socrates is best understood as a disagreement about Eros. Eros is a fitting subject for this contest, not simply because it happens to be the only subject about which Socrates repeatedly claims to be an expert, but also because Eros is said to be both a part of the human psyche and a god.

According to Nussbaum, Aristophanes' speech contains one of the two "most serious objections raised in the *Symposium* against Socrates' program for the ascent of love" (Nussbaum 1986, 171). In order to convey the power of Aristophanes' alternative account of Eros, one need only note the dispute about whether Plato preferred it to the one offered by Socrates. Bloom writes that "Plato makes Aristophanes the expositor of the truest and most satisfying account of Eros that we find in the *Symposium*" (Bloom 1992, 478, 485). Freud treats it as Plato's own account of Eros (Freud 1984, 46; 1985, 331–332). To emphasize Plato's respect for the speech, Plato has Aristophanes offer a response to Socrates' speech, thus indicating that Socrates' account of Eros is not simply Plato's last word (*Symposium* 212c).

Aristophanes presents his claim to be wise in erotic matters in the central speech of the *Symposium*. But before he speaks, Plato shows him afflicted with a case of the hiccups that leads to Aristophanes asking the pedantic doctor Eryximachus either to cure him or to speak in his place. Eryximachus recommends that Aristophanes try holding his breath, gargling, and sneezing to cure his affliction. While the poet tries these remedies, Eryximachus's speech reveals that he is a doctor who places greater trust in the healing power of medical science and the study of nature as a whole than in the power of prayer and incantation. In some respects he seems close to the natural philosopher ridiculed in the *Clouds* (Bloom 1992, 472). After both Eryximachus's speech and Aristophanes' hiccups conclude, the poet makes a joke at the expense of the doctor. Eryximachus spoke of a beautiful and orderly Eros present in every body, an Eros that can be instilled or shaped by art to cure the body of its pain and disorders. Aristophanes remarks that the cure for the hiccups was wonderfully orderly; that is, the joke is that the body is not orderly, but a bundle of disorders, disruptions, and convulsions which can cancel each other out with the help of art. The art of medicine prescribes sneezing to stop hiccuping. The beautified rational account of the harmony of nature turns out to be irrational insofar as it exaggerates the beauty and harmony of the body. When the insulted doctor threatens to watch over Aristophanes' speech lest he "prefer laughter to speaking peacefully" (189a7–b2) and commands him to "use his mind" and speak as though he were giving a *logos* (189b–c), Aristophanes explains that he does not fear provoking laughter, since it is both "beneficial" and "innate to his Muse," but fears instead saying laughable things (189b3–7).[1] This suggests that he does not regard his comedies as being absurdist or as celebrations of the irrational. Rather, his comedy exposes and debunks absurdity, showing as clearly as possible the irrationality of his characters' fears and hopes.

Aristophanes begins his speech by saying that human beings have been wholly unaware of the power of Eros. His proof of this is our neglect of the god. Had we perceived the god's power, we would have made the greatest sanctuaries, altars, and sacrifices to Eros. We should honor Eros because this god is the most philanthropic divinity, a "doctor" who tries to heal the illness that prevents us from enjoying the greatest happiness (189c–d). He will try to initiate everyone at the banquet into the power of Eros so that they in turn can teach others (189d4). While the others hesitate to have their speeches broadcast (173a8–b1, 176e, 218b), he asks them to spread his teaching, for he is confident that he will neither offend nor harm the city.

Before he can offer his radical renovation in worshiping of Eros, Aristophanes says that his listeners must first understand human nature and its sufferings. There is something in human nature that is deeper than Eros and that affects Eros greatly. His remark that "our nature is not as it once was" (189d6–7) causes some to conclude he believes that human nature is mutable and still others to go further to suggest that we therefore lack natural standards of justice and human excellence (Rosen 1987, 137; Saxonhouse 1985, 21). One difficulty with this conclusion is that he does, after all, employ the term *nature* to describe our species, a term which refers to that which is permanent and unalterable (e.g., Burnet 1930, 11). To say that our nature is mutable is to suggest that we have no lasting or unalterable character. But were this Aristophanes' implication, why speak of a nature at all? His assertion that we must learn about our "ancient nature" in order to understand our Eros today implies that there is something in that ancient nature that lingers with us today—and hence that our nature is not simply changeable.

Aristophanes' account of this ancient nature begins with his revelation that there were once three genders or "races," since there existed alongside men and women a third race of human beings who had the characteristics or "look" of both male and female. All three kinds were round, with their legs in a circle, with four arms, legs, and ears, and with two faces, two sets of genitals, and, in short, with twice the number of body parts which we have, except that they shared one head and neck. They walked upright and moved "freely" in whichever direction they wished, but could run very quickly by extending their eight limbs and tumbling like acrobats. They descended from three different celestial gods: males from the sun, females from the earth, and androgynes from the moon, which, he says, partakes of both the male sun and female earth. Like their divine forebears, the original human beings were shaped like globes and kept to an orderly circular motion (189d–190a). Moreover, they were awesome, mighty, and had great and proud thoughts. Because of their power and greatness of mind, they were not content to keep their orderly places in the cosmos but went into heaven to attack the gods in the manner of Homer's Ephialtes and Otus (190b5–c1; Homer *Iliad* 5.385 ff.; *Odyssey* 11.305 ff.). Aristophanes does not say exactly what the ancient ancestors wished to accomplish by assaulting the gods. Did they want to rule in their place? The very absence of a stated or clearly implied reason for their assault on the gods raises the possibility that they are, more than anything else, unwilling to be ruled, by nature rebellious, less eager to command than angry at being lorded over. If so, they are beings whose deepest desire is to "overcome," to assert themselves proudly against something in opposition, something apparently more powerful and higher. At heart, they are moved by the hope that they can overcome whatever opposes them. While a Socratic might call them "thumotic" or spirited, Nietzsche might understand them to exhibit the "will to power."[2]

Aristophanes says that when the ancients rose up against the gods, Zeus and the other gods deliberated about what they should do and were perplexed for a long time. The gods did not know how they could put an end to our licentiousness without having to kill us all just as they had killed off the giants. They spare us not because they love us but because they need the honors and sacrifices we provide them (190c1–6). Zeus then "thought hard" and declared that he had a device to weaken the human race without killing it, so that we would no longer be licentious. After warning us that we must be quiet and stop acting licentiously or else we will be cut in half again so that we will jump on one leg, he began to slice our ancestors into two halves "as one cuts apples or eggs." He then had Apollo sew us up and turn our heads so that we would see the wrinkles and scars that he left on our bodies (the lines on our chests and our navels) and be more orderly, remembering that we are at the mercy of the gods (190c–d). Yet after we were divided, something occurred which Zeus did not anticipate: each half desired its other half and entangled with it in an effort to grow back together (191a). In their effort to make humanity more fearful and orderly, the gods inadvertently gave rise to Eros. But since Eros came into being simply in response to human needs and is unlike other gods insofar as it cares for our well-being, one is compelled to wonder whether it is, in fact, a god at all. In order to shed more light on this issue, one must look more critically and more generally at this account of the gods, human nature, and Eros. Aristophanes presents the gods as needy beings who require our sacrifices (*Birds* 185–193) and who have the power to alter our very nature in order to make certain that we give them that respect. Yet if the gods can reshape us at their will, are they not manifestly bunglers? Zeus, the god with the greatest kingly wisdom, has difficulty thinking and devises a scheme that makes us not pious but erotic. Aristophanes suggests, in other words, that considering how poorly we behave toward the powerful and wise gods who demand that we be pious, the gods must be inept and hence boasters about their great powers and wisdom and hence laughable subjects of comedy (Bury 1932, 59). But if our reflections on our beliefs about the gods leads us to laugh at those gods, if our opinions about the gods belie their claim to be fearsome, awesome, and philanthropic, then these gods do not seem to be what we implicitly believe gods must be. Does Aristophanes consider these gods to be genuine gods? Simply by saying that the gods *need* our honors and sacrifices (190c4–5), Aristophanes indicates that they are not complete beings. Perhaps he implies that we are beings who by nature imagine superhuman beings who oppose, need, and rule us. On the other hand, simply because Aristophanes presents a funny and impious account of Zeus does not prove that he is an unbeliever. After all, these gods may seem incoherent to us because they are essentially mysterious. One can, however, safely say that Aristophanes is not an unquestioning defender of traditional piety and that we need to bear in mind the question of his piety.

Whether or not Aristophanes is a believer in the Olympian gods, he cannot think that the story of Zeus splitting us in two is a literal account of how we came to be as we are. But what then does he mean when he says that we once had an ancient nature which was altered by Zeus? As was noted above, the fact that he must discuss the character of the ancient ancestors to explain our nature indicates that the ancient nature is not lost in the past, but an important aspect of who we are now. The splitting refers not to our species's transformation through time, but to our nature's various depths or levels, to a hierarchy of powerful desires and proclivities always present in the psyche. Somewhere in our heart of hearts, in what is most ancient or most fundamental to us, we are—or think we are—the strong, free, and proud beings referred to in the speech. The "splitting" that brings about our "modern nature" refers not to an act of divine punishment, but to the fact that we find ourselves naturally subject to "Olympian" gods whether or not gods such as Zeus or Apollo actually exist (Neumann 1966, 422; Rosen 1987, 142). If, however, we harbor within us the ancient nature, if we are profoundly rebellious and freedom loving, why and by what psychological process would we make ourselves subject to such hostile and brutal deities? The answer is that it arises from our ancient nature: Somewhere deep within the soul, we understand ourselves to be as powerful and as deserving as the ancient ancestors; but because we lack their prowess and freedom, our desires and ambitions are constantly frustrated. In keeping with our rebellious, spirited, even willful nature, we lash out in anger, seeking someone or something to blame for opposing us, for robbing us not only of the object of our desires, but also of our strength and dignity. The greatness of our pride leads us to the thought that we can only have been weakened and are lorded over by powerful, misanthropic beings. We regard our suffering to be proof that gods exist (*Knights* 32–34). In the *Clouds*, even the chorus, led by Aristophanes, calls Zeus a tyrant (*Clouds* 565). The more aware we become of our weakness and of the power of the gods who impose on us, the more angry and terrified we become of them. This profound arrogance, fear, and anger is one "natural" source of our piety.

Because we are fundamentally proud but weak and hence angry beings, we cannot bear our piety well or for long. We respond to our miserable subjugation to the gods with Eros, which Aristophanes characterizes as a desire to be reunited with our own, particular "other half." This image seems to refer to the fact that Eros convinces us that somewhere in the world there exists a true kindred-spirit, a soul mate. Eros tells us that each of us is meant to find a beloved who is as akin to us as the left halves of our bodies are akin to the right. Lovers behave as if they shared a common good with an other half to the point that they do not believe that they have a good apart from that other half. When in love, we wish to lose our individual identities and become new beings—but not entirely new, for at the heart of Eros lurks a love of and respect for what is "one's own" (*oikeioteti*, 192c1). We inevitably equate that which is our own with that which is good. When we sense our incompleteness or deficiency, we do not simply conclude that there is something wrong with *us*; rather we believe that we need "more of ourselves" and hence seek out someone who is like us. Eros seems to end in union—yet this is only the beginning. Were this Eros for our other half satisfied, we would regain our ancient wholeness, strength, and daring and thereby presumably assault the gods once again (Carson 1986, 68). Through the emergence of Eros, we see another aspect of our psychological makeup: We are not only deeply fearful and angry, but also hopeful. Our Eros to reunite, to become whole and to overthrow the gods, is akin to the hopeful, even fantastic, projects carried out in Aristophanes' comedies.

One obvious objection to Aristophanes' thesis is that we do not love the kindred so much as the beautiful. Although he never mentions the word *beauty* in his speech, he does offer an explanation of where our longing for a beautiful beloved originates. When he first describes our ancient ancestors as circular beings with twice the number of body parts that we have, they sound grotesque; but then he mentions that they were symmetrical and globular because they descended from the symmetrical and globular celestial beings. By reminding us of the grace and beauty of the divine sun, moon, and earth, he suggests that the ancient human beings seem so ugly only because they look so unlike us. Compared to them, we are asymmetrical, wrinkled, and scarred. We are more inclined to perceive beauty in beings that are similar to ourselves than in beings with ostensibly more beautiful qualities. He does not say that the beautiful is merely a projection of our love of ourselves on the world. He does not deny that some things are intrinsically beautiful. But our sense of the beautiful is deeply tinged by anthropomorphism and perhaps even ethnocentrism. Instead of loving human beings on the basis of some objective sense of beauty, we love those who are kindred and perceive an illusory beauty in their kindredness (Nietzsche *Genealogy of Morals* 1:5–6; *Twilight of the Idols* "Expeditions of an Untimely Man" 19).

Aristophanes says that when our ancestors were first split, they were inactive and unwilling to do anything or part from each other. When the longing for completion first consumed us and prevented us from caring for our other needs, the whole human race began to perish (191a5–b1). When one lover died, the other would look for another "other half" to entangle with rather than live alone or perish (191b2–5). He does not say that lovers embrace their new beloveds with any less intensity than they embraced their old ones; it is as if each lover looks on his or her new other half as if it were the original. Just as our ability to live without our other halves testifies that we are not literally halves of one being, our capacity to love new beloveds suggests that erotic attraction is based not on true and perfect "complementarity," but on a recurring illusion that such complementarity exists. As he says at 191d5, lovers are *always* in search of their one and only; the perfect complement for whom we search is never to be found (cf. 193b5–6). The claim that we have been sliced from a single being illustrates exactly how difficult it is to find someone who could fulfill our erotic desires: We would have to have been sliced from a single body if we were to be as perfectly matched as we hope. Love affairs eventually fail because no one turns out to be the true one and only. Eros inclines us all to adultery rather than to lasting marriages (191d7–e2).

Having alluded to the illusory and adulterous character of erotic love, Aristophanes deepens his discussion of the relationship between sexuality and Eros. He says that in ancient times erotic coupling involved neither sexual gratification nor reproduction. Human beings had their genitals on their backs and reproduced by laying and fertilizing eggs in the earth, as grasshoppers do. Consequently, when human beings locked in erotic embrace, their genitals did not meet. But Zeus moved the genitals from the back of the body to the front to facilitate both reproduction and sexual gratification, the former to regenerate those who perish and the latter to relieve eros long enough to permit them to get on with their other deeds (191a–c). Eros is not rooted in sexuality; rather, sexual gratification is a device which allows us to overcome the debilitating effects of Eros. Nor does Eros grow from a desire to reproduce—this is incidental to sex. If Aristophanes does not believe that Zeus literally performed this sexual alteration, he suggests that prior to our awareness of and submission to the gods, human sexuality is arbitrary and licentious. Yet something within us makes us wish to leave this natural condition and become subject to the gods. The concern that leads us to yield to law is the desire to live in the family, yet another form of love of what is "one's own." Aristophanes powerfully illustrates the strength of this love in the *Clouds*, when he depicts Strepsiades being horrified at his son's suggestion that he will beat, and even have intercourse with, his mother (*Clouds* 1332–1343, 1370–1377, 1443–1451; Nichols 1987, 25; O'Regan 1992, 118; Strauss 1966, 40, 43). Strepsiades is outraged not at the thought that he might thereby lose his wife's affection (it is already lost), but at the prospect that through his son's incest with his wife he might lose his place in the family altogether. Fearing that he will lose his relation to his son, Strepsiades turns to the Olympic gods, demanding that they uphold the law that protects the family (*Clouds* 1468–1469, 1478ff.). At the heart of our abhorrence of incest and of adultery is the fear that these things will obliterate that which makes one's family one's own.[3] Because the untamed sexuality of those who love "their own" leads to incest and adultery, it must be suppressed by laws and by gods who uphold the family. In saying that Zeus "turns around" the *aidoia* (191b5–7), Aristophanes means not that Zeus literally moves the genitals from back to front, but that our belief in Zeus leads us to regard sexuality and sexual generation with shame and with awe. Once Zeus makes us to look upon generation in this way, our reproduction becomes orderly and recognizably "human" (190c7–d1, 191b–c). Thus, human nature is further sundered: we are beings whose pride demands freedom and yet who also need legal justice, the subjugation of ourselves and our families, to safeguard what is our own.

Following his account of the origin of Eros, Aristophanes returns to his assertion that the human race has descended from three different races and focuses on those who are male halves of the "whole male." Unlike heterosexuals, these men are halves of a being that is thoroughly manly and hence best. Aristophanes argues that their willingness to sleep with men is not shameless; even as boys their affection for men shows "boldness" and "courage" and "masculinity" (191e–2a). The singular proof that such youths are not shameless is they are the only youths who grow up to be politicians (192a5–7). This assertion that political ambition demonstrates both shame and manliness is puzzling, for one would expect their boldness and ambition to reflect their freedom from shame. The solution seems to be that a proud ambition implies a sense of shame. The proud attempt to show their strength by ruling in the belief that if they do not pursue rule they will show themselves to be weak and shameful. Their political ambition is distinct from Eros. While lovers seek their ancient strength through erotic union, the politicians assert themselves proudly, as if they possessed that strength already. Aristophanes adds that the politicians would, by nature, be content to live with their beloveds, but they are compelled by the law to pay attention to marriage and procreation (192a7–b3). It is not that politicians are immune to the pangs and hope of Eros. Both their Eros and their political ambition are rooted in a desire to demonstrate their strength and overthrow the gods. But Eros differs from political ambition in that when one is in love one is painfully aware of one's weakness and of how much strength and wholeness one has yet to recover. But those who seek to rule can put aside their feelings of need and can experience a sense of power and mastery that is akin to that of the gods (190c1–3). Because these are the most manly human beings, they have the strength to make and submit to laws that compel them to resist Eros so that they might give fuller scope to their passion to rule. Just as these politicians help promote the family by upholding laws that suppress adultery and incest, they also empower themselves by making laws that forbid pederasty.

The more one thinks through the comic poet's presentation of Eros, the more one discovers its grim, even tragic, undercurrents (Plato *Symposium* 223d; Bloom 1992, 483; Neumann 1966, 426; Nussbaum 1986, 173; Rosen 1987, 157; Saxonhouse 1985, 17–18; Strauss 1966, 78, 312). In response to our weakness, fear, and resentment at gods (whom we would imagine if they did not exist), we hope to find another half which, in fact, does not exist. Because Eros distracts us from all else, including the family, it seems that one must suppress it with law. Yet since Eros arises from the frustration of desire, any attempt to restrain it merely strengthens it again. Having related our burdensome natural condition, Aristophanes discusses the difficulty we face in recognizing and comprehending our Eros and nature. He says that lovers are willing to stay with one another through life even though they cannot say what they want from each other. Whatever lovers seek from their beloveds, no one would say that they enjoy being together so intensely simply because they want sexual intercourse. It could be rooted in mere physical desire only if each of our bodies were actually one half of another body that is separated from and wants to reunite with its own, particular other half. Thus, Eros finds its origins deep within the murkiness of the psyche. Aristophanes says that when we are asked what we love, the soul "divines" what it seeks and speaks in "riddles" (192b–d). The turbulence of the soul, its cacophony of rebellious pride, anger, fear, shame, and hope, exaggerates our strength, distorts our sense of beauty, and magnifies our sense of kinship with others to the extent that we cannot plumb its depths with clarity or certainty.

We can only guess at what we seek and who we are. Aristophanes' insights are fortuitous discoveries that cannot be made merely by following out the implications of our conscious beliefs and experiences. Aristophanes must confirm his insights as best he can, by exposing what seems to him "laughable" or problematic about our fears and ambitions and watching to see if others laugh. By showing that even his own account of the psyche is provisional, Aristophanes implies that we must not take for granted that our erotic, pious, and moral experiences have merely "psychological" causes and explanations and that we should not rule out the possibility that Zeus or some other, more plausible, providential gods rule over us.

Following these bleak reflections on the human condition, Aristophanes asks us to imagine the god Hephaestus standing over lovers as they lie together and asking them what they want from one another. He says that lovers could not tell Hephaestus what they want; but none would refuse an offer to be fused together in order to live as one both in this life and in Hades (192d–e). Only a providential and personal Olympian god could satisfy our deepest longings. Yet everything that we have learned indicates that Olympians would never fuse us together forever, for it would restore us to our impious wholeness. Because neither gratitude nor fear is as profound as our ancient rebelliousness, the Olympian gods will not fulfill us, either. Aristophanes does not, however, leave us with this disappointing insight. In the remainder of the speech, he speaks in a new way about what we can expect from the gods in hopes that this new account will make it easy for us to bear our "pious" subjugation and erotic longing. This may be a serious or half-serious recommendation as a religious innovation that is in keeping with our original nature. He begins by repeating that we long for a lasting union with our other halves because our ancient nature was once one and whole. He then says for the first time that we were taken apart by the god "through injustice" in the same way that the Arcadians were dispersed by the Spartans (193a1–3).[4] He adds that there is fear that we will be split again into four quarters and go around "sliced through the nose" like bas-relief statues if we are not orderly in our behavior to the gods. But for the first time he offers us grounds for hope: If we are pious, we may be reunited with our true other halves. Everyone should befriend and be reconciled to Olympians in hopes that the gods will allow us to find our own beloveds, which, he says, few at the moment do (193a–b). But on what new grounds can we hope that the Olympians will satisfy our rebellious Eros for unity and independence? Will we not continue to resent them for our weakness until we are strong enough to overpower them? To reconcile us to the Olympian gods, Aristophanes revises his account of the change in our nature. Even though he indicates at 190c that the gods weakened us out of their self-interest, he now raises the possibility that we are weak, unhappy, and erotic because of *our* injustice. But how could teaching us to blame ourselves for our condition make it easier for us to bear our condition? Because by attributing our suffering to our guilt, by taking on moral responsibility, we could begin to hope that we can act to end that suffering. Turning inward the same spirited anger that makes us blame our sufferings on the gods, we might find new grounds for a more hopeful piety. The more we would suffer, the more we would understand it to be rooted in our guilt; hence, the more pious we would become to atone for our guilt and to put an end to our suffering. Although we would be more pious, our primordial fear and resentment at the gods would be mitigated by our internalized anger and hopefulness, so that Eros would not spring up again as powerfully or as readily. He concludes that it would be just to sing hymns to Eros who benefits us the most by bringing us to what is our own. In the future, when we are pious toward all the gods, Eros will give us the greatest hopes that we can be restored to our ancient nature and become blessed and happy (193c–d).

## THE CRITICISMS OF SOCRATES IN ARISTOPHANES' *CLOUDS* IN LIGHT OF PLATO'S PRESENTATION OF ARISTOPHANES

Having examined Plato's account of Aristophanes' view of Eros, human nature, and the gods, we are in a better position to understand how Plato understood Aristophanes' criticisms of Socrates in the *Clouds*. The only character in the *Clouds* who seems remotely "erotic" (in the sense Aristophanes uses the term in the

*Symposium*) is the rustic Strepsiades, for near the beginning of the play he mentions that he was once very much sexually-erotically attracted to his wife (*Clouds* 40–54). But by the start of the play, his sole affection is fatherly love for Pheidippides. In order to escape the debts into which his son has plunged him, Strepsiades tries to learn from Socrates a kind of rhetoric that lets one evade the law. Although initially distraught when he fails to absorb Socrates' lessons, Strepsiades is later filled with joy at the prospect that his son might learn the rhetoric that lets him look down on the law (*Clouds* 808–809, 1201–1205). After Strepsiades discovers that Socratism threatens his own family, Strepsiades returns to law, justice, gods with a vengeance. The Clouds, however, urge Strepsiades to blame his misfortunes on his "eros" of evil deeds (*Clouds* 1459). The Clouds apply the term *Eros* not merely to the overwhelming attraction to one particular beloved but to the deeper passion behind the superficial attraction, to the desire to overthrow the law and the gods who uphold the law.

Socrates, on the other hand, never seems to have been in love with any other human being. The key to understanding Socrates' character lies in the Clouds' remark that they especially love him for his swaggering pride and ability to endure any hardship with manly toughness (*Clouds* 358–363). The Clouds draw our attention to Socrates' endurance because this shapes his thinking. Unlike ordinary men, Socrates possesses endurance or continence that permits him to ignore the body's needs. He expects his "student" Strepsiades to think with utmost clarity when lying on a mattress infested by fleas; but when Strepsiades lies on that mattress, either he is tormented to distraction by the insects or else his mind wanders to sexual matters (*Clouds* 412–417, 707–730, 733–735; Strauss 1989b, 125). But since Socrates has incomparable endurance or continence, he never succumbs to the feelings of great weakness and need that cause others to fall in love. In addition to calling our attention to Socrates' endurance, the Clouds also underscore his pride; his continence leads him to be fiercely proud. While the manly politicians of Aristophanes' speech in the *Symposium* resist their Eros with the help of laws in order to imitate the gods, the even manlier Socrates is able to ignore Eros and carry out an assault on the gods through natural philosophy. Unlike the relatively weaker and less continent

Strepsiades, Socrates' mind can roam freely, become "abstract," and mix with its "kindred," the air (*Clouds* 227–232, 700–706, 727–729, 740–745). While Socrates does not spell out the meaning of his allusion at lines 229–30 to mind mixing with air, among the pre-Socratics the mind is often associated with the element "air" on the grounds that to think clearly is to rise above "wetness," to transcend sensuality, emotionalism, and all that is human, in order to apprehend dryly, lucidly, and purely the nature of all things (*Clouds* 230–236; *Birds* 687–688; Diels 1985, Heracleitus 13, 36, 77, 117, 118; Diels 1985, Diogenes of Apollonia 4, 5). As a result of Socrates' "high-flying" thinking, he believes he has "seen through" the gods. He claims to have discovered that the cosmos is governed not by willful, spontaneous, mysterious, gods such as Zeus but by "vortex," a purposeless yet fully intelligible movement which regulates the whole according to necessity (*Clouds* 376–381). As Socrates' companion the Unjust Speech explains, we ourselves are governed by "natural necessities" (*Clouds* 1075), although we commonly conceal this by law (*Clouds* 1079, 1399–1400, 1421–1422, 1427–1432). Socrates himself openly teaches that providential gods like Zeus are imaginary and that justice has no innate or necessary power in the heavens or in the soul other than what it derives from convention (*Clouds* 367, 901–905, passim; Diels 1985, Antiphon 44; Aristotle *Nicomachean Ethics* 1094b14–17, 1141a20–b8; Diels 1985, Heracleitus 102; Plato *Apology* 26d; *Laws* 889e3–890a2;).[5] Proud of his ability to comprehend the cosmos, Socrates assimilates himself to the cosmic beings, looking down on gods and "ephemeral" human beings (*Clouds* 218–234), much like the proud ancient circle men of the *Symposium*.

Yet no matter how convinced Socrates may be that he knows the cosmos, he does not know himself. He is not erotic in the sense that he loves one other person; but while he believes himself to be radically detached from ephemeral human beings, his needs show through in his eagerness to teach others to think and act like himself. By encouraging his students to resemble him and to regard him as their authority, Socrates reveals that he loves what is "his own" (*Clouds* 120, 186, 503, 1112, 1170–1176). In addition to failing to see how much he wants to shape others, Socrates also ignores how he owes his extraordinary ability to think clearly to his strange continence and endurance. He does not understand that others are too fragile, too needy, too prone to delirious hopes and expectations, to lead a philosophic life. Socrates is likewise unaware of how powerfully love of one's own manifests itself as love of family and is thus oblivious to the likelihood that someone such as Strepsiades will turn to and feel the power of law and justice and Zeus. From a practical point of view, Socrates is unwise to teach atheism and conventionalism to those who cannot absorb these lessons. But, more importantly, he is unwise to assume that Zeus is a superstition and that justice is mere convention when in fact the manifest disorder of the psyche prevents anyone from knowing decisively that the gods or justice are only products of human imagination. Even though Socrates regards the Clouds as mere rhetoric, they prove to have a life of their own. The Clouds show their independence from Socrates by blaming Strepsiades for being erotic about evil things and by claiming to have been teaching him a lesson all along. They eventually permit Strepsiades to blame Socrates for all his troubles (*Clouds* 1304, 1458–1461). They are not mere words to be manipulated by those who understand natural necessities; in fact, they are willing, thinking beings who bring to sight the "necessities" of family, justice, and the gods. Inspired by the Clouds and by the Olympic gods (*Clouds* 1505–1506), Strepsiades sets fire to Socrates' school. By turning on Socrates and upholding the Olympic gods and their justice, the Clouds vindicate their claim to divinity in Athens. As one of the Clouds and as playwright, Aristophanes says "just things," defends the city and its gods while revealing Socrates' ignorance of their suprarational power. By revealing the superficiality of Socrates' account of human and divine things, Aristophanes means to reveal to Socrates how deeply he has misjudged love of what is one's own and overlooked the possibility that there are providential gods who care about justice and the family. The Aristophanic Socrates is carried away by spiritedness or pride. Because he is seldom reminded of his essential limitations by physical or erotic desires, he exaggerates his ability to comprehend the cosmos. In fact, he may even suffer from the deepest ignorance and be guilty, in a sense, of corrupting the young.[6]

## PLATO AND ARISTOPHANES ON THE WISDOM OF COMIC POETRY

Both Plato in the *Symposium* and Aristophanes in the *Clouds* present Aristophanes' life of wisdom as a serious alternative to the Socratic life. While I do not believe that Plato is persuaded by Aristophanes, I think that he expects his readers to appreciate the power of the Aristophanic alternative to Socratism. My purpose here is to sketch that alternative and its claims to superiority to philosophic life. Aristophanes' speech in the *Symposium* mentions neither philosophy nor poetry. Yet Plato's overall presentation of Aristophanes provides us a new view of the poet's way of life. In the *Symposium*, Aristophanes is the only character at the banquet who is not accompanied by a companion, by a lover or beloved (Friedländer 1969, 19), thus suggesting that the laughing, irreverent (189b3) poet has been freed by comedy from the erotic longings suffered by others. In the *Republic*, Socrates notes that laughter signals a "great change" and must be banished from a city that is devoted above all to inculcating respect for the most austere virtues (*Republic* 388e), since laughter follows from the sudden recognition that what we have greatly feared or greatly revered is not as fearsome or respectable as we imagined (e.g., Hobbes *Leviathan*, chap. 6). In saying that Aristophanes is devoted to Dionysus (177e1–2), Socrates seems to mean that he is devoted not only to the god of theater, but also to the deity most associated with drink (176b). Like laughter, drunkenness is a pleasure that produces an exhilarating, if momentary, liberation from shame, fear, and suffering (*Laws* 649d–e). In saying that Aristophanes is also devoted to Aphrodite, Socrates indicates that the poet is likewise dedicated to sexual gratification and to the exhilarating sense of freedom that accompanies it (191c). In other words, the Aristophanic life consists of using comedy, wine, and sex to break free from the inevitable anger, fear, piety, and hope that continually oppress us. As Nietzsche recognizes, at the heart of Aristophanic comedy is a longing for overcoming or for liberation from powers which burden us. The characters in Aristophanes' comedies who represent the comic poet, such as Dikaiopolis of the *Acharnians* and Euelpides of the *Birds*, seek neither erotic fulfillment with one true love nor political office; instead, they aim for a private life filled with simple, sexual, gastronomic, and alcoholic pleasures that one can enjoy without depending on the city or the gods.

More liberating than these delights, however, are the *insights* that underlie Aristophanic comedy.[7] There are even indications that Aristophanes has learned valuable lessons from studying natural philosophy with Socrates.[8] Alcibiades says that Aristophanes has shared in "philosophic madness" with Socrates (*Symposium* 218b). In fact, there is a discernable likeness between Pheidippides and Aristophanes suggested by *Clouds* 877–882. Aristophanes may have been freed from an unthinking acceptance of orthodoxy by studying natural philosophy with the "historical" Socrates—for even Plato admits that his Socrates knew the teachings of natural philosophers such as Anaxagoras (Plato *Phaedo* 97b; Aristophanes *Clouds* 365 ff.; Strauss 1966, 143). As one can see from Plato's juxtaposition of Aristophanes with Eryximachus in the *Symposium*, the comic poet has something in common with that practitioner of the medical art and student of nature. According to Eryximachus, the medical art possesses a thorough knowledge of the beautiful, harmonic motions that govern all bodies (186a–c). But as Aristophanes remarks at the finish of Eryximachus's speech, those motions are far less beautiful and harmonious than they appear. As is implied by the fact that Aristophanes' hiccups are cured only by sneezing, the disorders of the body are treated only by inducing other disorders (*Clouds* 189a). Behind Aristophanes' joke is the implication that, like the body, the psyche is a bundle of opposing, noisy urges, disruptions, and convulsions that require counterconvulsions to come to rest. Neither body nor soul is governed by an innate longing for harmony or health. Rather, we are able to infer from the disorderliness of body and soul the possibility of an order or harmony and to bring it about through art. To the extent that the artisan can produce rest or harmony in body or soul, he would appear to know its motions through and through. But while these arts can alleviate our afflictions, they cannot cure them once and for all. Recognizing the unavailability of a cure, Aristophanes relies on an ever changing variety of pleasures, of sex, wine, and thoughts (*Clouds* 547–548) because there is no complete and final liberation from the passions and beliefs that delude us. In the end, the failure of these pleasures to liberate us once and for all from anger, fear, hope, eros, ambition, and piety reveals the profound turbulence, irrationality, and obscurity of the psyche. Aristophanes' comic account of the psyche does not claim to be a fully demonstrable insight into the psyche, but informed speculations that need the confirmation of laughter from himself and from others.

By making the god Eros the subject of the dispute between Socrates and Aristophanes, Plato calls our attention to the beautiful cosmology and theogony laid out in the *Birds*, in which Eros plays a crucial role. In Aristophanes' presentation of Eros in the cosmology set forth in the *Birds*, we see that Aristophanes is skeptical not only of the philosophers' claims to know the psyche but also to their claims to comprehend the cosmos as a whole. Unlike the chorus in the *Clouds*, the chorus of birds does not include a figure who identifies himself as the playwright. In the first parabasis, the chorus speaks to the audience in the same terms that Socrates uses to speak to Strepsiades: They refer to human beings as ephemeral and look down upon them from the eternal perspective of ether or of intellect (*Birds* 685–689). Claiming to possess a complete or divine wisdom by which they can explain the nature of birds and the coming into being of the gods, rivers, Erebus, and Chaos, they assert that they have always existed, which makes sense insofar as only such beings could have definitive knowledge of the causes or principles that constitute the intelligible whole. At first there was dark Chaos, dark Erebus, Tartarus, and a whirlwind; but no earth, no sky, no heaven. There was Chaos, insofar as nothing was differentiated (Aristotle *Metaphysics* 989b), until Erebus and whirlwind gave birth to brilliant Eros, which is like a "vortex" (cf. *Clouds* 376–381). Eros is the "first cause" or principle, for it illuminates or differentiates and hence gives existence to heaven, ocean, earth and the deathless gods. But there are grave difficulties with the birds' theogony. Firstly, if Eros is the cause of everything, including the gods, then are the gods really what we mean by "gods"? If the gods are the first things, as Hesiod, for example, teaches, then the gods *are* the principles or starting points according to which we must judge and praise all things. If, on the other hand, there is a non-divine principle that is more fundamental than the gods, then the gods do not govern absolutely what comes into being and hence they lack the powers we attribute to divine beings. Their theogony can, with some thinking through, become atheistic and thus become a cosmology that would be acceptable to the Aristophanic Socrates. Secondly, if the birds were caused by Eros, they were not present from the beginning and hence cannot know beyond all doubt the causes or principles of all things. Moreover, when and how does ether, the element of mind, come into being (Strauss 1966, 171)? Can mind or soul be explained simply on the basis of the non-divine and sub-human cosmic principle Eros or vortex (Plato *Laws* 896ff.; for further difficulties with the cosmology, see Hubbard 1991, 165–166). By exposing us to the problematic cosmology of the birds, Aristophanes indicates how much natural philosophy takes for granted in claiming to comprehend the whole. Natural philosophers, it would seem, are so carried away by their pride in seeing through the gods that they fail to pay sufficient attention to the rational obstacles to doing so.

By laying bare the uncertain foundations of natural philosophy's psychological and cosmological claims, Aristophanes forces one to ask how one is to know, once and for all, whether we believe in gods simply because we are subject to pride, fear, anger, and hope or whether belief can also arise out of a genuine experience of something divine. In light of Plato's presentation of Aristophanes in the *Symposium*, Aristophanes seems to think that human beings are unable either to believe in or to dispense with the gods. No matter how liberating it may be to recognize the absurdity of certain beliefs about Zeus, we lack sufficient grounds for believing ourselves free from all such illusions or even for thinking that we have proven that "Zeus is not." Plato's Aristophanes does not so much imply that there is an essential conflict between the philosophic way of thinking and a poetic as that philosophers are thinkers who overreach their grasp by claiming to have comprehended and resolved experiences and beliefs that continue to elude them.

Based on Plato's presentation of Aristophanes in the *Symposium* and on Aristophanes' self-portrait in the *Clouds*, it seems that Aristophanes' circumspection about the limits of human wisdom leads him to use comic poetry to help moderate and guide the city. Like tragedy, his comedies explore mankind's fondest and most hubristic dreams, only to show us their impossibility and undesirability. Furthermore, by showing those who are hated or feared, such as Socrates and Cleon, to be ridiculous, imprudent boasters, Aristophanes softens the city's passions. Finally, comedy is able to offer political advice not only on a general, allegorical level, as one finds in tragedy, but also in manner far more personal, *ad hominem*, and hence with greater particularity and practical effect. While Aristophanes makes every effort to free himself from the conventions, passions, and opinions that rule his fellow citizens, he does not despise his fellow citizens. Unlike Socrates and Nietzsche, he sees a universal frailty that produces in him a certain sympathy or humanity that is reflected in his poetic efforts to protect the city, the family, and their gods (*Clouds* 549, 575–594). As Nietzsche recognizes, Aristophanes' account of the psyche prefigures something of his own. Both present human beings as unable to distinguish either the good or the beautiful from "one's own," as born with an irreducible sense of the "sacred," and as moved by a will to overcome. But contrary to Nietzsche's claim, Aristophanes' account of Socrates is based not on "mere" instinct, but also on a fuller and properly circumspect understanding of the psyche. Moreover, Aristophanes' far more moderate political posture points to another great difference: Aristophanes' comedies raise the possibility than certain human pleasures can free us, if only momentarily, from the captivity of our boastful ambitions and oppressive illusions and bring us a fleeting harmony or health of psyche. Yet Aristophanes is so alert to what is problematic about our knowledge of the psyche and the cosmos that he sees, more clearly than contemporary theorists, that these very problems require us to take seriously the possibility that "Zeus" and his justice do, in fact, exist. His plays reflect a subtle and searching examination of the claims of "faith," of "revelation," and of the "godness of the gods" (Strauss 1966, 313). Furthermore, while Aristophanes is perfectly aware of fundamental differences between a Socrates and a Strepsiades, he emphasizes the commonality of our nature, its essential limits, its suffering and illusions in a manner that elicits in him and his readers a deep sympathy and humanity.

By helping us see the power of Aristophanes' critique of and alternative to Socratic philosophy, Plato urges his readers to take seriously the charges raised by the *Clouds* and to ask whether

Plato's Socrates adequately comprehends the gods and the justice they uphold. We are compelled to demand of Plato's Socrates that he demonstrate that philosophy can bring to light the character and importance of our deepest erotic, political, and religious experiences as they present themselves, on their own terms, without indulging in the overconfidence, abstraction, and reductionism of which Socratic philosophy has always been accused by its critics.

# CHAPTER 5

# *Socrates' Education in the Erotic Love of the Noble*

Socrates and his great critic Aristophanes appear together in the *Symposium* as guests at a banquet honoring the tragic poet Agathon. When one of the other guests suggests they spend the evening competing to make the best praise of the god Eros, Socrates vigorously endorses the proposal. He claims, in fact, that he has expert knowledge of nothing other than "erotic matters" (Plato *Symposium* 177d7–8, 212b5–6; also *Theages* 128b1–4, *Lysis* 204b5–c2, *Charmides* 155d4–e2; *Phaedrus* 257; Xenophon *Memorabilia* 2.6.28). Socrates volunteers that Aristophanes will also agree to praise Eros. Socrates does not, however, aver that Aristophanes is also an expert in erotic matters; he merely asserts that Aristophanes will agree to speak because he is devoted to the gods Aphrodite and Dionysus. At first, one is likely to overlook the significance of Socrates' claim to know erotic matters. But in the course of his speech, Socrates' claim to know erotic matters will extend to knowing what moves, gratifies, and perfects the soul. Socrates says in the *Symposium* that he derives his knowledge of these matters from conversing with a foreign priestess named Diotima. These conversations provide him with the core of his education because they lead him to recognize, cultivate, and gratify his erotic longing for noble virtue and happiness. The *Symposium*'s account of Socrates' education in erotic matters thus gives us access to the thinking that took place during the famous "Socratic turn" described in the *Phaedo* (96a–100b) and *Apology* (20d–22e) or, in other words, during the birth of Socratic and therefore of classical political philosophy. The tradition credits Socrates with having founded political philosophy by calling philosophy "down from the heavens" and by compelling it "to inquire into life and character and issues of good and evil."[1] By retracing how Socrates responded to Diotima's teaching, we can begin to recover the insights and evidence that convinced him that philosophy is essential to virtue and happiness.

Socrates prefaces his speech about eros by explaining how he will describe it and thus how one should interpret it. He will not embellish eros by attributing anything to it that it lacks; yet in confining himself to the beautiful parts of eros (198d), he nonetheless exaggerates its beauty.[2] In order to understand the full truth about eros, one must supplement his explicit praise of eros. But how can one supplement his speech without imposing one's views on the dialogue? The key is that Socrates does not make a speech, but constructs a conversation between Diotima and himself as a young man. Within this conversation, Socrates recounts not only Diotima's teaching about eros, but also his own questions and objections to that teaching. He presumably includes these doubts and skeptical protests to give us the proper perspective from which to scrutinize Diotima's excessively beautiful account of eros. But how reliable is that youthful perspective if he has not yet been educated in erotic matters? Neither Socrates' immature skepticism nor Diotima's overly beautiful teaching can, by itself, provide one with the full truth about eros. One must recall that both he and Diotima are characters in a drama and that neither can be counted on to speak for Plato. If we are to recover Socrates' "erotic education," we must seek the path he took, bearing in mind his youthful concerns and perspective and asking how he responded to and learned from Diotima's teachings. Only then can we approach his full, mature understanding of "erotic matters."

We begin to hear how the young Socrates conversed with his teacher, the priestess Diotima, before we realize it, for after he finishes speaking with the tragic poet Agathon, he informs us that his conversation with the tragedian is almost identical to the opening stages of his conversations with Diotima many years ago (201d).[3] As he interrogates Agathon in the conversation at 199c–201c, Socrates explodes the poet's assertion that eros is beautiful and provides us with all the beautiful and good things. Socrates asserts that eros is not love of the kindred (199d) but, instead, a desire to possess the things we need and lack (200a–e).[4] If this is so, Socrates contends that to love the beautiful and good things is to lack beauty and goodness.

According to Socrates, after Diotima leads him to concede this point, he asks her if she believes that eros is ugly (or base) and bad (201e6–9). In other words, Socrates asks her if she thinks that eros is degrading and harmful, incapable of leading us to the beautiful and good things, such as pleasure, ambition, expertise, and fame, which Agathon says come from eros (196c, 197a–b). Diotima tells Socrates not to speak blasphemously and argues that something can be neither beautiful nor ugly (or neither noble nor base) in the same manner that someone can be neither wise nor wholly ignorant. Diotima suggests that one can have correct opinion without being able to give a reasoned account and that this is neither to know nor not to know. Insofar as this correct opinion appears to be a kind of knowledge, it would neither be irrational nor simply a lack of learning (202a2–a8). To have "correct opinion" means to have stumbled on the truth without being able to explain why what one has learned is true. An example of correct opinion would be learning, for instance, that heavy objects fall to earth, without knowing why they fall. If we cannot explain why what we have learned is true, our learning is still uncertain and hence somewhere between wrong opinion and knowledge.

The young Socrates appears to agree with Diotima that correct opinion is somewhere between prudence and lack of learning (202a8–9) and that eros can be somewhere between that which is ugly and bad and that which is beautiful (or noble) and good (202b1–5).[5] But he has reservations about whether eros has this intermediate status and questions Diotima by reminding her that everyone agrees that eros is a great god (202b6–7). He uses her argument that correct opinion is a kind of learning against her by asking her to acknowledge that since eros is commonly believed to be divine, it must be beautiful and good. He seems to reason that we hold an opinion to be correct when it seems true and when we are unaware of any counterexample which calls its truth into question. Thus, what seems true to everyone counts as a correct opinion. If, as Diotima says, correct opinion is a kind of learning, then she should yield to the common and therefore correct opinion that eros is divine and thus beautiful and good. But Diotima argues that "those who know," including Socrates and herself, deny that eros is a god. To prove this to Socrates, she asks if he denies that all gods are happy and beautiful. After Socrates responds with an emphatic "no, by Zeus," he goes on to agree that "the happy" are those who possess the good and beautiful things. Having agreed that eros needs and desires what is beautiful and good and that gods do not need what is beautiful and good, Socrates concludes that eros cannot be a god (202b8–d8). Through Socrates' challenge, Diotima admits that correct opinion, as such, is unreliable. When confronted by contradictory "correct" opinions, Diotima brings them together and invites Socrates to choose among them. She leaves it up to Socrates to say whether he is more certain that the gods can lack anything beautiful and good or that eros is a god. Upon a moment's reflection, he readily finds that he is more firmly convinced that the gods are beautiful and happy than he is that eros is a god. As much as eros may seem to be brought on by the presence of a god, he cannot conceive of a god who is not beautiful and happy. By working through Socrates' contradictory opinions in this way, Diotima cannot, of course, demonstrate the complete truth about the gods.

This sort of dialectical conversation cannot be counted on to disclose any final, objective truths about the subject; yet it can reveal what Socrates most deeply believes is true. If he responds consistently, both in words and in action, he might reveal a priority or hierarchy of opinions that would enable one to say something about the rank of *his* beliefs and desires. Diotima's exchange with Socrates thus provides us with a model for scrutinizing the entire conversation: If his eros is based on contradictory "correct" opinions, then his education consists in working through the contradictions and disclosing what he loves and needs most deeply. This would not, of course, prove that he understands himself or that his desires reflect a universal and unchanging human nature: our opinions and desires might be decisively shaped by history or language or some other force. But Diotima's questions and observations reveal Socrates' deepest concerns and point to one of the most important uses of Socratic conversation.

Having been persuaded that eros is not a god, Socrates asks whether it is mortal. Diotima responds that eros is "between mortal and immortal" and that it is a "great daimon" that is between "god and mortal" (202d8–e1). Socrates then asks what power it has (202e2), perhaps because he suspects that the gods are too lofty and too perfect to care about us and wants to know if the quasi-divine daimons have the power to help us or perhaps because he finds it unintelligible to speak of beings who are "between" mortal and immortal. Diotima replies that the daimons have the power to interpret and carry to the gods our requests and sacrifices as well as to interpret and carry back to us the gods' orders and "exchanges for sacrifices."[6] Confirming her earlier implication that she thinks the gods are too perfect to interact with man, Diotima notes expressly that "a god does not mingle with a human being." Rather, "the whole communion and conversation of gods with human beings" takes place through the daimons who "bind up the whole" (203a1–4). Socrates next asks Diotima to tell him who the father and mother of eros are. By asking about the genealogy of eros, Socrates points to a difficulty with saying that the daimons are between the mortal and the divine. Diotima's answer suggests that his father, Resourcefulness, is a god, and his mother, Need, is not a goddess. But this reply points to a difficulty: if the gods are too perfect to "be with" or have intercourse with mortals, why would Resourcefulness have intercourse with Need or with any other daimons? Recognizing this difficulty, Diotima says that to seduce Resourcefulness Need had to wait until he became drunk and sleepy (203b5–c1). Only if the perfect beings become drunken and imprudent can lesser beings have intercourse with them. In light of these difficulties, Diotima offers the young Socrates an account of eros that does not require that he regard it as an independent, willful, supernatural being. Eros may be "between mortal and immortal" in that it is an "immortal" attribute in the "immortal" species of mortal man. Nonetheless, Diotima avers that eros links us to the gods.

## THE BIRTH AND NATURE OF EROS

At 203b, Diotima and the young Socrates begin to discuss the birth and nature of eros. Contrary to Nussbaum and others who suggest that Plato uses the term *eros* to mean desire in general (e.g., Cornford 1971, 123–124, 129; Gould 1963, 110–111, 176–177; Santas 1988, 33–34, 172), Diotima speaks of eros as a single, particular desire, linked to but distinct from human sexuality and rationality. Eros is sexual in part because it begins at the "birth of Aphrodite" or at the inception of sexuality (203b2–3).[7] When we are children, we neither long for things with erotic intensity nor make noble sacrifices for the sake of beauty. Instead, we tend to be narrowly and even shrewdly concerned with ourselves. But when we begin to have sexual longings, the soul enjoys a sort of feast, a dreaminess and drunken confusion (203b3–7). Children who were once sensible become not simply disoriented, but also strangely troubled.[8] Diotima suggests that this adolescent melancholy is the first stirring of an inchoate but nonetheless profound sense of need. There is a specifically *erotic* need in the soul prior to the emergence of sexuality which we either do not sense or else dismiss until we become intoxicated and lulled by sexual desire. At this point, the separate and preexisting need "seduces" our resourcefulness and together they "conceive" eros, bringing into being the state of soul in which the mind becomes concerned with meeting this particular need (203b7–c1). Moreover, sexual desire provides us with a strong sense of what is beautiful. Thus, even though our erotic and sexual desires reflect separate needs, they often share the same beautiful object.

But while eros emerges through sexuality, it always depends on beliefs or opinions. We love only what we believe we need and what we believe we have the resourcefulness to acquire. Should we believe that we are not in need or that we are powerless to acquire what we need, our eros dies (203d8–e5). While all lovers hold beliefs about what they need, some experience a kind of eros that emerges through an awareness of ignorance. This eros resembles Socrates: it is poor, dry, tough, shoeless, courageous, crafty, and a powerful hunter who "plots to trap the beautiful and good" (cf. 203c–d with 175a–b, 214a, 220bff.). Just as Socrates describes his knowledge of ignorance in the *Apology*, Diotima says that this eros is philosophic and "between" ignorance and wisdom. It appears to be wise insofar as it knows that it lacks wisdom and prudence about what is "beautiful and good" or about what is required to be a "moral man" or "gentleman" (203e–204a; cf. *Apology* 21d).

Upon hearing this account of eros, the young Socrates asks Diotima to explain who the philosophers are if they are neither ignorant nor wise (204a7–8). This question seems odd, as if Socrates did not hear her description of philosophy. Or perhaps he asks her to restate the relation of philosophy to eros because he does not yet understand how philosophy can be a form of eros. Socrates' suspicion or puzzlement about eros emerges more clearly after Diotima assures Socrates that eros is philosophic on the grounds that eros loves beautiful things and therefore loves the beauty of wisdom; Socrates next asks her to explain how this sort of eros is useful for human beings (204d3–11). He asks her to explain our passionate concern with *to kalon* (the beautiful or the noble) because he finds this particular aspect of erotic love unaccountable. He asks how it is useful because he understands why we love good things, for they are manifestly a means to our own happiness; but he does not understand why we care for beautiful or noble things, for they bear no obvious relation to our own well-being (204d1–205a4).[9] Far from dismissing our willingness to put aside our good for *to kalon* as foolish, Socrates seeks out Diotima because he knows that he cannot account for this willingness on his own (206b5–6). He turns to a priestess for guidance because he wonders if eros is a divine power that moves us to love things other than our own well-being in a way that is beyond the ken of merely human reason.

Diotima, however, denies that eros is beyond our understanding and claims instead that it follows from our most fundamental erotic desire for good things as a means to our own happiness (205a–206a). According to the priestess, eros for *to kalon* leads us to a happiness that is complete. Because we naturally cast our thoughts to the future, we begin to desire a happiness that lasts; consequently, we also come to desire immortality as a means to that end (200d, 206e–207a). We love beauty because it is a means to the immortality that is itself a means to lasting happiness. Diotima's explanation of why we love beauty depends on the assertion that each of us is "pregnant" in body and in soul and that in giving birth we become immortal. We find beauty useful because in its presence we can give birth. Strictly speaking, we love not beauty, but the immortality which beauty makes possible (206b–207a). This does not, of course, satisfy Socrates (206e6), for Diotima has not explained what it means to be pregnant in the soul, nor how giving birth makes us immortal, nor how beauty helps us give birth.

## EROS AS GENERATION

Yet, instead of discussing eros for beauty, or even eros in human beings, Diotima begins the second part of the discussion by drawing Socrates' attention to the strange disposition of animals whenever they procreate. She describes eros as a bestial, subrational instinct in animals to have sexual intercourse, procreate, and nurture their offspring even if they must fight, starve, and die in order to do so. Diotima does not say directly that human beings have this animalistic eros, but only that one might suppose that we are erotic in procreating and caring for our offspring from calculation (*logismou*) (207b6–7). Leaving aside for the moment why we sacrifice for our children, she asks Socrates what causes this "erotic disposition" in animals. When Socrates cannot explain it, Diotima asserts that we are willing to sacrifice ourselves for our offspring because of our "mortal nature." In man as in beast, the "mortal nature" seeks to exist always and to be as immortal as possible. This mortal nature is capable of achieving immortality only through a process of generation that always leaves behind a new, young replacement of the old (207c8–d3).

She says that our mortal nature strives for immortality and not only generates our children but also regenerates "us" at virtually every moment of our lives. We are far more mortal than we realize: Although we say that "each animal lives and is the same," each animal is always "becoming young" in some ways while "suffering losses" of hair, skin, bones, blood, and the whole body. We change so frequently that we do not fully or truly exist from moment to moment. It is somewhat fictitious to speak of a particular man as if he were the same individual from when he is a child until he is an old man, for he is never quite the same (207d4–6). We change constantly not only in body, but also in soul. Our "ways, character, opinions, desires, pleasures, pains, and fears" are "never present as the same for each," but are "partly coming to be and partly dying." Because the things we experience in the soul change continuously, our mortal nature wants to restore all our former "ways, character, opinions, desires, pleasures, pains, and fears." What is even more strange, we continuously lose and gain not only different branches of knowledge, but also every particular piece of knowledge.

Although we may think we retain a lasting body of knowledge, all our thoughts are new thoughts masquerading as their predecessors (207d6–208a7).

Diotima says that each mortal thing preserves itself through the "device" of leaving behind "another young thing that is as it was" so that "the mortal" can share in immortality "in body and in all the rest" (208a7–b3). "The mortal" is a powerful love of things that are like what we are and what we have been that urges us to procreate and rear children who are like us so that it can live on in someone who is like us but who does not die when we do. Since our bodies, souls, and thoughts are always dying and being reborn, our actual "deaths" do not change our condition as significantly as we imagine. From the point of view of "the mortal," giving our lives for our children is not so different from an old hair falling out to make way for a new one. The sacrifices we seem to make of our bodies, souls, and thoughts are not sacrifices at all but, instead, "the mortal's" means of immortality.

Diotima concludes this part of her argument by saying that "everything honors its own offspring naturally" because "this seriousness and eros" attend everything for the sake of immortality (208b4–6). But Socrates is so astounded that he asks her, "really, wisest Diotima, is it truly like this" (208b7–9).Why does Socrates ask her if she is telling the truth? Having been convinced that we love the good for the sake of happiness, Socrates may doubt that lovers are moved to sacrifice themselves for their offspring for the sake of "the mortal's" immortality. Insofar as we have natural needs and desires, we want not merely to stay the same, but also to satisfy our needs, ease our pains, and improve ourselves. Instead of being the mere epiphenomena of "the mortal's" longing for lasting sameness, we are living beings who want happiness. Moreover, insofar as we are conscious of ourselves as subsisting beings who are distinct from our children, Diotima understates the significance of our deaths. Death seems terrible to us not only because it ends our experiences and thoughts, but also because we do not know whether we will still exist in some way after we die and whether we will be happy or miserable (*Apology* 42a, *Republic* 386b–7d). Moreover, Diotima has pointed to significant problems with the belief that we can attain the immortality that would make our sacrifices for our offspring acceptable.

Diotima describes the soul as if it were the same as our "ways, character, opinions, desires, pleasures, pains, and fears." The things we experience in the soul, our "ways, characters, opinions," and even our thoughts, are experienced through the perception, desires, pleasures, pains, and fears that we feel because we have human bodies. Even if our souls are immortal, the mortality of our bodies means that when we die we lose the physical experiences which make us what we are. Insofar as we have a deep and powerful love of what we are, of all our own things, death is necessarily a great loss. By understating the significance of death, Diotima understates how remarkable it is that we are willing to die for our offspring. Since we are thinking beings (207b7) and aware of our mortality, why do we love our children so much that we are willing to die for them? It cannot be that we simply do not care about dying or that we completely identify ourselves with our offspring. We have a fundamental desire to preserve and improve our own selves, our own bodies, souls, and thoughts, as long as possible. No merely physiological or biological account of eros can explain why we human beings are willing to die for our loved ones, because no merely scientific account takes into consideration our thoughts about death, our hopes about the future, and our concern with beauty. This account's failure to explain why lovers sacrifice for their beloveds or what role beauty has in eros apparently provokes Socrates' challenge.

## EROS AND COMPENSATION FOR DEATH

Diotima begins to present her full explanation for why we love *to kalon* at 208c, where she says that we take risks, exhaust wealth, work relentlessly, and even give up life itself because we love honor, renown, and "immortal fame" above all else. Would Alcestis have died for her husband, she asks, or Achilles died to avenge Patroclus, or the Athenian king Codrus died to save his kingdom, if they did not believe that there would be an "immortal remembering" of their virtue (208d)? Some commentators have been shocked by Diotima's assertion that heroes perform magnificent acts on the condition that they be honored. Dover, for example, remarks that "the notion that she [Alcestis] would not have died for Admetus had she not been sure of posthumous fame" seems "grotesque" to us (1980, 152). Surely, those who seek mere fame must be distinguished from true lovers of *to kalon*. Yet Diotima stresses that everyone does everything for the sake of immortal virtue and for the reputation it brings and that the better one is, the more one acts in this way (208d–e1)—in fact, she will later claim that even those who pursue *to kalon* itself love some things because they are more honorable than others (210d). Moreover, Socrates does not make any objection to this argument, even though he questions her previous argument by asking bluntly if she is telling the truth (208b).[10] Why might Socrates or Plato accept such a teaching? When one looks carefully at Diotima's statements and examples of those who love fame, one discovers that she does not claim that heroes like Alcestis act solely to win honor. Like Phaedrus (179b3–c3), Diotima says that Alcestis also died for the sake of both virtue and her husband Admetus (*huper Admetou apothanein*) (208d2–4). While one could object to Diotima that noble virtue is choiceworthy for its own sake and should be pursued without regard for fame, one must also concede that we are deeply distressed at the thought that someone might die for the sake of virtue without being remembered or memorialized in any way. While we do not admire glory hunters, we sense, like Phaedrus, that those who sacrifice for virtue or to save others deserve to be honored rather than cast into oblivion. Diotima merely contends that heroes recognize the enormity of their sacrifices and would find them unbearable were it not for the consolation they find in the belief that their decision to die will not be utterly forgotten. They do not die to become famous; rather, the small consolation they take from being remembered helps them find the strength to die for virtue or for their loved ones. Remembrance is a necessary but not sufficient condition for heroism.

If Diotima offers this account of eros for heroic virtue and fame as a paradigm for erotic love, then eros appears to be a response to the prospect of death. Although we do not face death as directly as Achilles and Alcestis, we are moved by their dilemmas because we are dimly aware that we, too, must die. Shaken by this, we take comfort in the heroes' courageous decision to die nobly rather than to preserve their lives, for they conform to our sense that death is not the worst of all fates and that one can be stronger than death. Like the hero, we find beauty or nobility appealing, not because it provides us with "literal" immortality, but because through caring for it we somehow find death bearable. Qualifying her earlier teaching that we love *to kalon* because it is a means to immortality, Diotima now indicates that we love it because it compensates us for mortality. But exactly what solace does beauty provide that makes death easier to bear? How do we come to be moved by or eager to be *kalon*? The provisional answer seems to be that by nature we seek good things as a means to lasting happiness (200d, 206e–7a) until we confront our mortality. Without being fully aware of it, our anguish at the prospect of death makes the pursuit of merely useful or good things seems fruitless and mundane, a wearisome treadmill. As our erotic desire for something more than the useful grows stronger, we turn our attention to things which seem beautiful, appealing in their own right (e.g., *Republic* 357b; see Pangle 1988, 292–293 n. 8). Thus, it is only after sexuality gives eros its opportunity to emerge, and provides us with an experience of something beautiful, do we begin take beautiful things with the great seriousness that is characteristic of eros.

Eros, however, is not merely a desire to possess beautiful things, but also a desire to perform beautiful actions that would lend beauty to our lives. In what sense are actions beautiful? When we see someone react to danger not with fear, but with calm assurance and by keeping one's wits about one, we find this courage appealing, attractive, even beautiful; similarly, we find cowardice somewhat ugly and pitiable. Given this sense that some actions are beautiful, some of us, shaken by our awareness of mortality, seem to think that if acting prudently cannot bring us lasting happiness, then perhaps acting beautifully can, if only for a moment, endow our lives with some meaning, some resplendent quality, some virtue, that would make life beautiful and worthwhile in itself. Some therefore desire to act beautifully in the hope that this permits them to transcend their insatiable desire for lasting happiness. In fact, men and women like Achilles and Alcestis desire to become *kalon* so much that they willingly lay down their lives in magnificent acts of heroism. These men and women are not lovers of fame, but lovers of beautiful or "noble" virtue who nonetheless find death terribly anguishing and who assuage their grief with the thought that their deaths at least permit their names to survive, even if they themselves cannot.[11]

Insofar as erotic love provides a powerful desire to act nobly and to win esteem, it is not surprising that it can move men like Codrus to sacrifice heroically for their political communities. Yet the impact of eros on politics goes beyond this, for Diotima says that the best love affairs culminate in lovers who bring forth political vision. Some are pregnant in soul with *phronesis* or "prudence," the "practical reason" that indicates how to arrange and order "households and cities" and that is called "moderation and justice" (209a3–8). Longing to give birth to their political offspring, they seek out a beloved who is endowed with both great physical and psychic beauty. When they find such a human being, they are "fluent in speeches about what virtue is," about "what sort the good man must be," and about what he must do (209b7–c1). They do not, however, seek out such beauties merely for the opportunity to articulate their political and moral views. They try to use their notions of virtue and the good life to educate, transform, and perfect their beautiful but not yet fully formed beloveds (209c1–2). But the lover does not simply impose his understanding of virtue on the beloved. The lover also "engenders" his offspring (his virtue) by touching and associating with his beloved, so that they can generate the offspring "in common" (209c2–4). Lovers expect physical and psychic intercourse to let them share, magically, daimonically, in their beloveds' beauty (202e–203a, cf. 175d3–7), just as Alcibiades expects to share in Socrates' beauty (217–219). Insofar as eros is for *to kalon*, we love those who have a kind or a degree of beauty which we lack (219e; Santas 1988, 32). Diotima's remark at 206d that we suffer and cannot give birth until we are in the presence of beauty means that we are afraid to act heroically or to pursue noble ambitions until we believe we share in and are transformed by the beauty of those we love.

While some slake eros through heroism or political deliberation, the greatest erotic satisfaction appears to come from law giving. Diotima asserts that everyone envies poets and founders of cities whose "offspring" are more beautiful and "more immortal" than human children. Especially envied are Solon, Lycurgus, and other Greeks and barbarians who establish the law, for they not only perpetuate their virtue and names, but also are worshipped like gods (209e).

## EROS BEYOND POLITICS

One might conclude from Diotima's teaching that law giving provides the best possible solace for death and hence that Socrates emerged from this conversation with a powerful erotic desire to legislate in an actual city—except that Diotima adds that there is a different, arduous path, rarely taken, that may lead one to the perfect goal of eros (210e, 211b). The path is the famous ascent by which the lover pursues a series of love affairs with ever more beautiful objects until he or she finally encounters the "beautiful itself," the *monoeidos* of beauty. After having "intercourse" and procreating "true virtue" with it, one may be loved by a god and immortalized (212a). Because this brief, "mysterious" passage describes the culmination of erotic desire, because it discloses the ultimate object of eros, it has long been the focus of controversy. Some contend that Diotima is promising Socrates that if he apprehends the beautiful itself, he can know and instill true virtue in the souls of others and thus achieve posthumous fame and influence greater than that possessed by any poet or lawgiver (Hackforth 1950, 44; Kraut 1973, 339 n. 7). But this interpretation does not account for everything in the passage, since it does not explain how being loved by a god contributes to one's immortality (O'Brien 1984, 198). Moreover, if eros is a desire for immortality, it is not clear how achieving even the greatest posthumous fame and influence could be said to achieve the "perfect goal" of eros. Others interpret the passage to mean that philosophers achieve immortality by participating in the immortality of the ideas (Bury 1932, xliv–xlv; Schleiermacher 1836, 280; Shorey 1933, 196). As Rosen explains, the philosopher first possesses the immortal through "intercourse" with the beautiful itself, through a sudden, immediate apprehension of the immortal ideas. This temporary moment of immortality can be recovered by making "virtuous speeches of truth." Through this combination of apprehension and speech, the desire for immortality may be satisfied "without denying that man is essentially a resident of genesis" (Rosen 1987, 275–276). But like the first interpretation, this also fails to explain how being loved by a god plays a role in becoming immortal. In addition, if eros is rooted in the desire not to die, it is not clear how apprehending an immortal idea during one's finite life gratifies that desire or consoles our anguish at death. Finally, this interpretation fails to explain why the philosopher loves the idea of the beautiful in particular. Were Diotima claiming that one becomes immortal by participating in the immortality of the ideas, one would expect her to say that philosophers love the ideas for their intelligibility and immortality. Yet she stresses that they love the idea of the beautiful, the most beautiful of all ideas, more than any other (210e, 211c–d, 212a1). It is the surpassing beauty of this particular idea that promises immortality. The question recurs: How does beauty help one become immortal?

The only interpretation that accounts for the whole of the passage is offered by O'Brien, who takes Diotima to mean exactly what she says: if Socrates mixes with the beautiful itself and brings forth true virtue, a god might reward him with immortality (O'Brien 1984, 198–199). One achieves the perfect goal of eros with the help of a god, because only divine intervention could transform us into immortal beings (180b).[12] This revelation qualifies her earlier teaching that we love *to kalon* rather than the good because we wish to transcend our futile pursuit of lasting happiness. Although we may want to love something beyond our own good and beyond ourselves, we never fully surrender the hope that we do not have to die. The hero's longing for a lasting reputation, for merely a shred of immortality, signals an irrepressible hope that we can escape death.[13] But how does the lover of the beautiful itself escape death? What *kind* of virtue wins immortality? Is it active, political virtue? Do erotic philosophers want to rule actual cities? Or is true virtue apolitical (e.g., *Republic* 519d–e)?

Even though Diotima says very little about true virtue, she indicates its meaning by telling us that it comes from intercourse with the beautiful itself. Earlier, she claimed that we seek intercourse with a beautiful human being because we hope that it will enable us to bring forth virtue that shares in his or her beauty. She now suggests that intercourse with the beautiful itself would enable one to bring forth from within oneself a true virtue that shares in its true beauty. But what is so unique, so overwhelming, so true about its beauty? Diotima says that the beautiful itself is wholly separate, unchanging, and pure; it cannot be found in anything particular, such as in a body or action or speech, but is always "alone by itself and with itself," always in "one form," never changing even though all the other things that share in its beauty come into being and pass away (211a–b). Ross calls this the most transcendent account of an idea in all of Plato (Ross 1951, 21). Why would one find this extremely separate and transcendent entity so awesomely and surpassingly beautiful (210d, 211e)? In part, *because* it is so separate and transcendent. Diotima calls it "pure, clean, unmixed, and not infected with human flesh, colors or a lot of other mortal foolishness" (211e). True beauty is that which rises above the particular, the physical, the practical, the mortal, the human.

If one loves the beautiful itself for the same reason one loves beautiful human beings, then one loves it in order to share in its beauty and become like it. One assimilates to the beautiful itself by first loving beauty in a body and by then abandoning that love affair because it is contemptible and petty to care for only one body. After loving many beautiful bodies, the initiate next must love someone for the beauty of soul—because the soul is more honorable than the body. The initiate must next forsake loving human beings altogether and begin loving beauty in actions, laws, and sciences. One must subsequently stop loving all particular things, including all particular actions, laws, and sciences, since concern for them is "servile and slavish," and turn instead to the immense "sea of beauty." At this stage, one can practice the "one philosophical science of beauty" and encounter the beautiful itself (210d). As in traditional mystery rites, this ascent to philosophy is a process of purification. At each stage, the initiate becomes purer and more beautiful by loving purer and more beautiful things (Santas 1988, 43–45). Finally, one gives birth to true virtue when one casts off all concern with "worldly" things and devotes oneself to the universal, non-material, "non-practical," immortal, and "suprahuman." As a result, those who love the beautiful itself and manifest true virtue disdain politics and ruling. To turn one's eyes to politics, to the realm of the particular, the practical, the mortal, the human, is to lose that which makes life bearable and worthwhile, for life is worth living only when one gazes at and couples with the beautiful itself (211d–e, 212a). But should one have intercourse with the transcendent beautiful itself and give birth to offspring that share in its suprahuman virtue, one might be loved and immortalized by a god.

Is it possible that Diotima really teaches this apolitical and suprahuman account of true virtue? It sounds foreign to both the traditional Greek and as well to the Socratic treatment of virtue (as we know it from other Platonic dialogues).[14] On the other hand, this account of true virtue accords with what Diotima teaches about the gods, for if the gods do not mix with human beings (*theos de anthropoi ou mignutai* 203a), it makes sense that one must rise above one's humanity to be loved by them. While the mature Socrates may not accept this utterly apolitical and suprahuman account of virtue, perhaps the *young* Socrates, the "pre-Socratic" Socrates, did. On the day of his death, Socrates says that in his youth he was a student of nature and that he thought that knowledge of the causes of each thing was "splendid" or "magnificent" (*Phaedo* 96a5–10). He was in particular a student of the natural philosopher Anaxagoras (*Phaedo* 97b). According to the Athenian Stranger in Plato's *Laws*, philosophers such as Anaxagoras (cf. *Laws* 886d with *Apology* 26d) believe that the natural things are far greater and nobler than those produced by human artifice. Among these latter, merely "human" things they place the gods and justice. They regard them as mere conventions because human beings "are constantly disputing with one another and changing these things and whatever changes they have made at a given time are authoritative, having come into being by art and by the legal conventions, but of course not by any nature" (*Laws* 889e3–890a2; see also Aristotle *Nicomachean Ethics* 1094b14–17, 1141a20–b8; Antiphon 44; Heracleitus 102; Pangle 1976, 1065). The impious, apolitical, proud "Socrates" who is ridiculed in Aristophanes' *Clouds* is precisely this sort of natural philosopher or scientist (Aristophanes *Clouds* 94–104, 223–226, 367ff., 901–902, 1201–1203, 1399–1400, 1421–1422, 1428–1429). Thus, Socrates' admission that he admired Anaxagoras leads one to suspect that he once resembled the natural philosopher portrayed in the *Clouds* more closely than is ordinarily thought (Guthrie 1971, 102; Strauss 1959, 92).[15] In fact, the *Symposium* alludes to Socrates' familiarity with natural science and even contains an assertion that Aristophanes' depiction of Socrates in the *Clouds* is at least partly accurate (175d and 221b; also, e.g., *Lysis* 214a–b; Xenophon *Symposium* 7.4–5). Moreover, Socrates' account of the origin of his philosophic activity in the *Apology* claims that it began when the Delphic Oracle replied "no" to his companion Chaerephon's question whether anyone is wiser than Socrates; but this claim is inadequate, for it fails to explain what led Chaerephon to ask such a question. Since the *Clouds* identifies Chaerephon as Socrates' partner in the morally dubious study of natural philosophy, the implication appears to be that he posed the question because he was impressed by Socrates' "pre-Delphic" wisdom in natural philosophy (Strauss 1983, 41; West 1979, 107).

## *The Erotic Need to Philosophize About Political Things*

If the young Socrates were this sort of natural philosopher, he would share Diotima's belief that true virtue is apolitical and suprahuman (e.g., *Republic* 486a). In saying at 212b that he is persuaded by Diotima, Socrates indicates that he recognizes his own love of wisdom in her account of eros for the beautiful itself, that he is not only curious to know the causes of each thing, but also deeply in love with the *beauty* of wisdom (cf. *Parmenides* 130b–e). Moreover, by acknowledging the truth of her teaching, he concedes that he loves "beautiful" wisdom because he believes that his love for it makes him noble (Bruell 1987, 104–105; see, e.g., *Phaedo* 69b–e, 63e–69e passim, and *Republic* 500c–d.) If Socrates accepts the pious Diotima's account of eros as an account of his own, youthful love of the ideas, then he suddenly recognizes that his intense devotion to philosophy is at least partly based on a hidden expectation that philosophy makes him so noble that he deserves not to die and that there exists a loving and just god who will not let him die undeservedly.

Receiving this teaching from Diotima does not end Socrates' education in erotics; rather, his *response* to this teaching transforms him into the mature Socrates. As a young man, he may have accepted the natural philosophers' skeptical view that justice and providential gods are mere conventions, products of human hope and fear. Yet his discovery that he harbors beliefs about these things in his own heart confirms that natural philosophy alone does not comprehend and debunk them. Furthermore, although he may suspect that his eros for immortality is merely hopeful, he is too open-minded, too cognizant that he has just learned not to trust his conclusions without circumspection, to dismiss the possibility of that there are gods who reward us with immortality for noble virtue. Indeed, his own sense of justice and piety may be a divination or reflection of the existence of such gods. With clarity unprecedented among philosophers, Socrates now sees that his own immortality and well-being depend on a thorough investigation of the meaning and status of noble virtue, justice, and the gods who are said to uphold it.

The *Symposium* points us toward the next step in his erotic investigation. Prior to praising eros (198d), Socrates explains that his speech will be overly beautiful and implies that we need to think critically about it to recover his full understanding of eros. If Diotima taught him this excessively beautiful account, then he must have learned to question it on his own to become an expert in erotic matters. Desiring immortality, he must have eventually wondered whether his dedication to the beautiful itself would be likely to lead to immortality. His prospects for immortality depend on his claim to love nothing physical nor practical nor particular nor human. Yet does not his desire for immortality suggest that he still cares for his own particular existence? Even if he despises the body and wants to exist without it, it seems that the body is a source of the "desires, pleasures, pains, and fears" that shape our "ways, character, and opinions," which, according to Diotima, constitute the soul (207e, *Phaedo* 83b5–c8). In other words, his desire to be immortalized as a particular being, as *Socrates*, means that he has a lingering attachment to things that are rooted in the mortal body. One might argue that he could transcend concern for his own particular and physical existence were he to aspire to some kind of "impersonal" immortality. Yet Diotima indicates that our anguish at death is relieved only by the thought that *our* children or *our* fame or *our* influence will survive indefinitely (207–208). Even the initiate who ascends to the higher mysteries seeks to become more noble and more honorable (210d) by loving the beautiful itself, not merely because this consoles him or her for death, but because this promises the perfect fulfillment of eros (210e, 211b); and this perfect fulfillment consists in not having to die, in achieving the literal, genuine, immortality that only a god could grant (212a). The very aspiration to merit immortality as a *reward* for noble virtue implies that one hopes to enjoy that reward and hence to continue to exist in some intelligible sense after death. Should Socrates see that his relentless desire to live beyond death belies his claims to transcend concern for every particular thing and to love only the beautiful itself, then he will recognize that he cannot expect a just god to reward him with immortality.

The less likely it seems to Socrates that dedication to the ideas makes him immortal, the less he can love the ideas specifically for their abstract beauty. To the extent that he remains erotic, he must wonder if other ways of life or other kinds of noble virtue make plausible claims to a god's reward. But the more he reflects on the various forms of eros for *to kalon*, especially on the hopes that animate heroic and political virtue, the more evident it becomes that Diotima's account of eros for the "beautiful itself" not only reveals the "moral" roots of the philosopher's eros for the ideas, but also radicalizes the problem of eros for *to kalon*, as such. Insofar as we identify *to kalon* with self-transcendence and self-sacrifice, it is impossible for us to pursue *to kalon* at the same time we pursue our own good (203a, 220e–221a)—thus Diotima omits even to mention "the good" or happiness in the last part of the speech, which describes eros for *to kalon* by itself. It may be in light of this opposition between the noble and the good that Diotima says in the *Symposium* (203) that the philosopher must become a "hunter" of that which is noble and good and that Socrates says in the *Apology* (21d) that he knows of nothing, of no way of life, that is *both* noble and good. This is disturbing because, as the young Socrates says, we seek both *to kalon* and the good in order to be "happy and blessed" (202e). Yet the difficulty deepens as one recognizes that eros for immortality leads us to understand *to kalon* to mean not simply that which is intrinsically worthwhile, but that which entails self-transcendence and self-sacrifice, because we believe that these things deserve reward

(179c, 180b, 193a–b, 208d–e, 209e, 212a, 220d–e). At the root of eros for *to kalon* lies a hidden sense of justice, a conviction that great sacrifices made for the sake of virtue or to save others deserve and must receive some reward. Because of this confidence in justice, eros for immortality makes us love *to kalon*, not because it allows us to forsake good things, but because, without being fully aware of it, we think that *to kalon* permits us to acquire good things (immortality and happiness) that we cannot obtain on our own. If, as Diotima suggests, we love *to kalon* as *the* means to lasting happiness, then we never love *to kalon* alone, by itself. We believe that we can secure our lasting happiness by putting this concern out of our minds. But insofar as our love of the noble emerges from this beginning, we are compelled to ask if we can ever fully transcend it. Granting that we are inevitably concerned with our own well-being, perhaps we could do or pursue things that are *kalon* but which do not require us to sacrifice our own good. Perhaps we could understand *to kalon* to mean that which is both intrinsically good for us and yet also useful to us for other things (e.g., *Republic* 358a). Impressive qualities such as the ability to keep one's wits about one in a moment of crisis or the capacity to understand the causes of things may fall into this category. But at this point another disturbing, yet necessary, erotic question must be raised: are such beautiful qualities or capacities, strictly speaking, genuinely noble or deserving of just compensation? Can one expect to be rewarded by a god for dedicating oneself to *to kalon* if this dedication is fully compatible with one's own well-being? The more that Socrates comes to see the difficulty in claiming that his dedication to *to kalon* is noble or deserving of reward, the more he must doubt that he can do anything to earn or assure his immortality. But if he comes to believe that he has no means to immortality, must he ultimately despair? According to Diotima, he need not, for if one knows that one lacks the resourcefulness to gratify eros, then eros will die (203e1–3). By thinking through the problems with the arguments that underlie his hopes for immortality, by thinking through the "problem of the noble," Socrates may eventually become convinced that he lacks the means to deserve immortality and that he must, inevitably, die; and, having learned that he must die, having faced his mortality, Socrates would cease to love *to kalon* as a means to immortality. And it is this change in what Socrates himself loves after reflecting on his eros that would constitute the single greatest piece of evidence in support of Socrates' emerging understanding of eros.

Scholars have long recognized that the *Symposium*'s teaching that the soul is mortal conflicts with other dialogues, especially the *Phaedo*, which argues for the immortality of the soul; R. Hackforth wonders if Plato wrote the *Symposium* during a temporary moment of doubt (Hackforth 1950, 45; 1955, 21; Rosen 1987, 276 n. 157). Yet scholars now question whether the *Phaedo* seriously teaches that the soul is immortal. According to Jacob Klein, Socrates speaks of two kinds of immortality in the *Phaedo*. The first kind is that of a particular soul that exists through time, entering a body during life and departing for the next world at the approach of death. But Klein argues that the arguments offered in support of this type of immortality are neither fully cogent nor persuasive. Socrates never establishes the immortality of the individual soul through time (Klein 1965, 137–138, 146–148; see also Ahrensdorf 1995, 91–113; Bolotin 1987, 46, 51). The second kind of immortality is the soul's desire and capacity to apprehend the intelligible, permanent beings; there is a "part" of Socrates that exists after he no longer exists: it is human nature's enduring inclination and ability to comprehend the truth that transcends time and place (Klein 1965, 131–132, 149). But how, one wonders, could this ability to perceive the ideas gratify eros, which the *Symposium* identifies as the desire not to die? How does it ease one's anguish at the prospect of mortality? It is far from clear that our desire not to die is reducible or equivalent to the desire to apprehend the unchanging character of permanent beings. Perhaps Klein would explain that philosophy does not satisfy the individual's desire not to die; instead, philosophy provides Socrates with an "adult sobriety," a "serenity in gravity and jest," and a "pleasure in learning" that strengthen and console him to the point that he can accept his mortality and "learn how to die" (Klein 1965, 148; *Phaedo* 67d–e). But no matter how invigorating and comforting philosophy may be, the *Symposium* suggests that the hope for lasting happiness, the anguish at death, and the aspiration to win immortality through the noble are so deeply rooted in the soul that one may need to permit them to "surface," take them seriously on their own terms, and think them through before one can scrutinize and, if necessary, to the extent possible, correct them. Diotima's account of eros inflates Socrates' deepest and perhaps wildest hopes until, strengthened and consoled by philosophy, he cannot help but see their deficiencies.[16]

Yet if Socrates suspects that our eros for individual immortality cannot be gratified, why does he claim that philosophy gratifies eros? While explaining to Socrates why we love beautiful as distinguished from good things, Diotima describes eros as a desire for immortality that manifests itself in several ways: as the sexual, reproductive instinct that we share with animals, as a desire for beauty that can compensate us for dying, and finally as an ambition to be beautiful or noble enough to deserve immortality. But looking more carefully at the passage in which Diotima describes eros in a way that resembles the mature, Platonic Socrates (203), one notices that she does not say that it is a desire for the beautiful itself or for nobility by itself. Nor does she claim that eros seeks to procreate or to achieve immortality. Rather, she says that eros is a desire for that which is both *kalon* and good, for something whose beauty or nobility does not promise personal immortality but accompanies and adorns what is good for us. Perhaps Socrates becomes cognizant and desirous of this beauty as the result of his doubts or uncertainty about ever achieving the immortal bliss described at the end of Diotima's speech as well as the suprahuman wisdom said to be at the top of heaven in the *Phaedrus*. Even though he may be saddened to think that his progress toward perfect wisdom may be ended before its completion by death, he can still find enjoyment in reflecting on the extent of his progress toward that goal. By reflecting on Diotima's teaching, Socrates finds that the object of his own eros changes. And these changes confirm the most important elements of her teaching. They show that we do love what we believe we need and that we need not only what is noble, but also that which is good for us. He finds, in others words, that reason is able to comprehend and correct his eros for noble virtue. Reason is able to provide him with a kind of "psychology" of eros or of the soul. But this surpasses the sort of account of interior causes and effects which tends to characterize modern psychology. For in his process of *self*-examination, Socrates takes his bearings by his own sense of nobility and has thought it through "on its own terms." Based on his own experience and understanding of the noble, he finds that he loves the *kalon* not by itself but only in conjunction with what also makes him good. He thereby acquires a self-knowledge or wisdom that appears to him to be both splendid or admirable or noble on the one hand and useful or good on the other. In fact, wisdom seems to be one virtue in particular whose beauty is not diminished by the thought that it is pursued prudentially, out of the ever present need for what is good for oneself (cf. *Laches* 192d–193e; *Republic* 334b, 358b). When comparing what he knows with what others do not, Socrates finds his condition intrinsically admirable and takes pleasure in it, even if no one else recognizes it as such (*Apology* 21d1–3).[17] By making Socrates *kaloskagathos* in this sense, philosophy can be shown to gratify at least one natural desire that comes to sight through eros. The mature Socrates may thus enjoy and take pride in gathering particulars together and separating them into their natural kinds, since this is the kind of knowledge available to us in this life (*Phaedrus* 249c). If the mature Socrates ceases to love the ideas as a means to immortality, he need not stop loving them altogether; in fact, he may grow to love them in a "purer" sense, simply because they gratify his desire to understand the whole. Socrates will continue to speak and think in terms of universals, for both language and thought itself may lead one to do so. But Socrates will understand the universals more clearly, for he will no longer disdain to study particulars as a means to understanding the ideas nor avert his attention from those ideas which are not beautiful (*Parmenides* 130c–e). In notes appended to the second edition of his book on the *Symposium*, Rosen challenges Diotima's claim that the objects of philosophic thought must be beautiful and complains that she offers no argument for her contentions. He writes that Diotima fails to prove "the ostensibly beautiful nature of knowledge of things other than beauty" (Rosen 1987, 338 n. A). But perhaps Rosen cannot find Diotima's argument for her equating eros for "the intelligible" with eros for beauty because Diotima is not describing the eros for the intelligible or for the truth, regardless of its beauty, that animates a complete, mature philosopher. Her statements do, however, make sense if she is describing one who loves wisdom for its beauty and for the nobility or virtue which wisdom seems to confer on the knower. And it is precisely this eros for the beauty of wisdom which Parmenides attributes to the *young* Socrates and which he distinguishes from philosophy per se (in fact, earlier in their conversation at 204d, the young Socrates objects when Diotima identifies eros for the beauty of wisdom with philosophy). Parmenides tells the young Socrates that his attraction to only beautiful ideas, together with his revulsion at ideas of ugliness, prevents him from becoming a genuine philosopher (*Parmenides* 130c–d).

Socrates' transformation changes not only his love for philosophy or wisdom, but also his stance toward other human beings and their beliefs. Socrates seems to have learned erotic matters by discovering the problematic character of our unreflective love of *to kalon* and by awakening a desire to know what is truly beautiful and good; but how does he *know* that he has loved *to kalon* as a means to immortality? that reason now fully illuminates his needs? that he is not still driven by other longings whose influence remains hidden from him (*Phaedrus* 230a)? How does he know that his apparent transformation is not due to some veiled form of "will to power?" Or to some arbitrary quirk in his own character rather than to his having come upon the deepest needs of human nature? How does he know it is not a symptom of his corruption or fallen nature? Perhaps others have experienced inspirations or divinations that reveal more fully the true human situation.

Precisely because his education in erotics teaches him to be skeptical about his own thinking, he must become the "fierce hunter" who relentlessly plots to trap and take apart the "noble and the good" (203) as he and others understand it. Liberated from his youthful assumption that philosophy alone is noble and good, he now examines the claims of non-philosophers, of politicians, poets, craftsmen, and gentlemen, to be noble and good and to know of gods who oversee and reward their actions (*Apology* 21c–22c; Xenophon *Oeconomicus* 6.13–17). Freed from his youthful contempt for particulars, he tests his understanding of eros by conversing with particular human beings. The dialogues show him exploring in great detail how a variety of concrete, particular human beings experience and understand *to kalon*.

One indication that the mature Socrates has been transformed from the devout lover of the beautiful itself into a fierce hunter of noble virtue, justice, and the gods comes to sight as one reflects on how the mature Socrates describes his "expertise" in the *Symposium*. If he simply accepts Diotima's account of expertise in erotic matters, he would presumably agree that it culminates in apprehending the beautiful itself and in giving birth to wisdom that partakes of its beauty (210d6–e1, 211c3–d1, 212a5–6). But while Socrates twice claims that he is an expert in erotic matters (177d7–8, 212b5–6), he never claims to have seen the beautiful itself and tells both Agathon and Alcibiades that his wisdom is doubtful, disputable, and perhaps not even *kalon* (175e, 216d, 219a). His education in erotics has culminated not in beautiful knowledge of the beautiful itself but in the discovery that his wisdom may not be *kalon*, for he has learned the problematic character of *to kalon*, and in the further discovery that his wisdom is disputable, for he knows that his understanding may be distorted by unrecognized hopes and expectations.

The *Symposium* shows that not only the mature Socrates' arguments but also his actions are inconsistent with Diotima's teaching. If he believed that he might win immortality by devout contemplation of the beautiful itself and by disdaining everything particular, physical, practical, and human, how could he readily and cheerfully end his solitary thinking earlier than usual (175c) merely to go to a banquet? Would he eagerly seek out conversations with non-philosophers like Alcibiades (222b)? In fact, he seeks out such conversations because he has learned that he needs to scrutinize the relation between *to kalon* and the good and that he can do this best by confirming his thinking by examining the others who love *to kalon*. Alcibiades' description of Socrates points to the kind of testing that took place in those conversations: For example, to confirm that our opinions about *to kalon* guide what we love, he changes Alcibiades' opinions about what is noble and thereby changes what he loves (216a–b). Throughout the dialogue, Socrates' demeanor indicates that he is not deeply moved by *to kalon*. He is insultingly unimpressed by Agathon's "beautiful" wisdom (175e) and rhetoric (at 198c2–5 he compares listening to Agathon's speech to being in Hades) and by Alcibiades' youthful beauty (219c–d). Moreover, he openly concedes that he is not ordinarily beautiful but must "make himself beautiful" (174a) to attend the banquet. Although the *Symposium* shows Socrates making a beautiful praise of eros, it also contains Alcibiades' reminder of the character of most Socratic conversation: Socrates forever talks about "pack-asses, blacksmiths, shoemakers, and tanners" (221e). He relies on examples of the practical or useful to guide his conversations because he has learned the importance, even the primacy (205–6), of the good in our lives. Accordingly, he blames Alcibiades for neglecting his own needs (216a5–6) and praises him when he prudently pursues what is good for him (218d7–219a1). As one recognizes the difference between Diotima's presentation of philosophy as eros for the beauty of wisdom and the mature Socrates' "critical distance" from *to kalon*, one discovers a further reason why Socrates attributes his speech to Diotima. The speech is merely the beautiful part of the truth about eros (198d); although it truthfully articulates the hopes that underlie eros for *to kalon*, it lacks the critical scrutiny of that longing that marks Socrates' mature understanding of erotic matters.

Because Socrates' primary erotic goal is to examine how and why human beings love *to kalon* so that he might learn how to guide his own life, his arguments are not always be meant to teach or to advise. He makes abstract, implausible, contradictory, even irresponsible arguments that may be impractical for guiding one's life or one's city but that are very practical for revealing both his various interlocutors' concerns and also the practical power of rational argument to affect those concerns.[18] Even though the transformation in Socrates' eros focuses his attention on learning how he should live rather than on ascending to what Nussbaum calls a "world without happening" or on legislating for actual cities, he is now more willing to take part in actual politics than when he was young. No longer assuming that practical, political, human concerns are servile or base, he is free to assist his fellow citizens by showing them what is questionable about the city's dominant opinions about noble virtue, the gods, and justice. Equipped by the inquiry into the beautiful and good with a rich and subtle account of the *psyche*, the Athenian Stranger in the *Laws* demonstrates the general guidance a Platonic philosopher might offer to actual statesmen or lawgivers.

Yet certain difficulties remain. At the conclusion of Socrates' speech, the narrator of the dialogue tells us that while most of those present were impressed, Aristophanes was dissatisfied and wanted to respond (212c4–6). Explicitly in the *Clouds* and implicitly in his own speech, Aristophanes accuses Socrates of being ignorant about eros, offensive to the gods, and a corrupter of political life. Presumably, his rebuttal would explain how these charges have not been fully met by Socrates' speech. But before he can say anything, Alcibiades bursts in and absconds with the conversation. Although we do not know for certain what Aristophanes objects to, the very fact that Plato shows us that he has objections warns us not to accept Socrates' account of eros too readily. Aristophanes' explicit objections are not, however, lost. They are presented by that which substitutes for them in the drama: Alcibiades' praise, criticism, and reaction to Socrates. The notorious Alcibiades is said to be Socrates' beloved, lover, and student. Socrates' failure to educate Alcibiades to virtue raises questions not only about whether Socrates can educate others, but also about whether he is correct that the deepest need in human nature is an erotic desire to know how to be noble and good. Alcibiades' ultimate rejection of the Socratic life and frustration with Socrates may be due less to his own deficiencies as a student than to the inaccuracy or inhumanity of Socrates' understanding of the soul and its virtue. In order to satisfy the doubts of Aristophanes, of his fellow citizens, and of contemporary readers, Plato must explain how Socrates' manifest failure with Alcibiades does not undermine but somehow affirms that Socratic philosophy is needed to comprehend, gratify, and perfect the soul.

# CHAPTER 6

# *Alcibiades' Education to Virtue*

Alcibiades is one of the most prominent characters in the Platonic corpus. In fact, after Socrates himself, he may be the most significant character in all of Plato's writings. He is the only person whom Socrates ever claims to love (*Gorgias* 481d; *Protagoras* 309a–b; *Symposium* 213c). He is the only person whom Socrates assiduously tries to educate and who eventually goes on to a prominent political career. Because the dramatic date of the *Alcibiades Major* is the earliest of all Plato's dialogues, it appears that Socrates chooses to speak with Alcibiades in his first significant conversation as a mature, dialectical, political philosopher.[1] Finally, Alcibiades' many years of close association with Socrates entitle him to give, in his speech near the end of the *Symposium*, the single most memorable praise of Socrates' way of life.[2]

While Plato draws our attention to Socrates' enduring interest in Alcibiades, the lessons we are to take from it are ambiguous and even troubling. For the object of Socrates' great and persistent attention appeared so lawless and ambitious to his fellow-citizens that even though they recognized his outstanding political skills and followed his advice, they nonetheless accused him of impiety and treason and condemned him to death (Thucydides 6.27–29). In fact, Socrates' influence on Alcibiades seems to be a principle reason that Socrates was condemned of corrupting the young (Plato *Apology* 33a–b; Xenophon *Memorabilia* 1.2.12).[3] Plato's presentation of Socrates' association with Alcibiades does not obviously or simply exculpate Socrates from the corruption charges. Plato portrays Alcibiades not only as passionately concerned with acquiring noble things such as glory and virtue, but also as very eager to follow Socrates' guidance. But Plato's Socrates does not seem to act very responsibly or kindly in his dealings with Alcibiades. Socrates convinces Alcibiades that he needs Socrates' help by stirring the young man's ambition to rule the world while denigrating the authority of Athenian law and democratic approbation. In the end, Socrates never teaches him what he needs to know but seems only to mock Alcibiades' weakness. It may, of course, be Alcibiades' rather than Socrates' fault that Alcibiades fails to understand what Socrates tries to teach him. But even if this proves to be the case, Alcibiades' failure to absorb a Socratic education calls into question whether those who passionately desire the noble things in fact need a philosophic education and thus whether Socrates knows human nature and its virtue. In either case, the existence of Alcibiades points to important problems with Socrates' claim that by nature philosophy is *the* means to genuine nobility and goodness. By bringing Alcibiades into the *Symposium* immediately after Socrates claims to know erotic matters, Plato reminds us that we cannot claim to know whether Socrates knows erotic matters until we consider the implications of his failure to educate Alcibiades to virtue.

The challenge that Alcibiades poses to the claims of Socratic education is not lost on Socrates' modern critics. According to Nietzsche, Socrates and Alcibiades represent two opposite human possibilities. Socrates, the first theoretical man, exemplifies the superficiality, the utilitarianism, the vulgarity, of rationalism. Alcibiades, on the other hand, is the outstanding example of antiquity's instinctual, healthy aristocrat. Nietzsche claims that great individuals such as Alcibiades do not emerge from aristocratic classes until the class as a whole has begun its descent. In an earlier age, aristocrats would have shrugged off Socrates' questions or merely played with them, as a new form of wrestling. But in Socrates' time, the aristocratic class was no longer instinctually healthy. The souls of the members of that class had declined into a painful and dangerous chaos that welcomed the tyranny of Socratic rationalism. Alcibiades, however, is a late but even stronger example of aristocratic greatness (*Beyond Good and Evil* 200). One sign of Alcibiades' outstanding virtue appears to be that he ultimately shrugs off Socrates' questions.

More recently, Garagin and Nussbaum have argued that the *Symposium*'s portrayal of the relationship between the philosopher and the young statesman reflects an insurmountable gulf between philosophy and human affairs. According to Garagin, Socrates' absorption into the higher reaches of philosophy prevents him from communicating with non-philosophic youths such as Alcibiades (Garagin 1977). Nussbaum argues that Alcibiades and Socrates are in the grip of two distinctly opposite and irreconcilable kinds of eros and thus that they possess two separate kinds of understanding and ways of life. Alcibiades is moved by an emotional, personal, particular love for Socrates as a "whole person." Socrates, on the other hand, flees unsteady emotions fraught with pain by devoting himself to the impervious joys of contemplating the abstract, universal beings. But in doing so, Socrates loses touch with the character of contingent things and thus becomes not only unwilling but also unable to provide Alcibiades with the human guidance he needs (Nussbaum 1986).

In order to understand Plato's account of Socrates' failure to educate Alcibiades to virtue, it is necessary to focus on two dialogues in particular, the *Alcibiades Major* and the *Symposium*. The *Alcibiades Major* recounts Socrates' initial meeting with Alcibiades and how Socrates convinced the young man of his need for a Socratic education. The *Symposium* recounts the breakdown of their association and helps us understand the obstacles that prevent Alcibiades from learning what he needs from Socrates.

## THE *ALCIBIADES MAJOR*

The *Alcibiades Major* was judged by ancient and medieval scholars such as Albinus and Farabi to be the proper introduction to the Platonic corpus (Forde 1987, 222; Pangle 1987, 3). Yet for over a century scholars have rejected the dialogue as spurious, not because they find internal, textual evidence of anachronism, but because they deem its substance unworthy of Plato. Schleiermacher, for example, says of the *Alcibiades Major*

> This little work, which, with those who are accustomed to admire in the gross, has been ever a subject of most especial commendation, appears to us but very insignificant and poor, and that to such a degree, that we cannot ascribe it to Plato, even though any number of those who think they can swear to his spirit, profess most vividly to apprehend it in this dialogue. (1836, 329–330)

More recently, however, some scholars have begun to reconsider this verdict and cite the dialogue in their surveys of Plato's political thinking.[4] It is the goal of this chapter to show that a sufficiently careful, dramatic reading of the dialogue reveals enough of the dialogue's subtlety and importance to explain why readers over the centuries considered it one of Plato's most helpful dialogues. I will try to show that even if the dialogue was not written by Plato himself, it reflects a sufficiently profound understanding of Platonic political philosophy to help us recognize the significance of what transpired when Socrates first convinced Alcibiades to become his student.

The dramatic date of the dialogue is approximately 430 B.C., when Alcibiades is in his late teens and Socrates, his late thirties (*Alcibiades Major* 131e). Socrates' stated reason for engaging in the earliest dialogue recorded by Plato is that Socrates is Alcibiades' first, most faithful, and truest lover and now hopes to win Alcibiades' love by offering to teach what he needs to know to rule the "Greeks and barbarians" (103a). Socrates explains that he has followed Alcibiades for years but has never spoken to him before because "the god" has up until now prevented him from speaking. Socrates notes that all of Alcibiades' other lovers have given up trying to seduce him. They left because they despaired of overcoming Alcibiades' extraordinary sense of self-sufficiency, which he displayed by reminding his suitors of his good looks, family, and wealth (103b). Socrates says that he differs from the others in that he believes that Alcibiades is not satisfied with these possessions (105a). According to Socrates, the sign of Alcibiades' dissatisfaction with himself is his ambition to rule the world. Socrates' attempt to win Alcibiades' love is based on the hypothesis that because Alcibiades is ambitious, he must be moved by an unrecognized but powerful and needy erotic desire. This suggests that there is more at stake in Socrates' proposition to Alcibiades than his romantic success. If Socrates' arguments can undermine Alcibiades' apparent self-satisfaction and can reveal a deeper need to know how to be noble and good, then Socrates will have taken an important step in verifying that human nature is fundamentally erotic, just as Diotima taught. But if Socrates cannot move Alcibiades, it would suggest that Aristophanes is correct, that men such as Alcibiades are driven by the spirited pride of our "ancient nature" or perhaps by something such as what Nietzsche calls "instincts." Socrates remarks at 105e that he alone can provide Alcibiades with the education he needs to accomplish his goals and that he hopes to be to Alcibiades what Alcibiades wants to be to Athens. Since Alcibiades wants to rule Athens, perhaps Socrates means that he wants to rule Alcibiades as a way of ruling Athens. Or perhaps he means that he wants to learn if he can make Alcibiades need Socrates' beauty in the same way that Alcibiades hopes to make Athens feel the need for his beauty.

After Alcibiades agrees to answer a few questions, Socrates asks him what kind of expert advice he plans to give the Athenians. Accepting Socrates' premise that statesmen need to give expert advice, Alcibiades answers that he will advise them about war and peace and more specifically about what is just and what is unjust. In response to Socrates, Alcibiades concedes that he cannot be an expert in justice if he has never learned it from others or experienced the need to study it on his own. Yet Socrates observes that Alcibiades has always thought he knows what justice is. He says that when he watched Alcibiades playing games as a young boy he observed how Alcibiades protested loudly when he believed he was treated unjustly. Alcibiades responds emphatically that he was right to complain when treated in an unjust way (*Alcibiades Major* 110b). Alcibiades' enduring indignation at his playmates' failure to respect the rules in a childhood game may seem trivial or petty, but it casts light on Alcibiades' understanding of justice. It tells us that he understands justice to consist in abiding by rules that limit us as we compete for our own advantage. The function of such rules seems to be to make the competition orderly; but if the object of the game is simply to win, why should Alcibiades be angry at those who surreptitiously break rules to achieve their goal? Why are they obligated to respect the rules when they have the opportunity to circumvent them? Alcibiades evidently believes that obedience to the rules serves a further purpose: He believes that obedience to the rules confers honors on one's playmates. By obeying the rules, he shows respect for others and expects them to do likewise to him. Obedience to rules not only makes games more orderly, but also confers mutual respect on all participants. This respect is the common good that one cannot acquire outside the game itself. Those who cheat are unjust in that they accept the good, the honor, that he pays them while failing to give him the honor that he expects in return. Applying this understanding of justice to politics, citizens would obey laws that restrict their individual advantage as a means to securing honor from one another. Were Alcibiades to doubt the importance of being respected by his fellow citizens, he would presumably be far less attached to justice and less restrained in pursuing his advantage.

Since Alcibiades must acknowledge that he has never doubted his knowledge of justice, it appears that he must also acknowledge his ignorance. But Alcibiades cleverly suggests that he absorbed his knowledge of justice from the people, much as he learned the Greek language (*Alcibiades Major* 110e). In response, Socrates induces Alcibiades to agree that even though the people may know some things, they cannot be presumed to know things about which they disagree violently, such as justice (112d). In the face of this argument, Alcibiades acknowledges his ignorance about justice, but he dismisses it on the grounds that even though the Athenians talk about justice and injustice they care only about their advantage (113d). When asked by Socrates where he learned what is advantageous, Alcibiades tries to deflect the question, thus suggesting that he is untroubled by his ignorance and that he is not, after all, moved by an eros to know how to be noble and good. In response, Socrates offers to prove to Alcibiades that the "just things" are advantageous and thus that his ignorance of justice extends to what is advantageous (113d–114b).

Socrates begins this proof by clarifying Alcibiades' understanding of the just, the noble, and the good. Alcibiades believes that all just things are noble but that there are some noble things that are bad and some shameful things that are good. Alcibiades may have in mind such things as his father's death in battle, which seems manifestly just and noble but, nonetheless, bad or disadvantageous (*Alcibiades Major* 116b). In order to investigate the relation between what is noble and what is good or advantageous, Socrates asks specifically about the nobility and the badness of rescuing one's friends and relatives in battle. Alcibiades readily agrees that courage is the noble thing that shines forth in rescuing friends and that it is readily distinguishable from what is bad about rescuing friends, namely, losing one's life. Socrates next leads Alcibiades to agree that noble courage is most desirable and one of the best things, along with life itself, and that base cowardice is one of the least desirable and worst things, along with death. Through a series of short questions, Socrates leads Alcibiades to agree that the nobility of rescuing friends (courage) is altogether good, while the badness that follows from rescuing friends (death) is altogether bad. Socrates also induces Alcibiades to agree that noble things produce only good things and that shameful things produce only bad ones. The implication of Socrates' argument seems to be that insofar as rescuing friends in war produces good things, it cannot also produce bad ones. In saying that rescuing friends in war is noble but bad, Alcibiades argues, in effect, that it is both good and bad. But having agreed that what is noble cannot be bad, Alcibiades must also acknowledge that nothing noble is bad and that nothing shameful is good (116b).

Even though Alcibiades goes along with Socrates' arguments in this passage, he does not seem to be altogether persuaded that noble things are never bad. His responses are guarded and grudging. While Alcibiades cannot put his reservations into words, it is not difficult to imagine why he may not yet be convinced by Socrates. For in addition to being abstract, Socrates' arguments seem somewhat tendentious. Socrates begins his refutation by suggesting that the nobility of rescuing comrades is readily distinguishable from the badness of such acts. It is true that what we admire in the courage of heroes is not that they are injured or killed but that they manifest great strength of soul in coming to the aid of others. Nonetheless, Socrates seems to mislead Alcibiades when he argues that courage is *utterly* separate from what is bad. For we do not recognize courage in others unless we see that they persevere in the face of great danger or suffering. Nor do we draw on our own courage unless we must endure hardship ourselves. We may admire the skill of those who save lives, but we are not moved by the nobility of their courage unless we see them working in circumstances that burden or threaten them. Insofar as courage manifests itself only to the extent that one experiences bad things, there is always some badness in showing courage no matter how much we desire it. Another aspect of this same problem emerges from Socrates' proof that courage is among the best things. Alcibiades understandably says that he wants to be courageous and counts it among the best things. When Socrates asks what price he would accept to give up his courage, Alcibiades says that he would choose to die were he a coward. Socrates then induces Alcibiades to say that courage and life are together among the best things and cowardice and death among the worst. But in equating the goodness of courage with the goodness of life, Socrates covers over the one bad aspect of being courageous, namely, that one may have to forfeit of one's life to manifest it. Similarly, in simply equating the badness of death with the badness of cowardice, Socrates conceals the one good consequence that seems to come from shameful cowardice, namely, that through it one at least remains alive (*Alcibiades Major* 115b).

After hurrying through this series of questionable arguments, Socrates offers another that claims to prove that the noble things are good (*Alcibiades Major* 116b–d). He begins by drawing Alcibiades' attention to the belief that to act nobly is "to act well" (*eu prattei*). He then notes that we say that to act well is to be happy, that having good things makes one happy, and that acting well and nobly makes one happy. He concludes that since to act well is thought to be both good and noble, the noble is the same as the good and is thereby advantageous. Since they have already agreed that justice is among the noble things, justice, too, must be advantageous. At this point, Alcibiades sees that his original argument that justice can be both noble and bad has been fully reversed, curses vehemently, and exclaims that he does not know what he has been talking about. Alcibiades is not comforted by Socrates' argument that the noble things are always good because he is not yet convinced that this is so. But he does recognize that he does not understand these matters as well as he thought. Socrates appears to confuse him by exposing a difficulty with Alcibiades' initial understanding of nobility. For Alcibiades regards some noble things, such as courage, to be most desirable even though they are in some respects bad for him. At the same time, he believes that being courageous and noble is an important part of leading a full and happy life. Because Alcibiades has never reflected on how noble courage contributes to our ultimate happiness, because Alcibiades has never reflected on what it means to be a virtuous or happy human being, he is unable to counter Socrates' arguments and must confess his ignorance.

In response to Socrates, Alcibiades acknowledges that he is not only confused but also poorly educated. Yet Alcibiades is strikingly unperturbed by this revelation. He accepts that his competitors are uneducated and concludes from this that he is certain to best them because of his superior nature (*Alcibiades Major* 119b–c). Because Alcibiades is not troubled by his ignorance of how to be noble and good, he seems to contradict Diotima's teaching that an awareness of such ignorance will spark erotic love. Rather than give up his investigation, however, Socrates reprimands Alcibiades for having forgotten that his rivals are not his fellow Athenians but the Spartan and Persian royalty. Socrates stops asking short questions and makes a long speech about the lineage, upbringing, and grandeur of the Spartan and Persian monarchies. Compared to them, Alcibiades' nature is undistinguished and very much in need of the compensatory effects of education. Socrates asks Alcibiades to imagine what a Persian queen would expect of a Greek who aspired to compete with her son for empire. Socrates says that she would expect the Greek to have cared for himself and to have acquired wisdom, acts at which the Greeks excel, and would be aghast to learn that someone like Alcibiades dared to rival her son. Socrates commands Alcibiades to obey him and the Delphic Oracle by learning to know himself, since this is his only means of acquiring the power he seeks. Socrates concludes by saying that if Alcibiades fails to care for himself, he will not satisfy his erotic longing for renown among Greeks and barbarians, an erotic longing that is greater than anyone has ever had for anything (121a–124c).

Upon hearing this long description of his relative natural deficiencies, Alcibiades is won over completely. He asks how he is to care for himself and affirms that Socrates speaks the truth. Having elicited this request, Socrates finally makes Alcibiades feel erotic. Alcibiades did not care that he could not explain what is noble and good because he was convinced that his nature was sufficiently noble and good. But when Socrates forces him to doubt the nobility and goodness of his nature, he is shaken and responds with a needy, passionate desire to learn how to be noble and good. This speech has two important effects. Firstly, it finally confirms Diotima's teaching that erotic love depends on the *belief* that we lack something we need to be noble and good. Alcibiades loves what he believes he needs but lacks. Secondly, this speech marks the beginning of Alcibiades' education to virtue. By awakening him to his ignorance and need, he begins to desire to learn what is truly noble and good. Yet the argument that shatters Alcibiades' confidence is problematic. For it is not clear from what Socrates says that the Persians and Spartans are endowed by nature or by birth with genuine virtue. In the course of describing the Persian monarchs' good upbringing, Socrates casts doubt on their good natures by mentioning that they have a whole class of servants whose job it is to "straighten limbs" (*Alcibiades Major* 121d–e). In order to prove the purity of the Spartan monarchy's lineage, Socrates notes that the Spartans scrupulously guard their queens to prevent them from committing adultery. But in order to prove the purity of the Persian line, Socrates points to the opposite practice, to the presence of guards, to demonstrate that the line must be untainted. Most importantly, in persuading Alcibiades of the superiority of his foreign rivals, Socrates emphasizes his rivals' extraordinary wealth (122e–123b). The fact that Alcibiades believes that wealth reflects virtue not only betrays Alcibiades' superficiality, but also raises new questions about the character of Socrates' erotic love for him. At the outset of the dialogue, Socrates claims to love Alcibiades because he sought rivals beyond Athens and never imagined that his wealth was anything great (103b–4c; 104e). But Alcibiades' youthful confidence is now shown to have rested on his belief that his superior wealth reflects his natural superiority to his fellow Athenians. One would expect that this would cool Socrates' eros for Alcibiades—and yet Socrates continues to say that he loves Alcibiades and converses with Alcibiades for years (*Gorgias* 481d; *Protagoras* 309a–b; *Symposium* 213c). This raises the possibility that Socrates continues to pursue Alcibiades, not because Socrates cares for him in the admiring way that most lovers care for their beloveds, but because talking with Alcibiades gratifies Socrates' erotic desire to know what moves human beings such as Alcibiades. For no matter how questionable Socrates' arguments may be, the fact that they undermine Alcibiades' helps to shed light on the roots of our eros to be noble and good. Vlastos claims that Socrates is guilty of "intellectualism," that is, of focusing entirely on the argument "without paying any attention to the deeds or actions of individuals" (Vlastos 1971, 54). Yet Socrates tells Alcibiades that he has been watching him for years without speaking to him (*Alcibiades*

*Major* 103a, 104d, 106a, 110b). Plato's dialogues reflect Socrates' deep, abiding interest in both the words and actions of his interlocutors.

Whereas Alcibiades seemed boyishly indifferent to how he contradicts himself throughout the earlier part of the dialogue, he now is alarmed at his lack of education about what is just and noble and good and advantageous. When he asks for help, Socrates replies that they must deliberate together about how to acquire virtue. At this point, Socrates confesses that he does not yet possess the knowledge that Alcibiades needs. He does, however, claim that his guide in this quest, the god or daimonic voice, is better than Alcibiades' guide, Pericles (*Alcibiades Major* 124c, 103b). In response to this, Alcibiades says that Socrates is joking. Socrates acknowledges that he may be joking, but he asserts once again that they need to take care about themselves.

After securing Alcibiades' agreement that they want to become as virtuous as possible, Socrates asks to which virtue they aspire. Alcibiades answers that they should have the virtue of those who are "noble and good" or who are "perfect gentlemen," a virtue which turns out in his view to be the virtue of knowing how to rule one's fellow citizens (*Alcibiades Major* 124d–125d). This statement casts light on Alcibiades' ambition. For it tells us that he has all along wanted to rule because he believes it will show that he is "noble and good." Prior to talking with Socrates, Alcibiades believed that he was by nature noble and good but had not yet displayed it. By exposing the sense of need that animates Alcibiades' desire to rule, Socrates raises the further possibility that Alcibiades wants to rule to answer his own, unrecognized, doubts about his virtue.

Accepting Socrates' premise that the good ruler must be "sensible" and have a certain kind of knowledge, Alcibiades explains that the good ruler knows how to give "good counsel" about managing and preserving the city. Just as the art of medicine brings health to a body, the art of ruling brings friendship and agreement to the city (*Alcibiades Major* 126a–c). But knowing the art of ruling entails not only knowing the goals of ruling, but also knowing how to accomplish those goals. Socrates notes that we rely on mathematics to agree with one another and even to agree with ourselves when confused about measurement. But in cities it is not clear how agreement is reached. Socrates secures Alcibiades' agreement that the friendship and agreement of a city is like that of a family insofar as it comes through a common understanding. But Socrates notes that even within the family there are divisions of labor and of expertise. As he has already implied, those who are experts in one art necessarily neglect the other arts (125a, 127a). If agreement depends *entirely* on knowing the same things, then specializing in separate arts would seem to undermine the agreement that holds the family together. Similarly, in cities friendship would vanish to the extent that each citizen "does his own things." But Alcibiades objects that cities are best managed when each citizen practices his own things. In fact, citizens are just when they "do their own things" rather than those of others and it is through this specialization that friendship comes into cities. At this point Socrates observes that Alcibiades has contradicted himself again by claiming that civic friendship comes both from knowing one thing and also from knowing different things. Alcibiades complains that he does not know what he is talking about and now concedes that he is in a most shameful condition (127b–d).

By weakening Alcibiades' conviction that he knows how to manifest virtue, Socrates makes Alcibiades feel even needier than before. Socrates' arguments not only demonstrate how Alcibiades' awareness of his ignorance inflames his desire to learn, but also point to a problem with Alcibiades' assumption that he can acquire virtue by learning only about justice. The city is based on a division of labor in which each citizen specializes in a specific art to provide for his or her own needs. If the citizens' friendship and agreement comes from specializing in practicing different arts and in learning how to bring about different goods, then to be just is to become an expert in securing a part, a fraction, of the whole human good. Thus, it would seem that the virtue of any particular citizen is but a fraction of the whole of human virtue (Aristotle *Politics* 1276b37–1277a14) and thus that one cannot become a good human being *solely* through being just. One might reply, as Aristotle himself suggests, that those who rule the whole city would not specialize in particular arts and could be in a position to know all the arts and the whole good (1277a14–25). But would not the ruler's failure to specialize in particular arts render superficial that ruler's knowledge of those arts and of the goods they produce? This difficulty is suggested by Aristotle himself, when he remarks that rulers require a special education. He quotes a king in one of Euripides' plays who says "No subtleties for me, but what is needed for the city" (1277a19). By adducing this quote, Aristotle indicates that even the ruler's special education is incomplete. If one seeks knowledge of the whole good, one must look beyond what one learns through justice alone. As Socrates tells Alcibiades, it is only after completing a suprapolitical education to virtue can one responsibly enter politics and attempt to lead others to virtue (*Alcibiades Major* 134c).

Upon recognizing that he does not know how to rule, Alcibiades curses, laments that he does not know what he has been talking about, and remarks that he has not even noticed his most shameful condition. Socrates reassures him that his is the proper age to discover his ignorance about himself and to care for himself (*Alcibiades Major* 127d–128a). In order to help Alcibiades learn to take care of himself, Socrates asks what it means to care for oneself. Socrates pursues this by drawing Alcibiades' attention to how the various arts care for what we own, but not for "the self itself." In order to discover which art allows one to care for the self, it is necessary to learn what "the self itself" is (129b). In searching for this, Socrates notes that in their conversation there has been a "Socrates" who uses speech to talk to Alcibiades and an "Alcibiades" who uses speech in reply. He also notes that this user appears to be something other than the body, since the body is sometimes sacrificed for the sake of something else. According to Socrates, that which uses speech and the body is the soul and thus the soul is the self. Socrates notes that the argument may not be conclusive, because instead of defining the self they have merely delineated each of the parts of the self (130d). In other words, Socrates is aware that he has not proven that there is one, fixed, autonomous, "centered" user of speech and of body that is the soul. Various forces, instincts, and even inspirations could shape the self in ways that belie Socrates' suggestion that the soul is the single, unified user. But Socrates' conversation with Alcibiades as a whole suggests that Alcibiades is moved by one thing above all, by an eros to know that one is noble and good. Alcibiades' response to Socrates' questions and speeches supports

Socrates' hypothesis that eros guides the soul and in that sense is the self.

Socrates encourages Alcibiades to look at himself with his own soul (130e). He notes that no one knows himself through any of the arts such as medicine, gymnastics, and farming (*Alcibiades Major* 131b). Socrates then identifies self-knowledge with the virtue "moderation" and concludes from this that no one can become moderate through the arts. Because one cannot acquire self-knowledge or moderation through the arts, the arts are base (131c). The money-makers, whom Alcibiades presumably regards as the epitome of vulgarity, care for money but do not care for their own things. Socrates compares them to lovers of bodies who love what belongs to their beloveds but do not love their beloveds' souls. Such lovers are inconstant because they love an inconstant thing, while lovers of the soul are steadfast because they love something lasting. Insofar as Socrates loves Alcibiades' soul, he is Alcibiades' only true lover (131e).

Socrates warns that his great, remaining rival for Alcibiades' eros is "the many" (*Alcibiades Major* 132a). Socrates does not explain why Alcibiades is likely to be tempted by their love. He may mean that Alcibiades will be tempted to believe that his doubts about his own virtue can be overcome by popular acclaim. According to Socrates, the antidote consists in remembering that he needs a suprapolitical education in order to rule. Otherwise he will never care for himself or for others. In order to learn to care for himself, he must first see himself. Yet it is impossible to see oneself directly. Socrates compares the difficulty of knowing oneself with the difficulty of the eye seeing itself. He says that the eye cannot see itself by itself, but must look at itself in the eyes of another. More precisely, the eye must see itself by looking at the place in the eye that sees. Similarly, the soul cannot see itself by itself, but most look into the soul of another and especially into the place in the soul that knows. To know oneself, one must look into the wisdom of others, for this is most divine virtue, just as the mind is the most divine part of the soul (133b).[5] Thus, Alcibiades needs to look to Socrates' wisdom to gain the self-knowledge he needs to rule and to manifest virtue. Now, Alcibiades goes along with this argument even though Socrates does not explain why it is impossible to know oneself directly or why one can know oneself only by looking into someone else's wisdom. One possible meaning of such claims emerges, however, when we recall what leads Socrates to confer with Alcibiades in the first place. Socrates needs to converse with others to confirm what he learned about eros from talking with Diotima. Because he does not know for certain that he is moved by an erotic desire to know how to be noble and good, he must test others to see if their concern with noble things is also rooted in this same erotic desire. By looking into Alcibiades' mind, Socrates finds that Alcibiades cares about the noble things to the extent that he believes he needs and lacks them. Insofar as Alcibiades appears to be moved by the same erotic desire to be noble and good that moves Socrates, Socrates is able to confirm his knowledge of the soul.

Socrates concludes by arguing that those who lack self-knowledge should not even rule themselves, but should be ruled by those who know. In response, Alcibiades vows that he will follow Socrates in order to learn moderation much as Socrates has followed Alcibiades for years (*Alcibiades Major* 135d). This final pledge offers yet another demonstration of Socrates' knowledge of eros, for it shows that Socrates is able to alter what Alcibiades loves by altering his opinions about what he needs and what is noble and good. On the whole, this conversation supports the "psychology" that Socrates derives from Diotima's teaching in the *Symposium*. But Socrates signals his full awareness that it is difficult to see the soul directly and decisively. Moreover, the very doubts about cause and effect that led him to question the decisiveness of natural philosophy (*Phaedo* 95e ff.) also call into question any merely psychological account of the causes and effects in the soul. Socrates' success in turning Alcibiades' soul around supports his hypothetical understanding of the soul, but it is imperative that Socrates take additional steps to support his belief that the philosophic life is the indispensable means to being noble and good. In light of this, Socrates must be curious to learn whether Alcibiades' own independent experience and understanding of what is noble and good differs from his own belief that wisdom is *the* preeminent virtue of the soul. Near the end of the dialogue, Socrates leads Alcibiades to agree that wisdom is the most divine virtue and that the mind is the most divine part of the soul (*Alcibiades Major* 131b). But does Alcibiades genuinely believe that this is so? Or is he merely swept along by the torrent of Socratic argument? It is plausible that Alcibiades believes that the gods are wise. But why should he agree that they are not equally courageous or just or moderate? Looking at Alcibiades' confusion about the nobility of courage as he understands it, we may discover a reason why he would not attribute that particular virtue to the gods. Insofar as Alcibiades believes that we manifest courage only when we are faced with death, he presumably thinks that courage in this sense is the preserve of mortal beings. The gods may be adamant, they may be caring, they may even suffer, but insofar as they never die, they cannot be said to experience the same anguish that mortal beings endure in facing death. Likewise, it is difficult to understand how and why the gods would be just according to Alcibiades' initial understanding of why human beings care about justice: if justice means abiding by an implicit agreement to limit oneself in competition with others so that all might garner mutual respect (110b), it is difficult to understand why sacred beings such as the gods would feel the need to make such an agreement to win our respect. Similarly, if we human beings turn to justice to meet our needs and practice justice by dividing up our labors and areas of expertise (126–127), it is difficult to understand why the gods would practice the same justice that we practice. Since it appears that Alcibiades himself would not claim that virtues such as courage or justice (as he understands them) are attributes of gods, and since Socrates easily wins his agreement that moderation is a form of self-knowledge, it seems that Alcibiades would not deny the Socratic claim that knowledge or wisdom is *the* preeminent, cardinal virtue of divine beings. Most importantly, Alcibiades' overall reaction to Socrates indicates that he needs and desires the kind of self-knowledge that Socrates appears to have acquired as he has thought through what he desires and loves. Thus, even were we to set aside the psychological insights that Socrates gains from talking with Alcibiades, we still see that Alcibiades does not advance and maintain any alternative to Socrates' understanding of virtue.

While Socrates ultimately fails to educate Alcibiades to virtue, his initial conversation vindicates much of Socrates' knowledge of the love of noble virtue. Even if the *Alcibiades Major* was not written by Plato himself, it nonetheless reflects a deep understanding of the purport of Socrates' first encounters with Alcibiades as Alcibiades describes them in the *Symposium*. It explores what transpired when Socrates first troubled Alcibiades deeply (*Symposium* 215c–e, 221e–222a). It depicts how Socrates made him powerfully aware of his ignorance and of his need to step away from politics and to seek a Socratic education (*Symposium* 216a–b). Despite all this, the *Alcibiades Major* shows signs that Alcibiades is not entirely persuaded by Socrates. For after Alcibiades agrees that he needs self-knowledge and wisdom before entering into politics, he remarks that he will next begin to study justice. It is at this point that Socrates expresses his doubts as to whether he will prove strong enough to save Alcibiades from the clutches of the city (*Alcibiades Major* 135e). The prospect that Socrates might fail to carry out Alcibiades' education to virtue raises important questions about the justice and prudence of the Socratic enterprise: If Alcibiades proves unwilling or unable to follow through on the education to virtue that Socrates proposes, Socrates will have undermined Alcibiades' initial motives for obeying the law and limiting his own advantage (110b–c) by weakening Alcibiades' respect for the judgment of the people (111e–112a) and by questioning the importance of winning the respect of his fellow citizens (120e ff.). In order to show that his own inquiries into erotic matters are politically responsible and just, Socrates must show that philosophy is able to lead one to justice.

# CHAPTER 7

# *Socrates and Alcibiades in the* Symposium: *The Failure and Triumph of Socratic Education*

While Schleiermacher disparages the previously venerated *Alcibiades Major*, he regards Alcibiades' speech in the *Symposium* not only as the crown of the dialogue but also as *the* single greatest account of the Socratic life in Plato's dialogues. He praises the way it

> exhibits Socrates to us in the unwearied enthusiasm of contemplation, and in joyous communication of the results, in the contempt of danger and exaltation above external things, in the purity of his relations, and in his inward divinity under that light and cheerful exterior; in short, in that perfect soundness of body and mind, and consequently, of existence generally. (Schleiermacher 1836, 278)

Despite Alcibiades' manifest admiration for Socrates in both the *Alcibiades Major* and the *Symposium*, the latter dialogue informs us that Alcibiades eventually gave up trying to learn from Socrates how to be noble and good. According to Alcibiades, his failure to learn from Socrates was not his fault. In fact, he promises in his speech in the *Symposium* not only to praise Socrates but also to take "vengeance" on him. On reflection, it turns out that the speech lays out a profound critique of the Socratic life. Alcibiades accuses Socrates of being hubristic and outrageous. He says that Socrates despises everyone and cruelly refuses to share his noble and divine secrets. He says that not even Socrates' virtues are worthy models of emulation, for they derive their strength from strange, inhuman powers. Perhaps Alcibiades bears most of the blame for being unwilling or unable to absorb what Socrates tries to teach him. But even if this were the case, Alcibiades' inability to learn from Socrates would cast doubt on his claims that human beings by nature are moved by an eros to be noble and good and that it is possible to cultivate and gratify this eros through philosophy. If Socrates cannot educate his gifted and erotic beloved to virtue, then perhaps Socrates cannot demonstrate that he *truly* understands eros. Perhaps our ambition to be noble and good is rooted in something "instinctual" or nonrational. Perhaps we seek a kind of knowledge that Socratic philosophy does not provide. Perhaps Socrates is liberated and gratified by philosophy only because he is not quite human (*Symposium* 215a, 221d; cf. Nietzsche *Twilight of the Idols* "The Problem of Socrates," 3). The goal of this chapter is to learn why Alcibiades fails to learn from Socrates and whether this casts doubt on Socrates' claim to know the soul and its virtue.

## ALCIBIADES IN THE *SYMPOSIUM*

To appreciate the significance of Alcibiades' speech in the *Symposium*, it is useful to recall the context of his entrance in the dialogue. Immediately after Socrates finishes recounting his education, Aristophanes tries to respond (212c4–6).[1] But before he can say anything, Alcibiades interrupts and prevents us from hearing Aristophanes' challenge. The very fact that Plato shows us that Aristophanes has objections warns us not to accept Socrates' account of eros too readily. The narrator of the dialogue, Socrates' disciple Aristodemus, infers that Aristophanes objects to Socrates' abrupt dismissal of his thesis that we love what is our own or what is kindred. Socrates had argued that our willingness to undergo amputation proves that we love "the good" rather than "one's own" (205d10–206a1). Aristophanes might respond that this very example proves merely that we will do anything for that which we consider most truly our own. We part with our limbs not because we are indifferent to what is our own, but because we want to keep our own selves alive. Aristophanes denies that we love others because we need nobility or immortality. Instead, we love the kinship we share with our other halves and would not be affected by thinking through our attraction to what is noble and good. According to Aristophanes, Socrates is thoroughly unerotic. He devotes himself to philosophy because of his spirited pride and hostility to the gods, whom philosophy debunks. In order for Socrates to give a truly satisfactory account of eros, he must account for the love of what is one's own in souls that reportedly long for noble virtue and happiness.

While it might appear that Alcibiades preempts Aristophanes' challenge to Socrates, on closer inspection it turns out that alongside Alcibiades' glowing praise of Socrates there can be found a serious critique of Socratic philosophy that Aristophanes himself might endorse. The opening of the dialogue is replete with literary touches that suggest that Alcibiades in part stands in for Aristophanes. Alcibiades enters the dialogue crowned with ivy, intoxicated and led by attendants, the very image of the god Dionysus (212d).[2] Alcibiades' resemblance to Dionysus links him to Aristophanes, not only because Dionysus is the god of theater, but also because Aristophanes claims to be the god's descendent in the *Clouds* (*Clouds* 509). Moreover, when Socrates accuses Alcibiades of trying to provoke laughter, Alcibiades, like Aristophanes, replies that he does not fear being laughed at as long as he tells the truth (214e). Alcibiades even quotes a line from the *Clouds* in order to convey Socrates' strangeness and inhuman coldness (221b). Yet Alcibiades stands in for Aristophanes, not only in some of the things he says about Socrates, but also in that he represents one of Aristophanes' deepest criticisms of Socrates. For Aristophanes' *Clouds* shows Socrates leading a young man (Pheidippides) who resembles Alcibiades in many respects into a life of lawlessness and impiety (compare *Alcibiades Major* 110b–c with *Clouds* 25; Thucydides 6.16 with *Clouds* 28; and Xenophon *Memorabilia* 1.2.40–46 with *Clouds* 1399 and 1400). Thus, our first impression that Alcibiades robs us of Aristophanes' challenge to Socrates is misleading, for Alcibiades dramatically raises questions about Socrates that Aristophanes intended to raise when he was interrupted.

After Alcibiades enters the dialogue, he takes wreathes from his own head to honor the tragic poet Agathon, who hosts the banquet to celebrate his victory in a dramatic competition. But soon he notices Socrates and exclaims that he has been ambushed once again by Socrates. Socrates asks Agathon to defend him and complains that his love of Alcibiades has become very troublesome. He says that his love of Alcibiades has been most troublesome because of Alcibiades' jealousy and envy when he looks at or converses with any other beautiful person. Socrates implores Agathon to reconcile him with Alcibiades or at least to defend him against Alcibiades' "madness and love of lovers" (213c6–d7).

Alcibiades insists that Agathon must share the wreathes he wears in honor of his victory in a recent dramatic competition with Socrates because Socrates defeats everyone in speeches, not as Agathon did the other day, but always (213d7–e6). Alcibiades compels everyone to start drinking as heavily as he has been. When Eryximachus begs Alcibiades to join them in praising the God Eros while they drink, Alcibiades at first declines, because it would not be fair for him to compete since he is drunk. He remarks, however, that no one should believe what Socrates says in praise of Eros, for Socrates does not permit anyone to praise any god or human being other than Socrates himself. In response, Socrates tells Alcibiades not to blaspheme by claiming that Socrates teaches young men not to praise the gods.[3] Alcibiades insists that he cannot praise anyone except Socrates when Socrates is present and resolves to "assail" and "take vengeance" against Socrates while he praises him. When Socrates asks if Alcibiades means to raise a laugh, Alcibiades, like Aristophanes, promises to tell the truth. With Socrates commanding him to tell the truth, Alcibiades orders Socrates to interrupt him if he says anything untrue while he tells of Socrates' "strangeness" (214d–e).

## ALCIBIADES' PRAISE AND BLAME OF SOCRATES

Alcibiades' speech begins by likening Socrates to two different images. The need for two images suggests that Socrates is incommensurable with any other being or thing. According to Alcibiades, Socrates is like no one person or thing ever to lived before. Socrates is both like the statues of the semidivine Silenus, statues which can be opened up to reveal inside them images of gods, and like the satyr Marsyas. Alcibiades explains that these images fit because Socrates is hubristic and looks like them. He is in particular like Marsyas because his speeches are musical, incredibly beautiful, and moving. Alcibiades' use of these images raises at least two important questions: Garagin notes that the term *hubris* is used in the *Hippolytus* to describe the ambition to be superior to the gods (*Hippolytus* 474–475; Garagin 1977, 25). What is the relation between Socrates' hubris and his inner divinity? And what is the relation between the outer, Marsyas-like beauty of his speeches and the beauty that can be found within him?

The speech is divided into three parts: the first describes the outward beauty of Socrates' speeches, the second, the inner beauty of Socrates himself; and the third, the outer looks of the speeches. Alcibiades praises Socrates' speeches not by recounting their substance but by describing their effect. He emphasizes that the speeches are powerful in themselves rather than through Socrates' manner of speaking or force of personality. Whether they are repeated by a woman or a man or a child, they have the same power over all who hear them. They are "divine," for they possess listeners and fill them with a need for gods and rites of initiation. Alcibiades says that he is far more affected by Socrates' speeches than by any other form of music or speech, including the political oratory of Pericles. Socratic speeches make Alcibiades so troubled and ashamed at his slavishness that he feels as if his life is not worth living (215c–216a). To this day, these speeches make him agonize over his willingness to care for the things of the Athenian people while he neglects his own self. Yet Alcibiades announces from the outset that through his own force of will he has stopped listening to those speeches. He explains that he ran away from Socrates "as if from a Siren," not wishing to sit next to him growing old in "idleness" (216a6–8; cf. *Frogs* 1491). Here we find Alcibiades' first explanation of why he forsakes his desire to have a Socratic education: To spend one's life listening to Socratic speeches is to withdraw not only from politics but from life itself. Like a siren, he lures people into a kind of perpetual, living death during which they never learn what they seek to know. Having found that situation unbearable, he avoids listening to Socrates' speeches and knowingly allows himself to be won over by the honor of the many (216a–c).

The core of Alcibiades' speech is his account of Socrates' inner beauty and virtue and of his attempt to share in it. Alcibiades claims that he alone understands Socrates inner nobility and magnificent hubris and will open up his hidden life to all. On the outside, Socrates always seems to be in love, struck with lightening by beautiful youths and "ignorant of everything" and knowing nothing. But Socrates' apparent eros for beauty and ignorance are merely the disguises of a Silenus. There is neither eros nor ignorance in Socrates' heart. He is, instead, full of "moderation" and indifference to the *kalon*. No one, says Alcibiades, would believe how Socrates contemns beauty. Socrates thinks no more of a beautiful human being than of someone who is wealthy or who has any other quality that is esteemed by the vulgar. Socrates thinks that all such things are "nothing" and that we are "nothing." Yet despite Socrates' inner moderation and unerotic character, he is always ironic and playful with everyone (216c4–e5).

Alcibiades says that he does not know if anyone has seen the images that lurk within Socrates when he is serious and opened up. But Alcibiades says that he once saw them and that they seemed so divine, golden, "all-beautiful" or "all-noble" and wondrous that he was compelled to do whatever Socrates ordered (216e7–217a2). Alcibiades says that he determined at that point that he must find out the whole of Socrates' knowledge—apparently believing that were he to share in Socrates' knowledge, he would also share in those qualities (217a4–5; Garagin 1977, 34). Alcibiades thought himself fortunate to possess great "youthful beauty" and resolved to use it to entice Socrates to drop his guard in a moment of intimacy and talk to Alcibiades as a lover talks to the one he loves.

After several failed attempts to let Socrates seduce him, Alcibiades finally decided that Socrates must be "set upon by force and not released" since he was already committed to the attempt and had to learn what was happening. He invited Socrates to dinner in the manner of a lover who plots to capture his beloved but was too ashamed to offer himself to Socrates. Even though he originally was Socrates' beloved, Alcibiades seems to have fallen in love with Socrates (217c, 222b–c). He apparently wants to "be together" with Socrates, partaking of his beauty and giving birth to his own beautiful virtue (206c–207a).

In his second attempt to seduce Socrates, Alcibiades was not so restrained by shame. He kept Socrates talking long into the night and insisted that Socrates sleep at his house (217a–d). Alcibiades offers three excuses for revealing the shameful incident that happened next. His first excuse is that he is drunk and cannot help speaking shamelessly. His second reason is that, despite the shamefulness, justice requires him to reveal Socrates' "magnificent arrogance." His third reason is that those who hear him have also experienced the pain that compelled him to act shamelessly and will forgive him (217e–218b). The pain comes from the "snakebite" of "philosophical speeches," speeches that bite more savagely than a snake whenever they grasp a young soul that is "not unfortunate by nature." He includes among those who have been bitten and experienced "philosophic madness" and "bacchic frenzy" all who are present at the banquet, including Phaedrus, Agathon, Eryximachus, Pausanias, Aristodemus, and Aristophanes.

On the night that he offered himself to Socrates, Alcibiades told Socrates that he considered Socrates to be his only deserving lover. Alcibiades explained that he thought that he would be foolish to deny Socrates anything that he wanted. For Alcibiades wanted to become as good as possible and considered Socrates to be the best at assisting him in this. He would be far more ashamed, he said, before sensible men for failing to gratify a man like Socrates than he would be before the "many and senseless" for gratifying him (217e–218d).

According to Alcibiades, Socrates' response to his offer was very "ironic," by which Alcibiades seems to mean that it was joking and playful and false. Socrates said in reply that he admires Alcibiades for resolving to become the best possible. He next remarks that Alcibiades' proposition implies that Alcibiades sees an "impossible" or "unworkable" beauty in Socrates. Socrates appears to mean by this that Alcibiades believes that he has no independent access to the sort of beauty that Socrates possesses. Granting for a moment that Socrates' beauty is beyond Alcibiades' grasp and must be given to him by Socrates, Socrates points out that the bargain would not profit him nearly as much as it would Alcibiades. He would be acquiring something "bronze," of little value, in exchange for something "golden," the most valuable of secrets (218d–219a). Thus, Socrates salutes Alcibiades' prudence but draws his attention to his failure to consider whether the exchange is prudent for Socrates. Subsequently, Socrates goes on to warn Alcibiades that he may not recognize that Socrates' own beauty or nobility may be "nothing" (219a). But Socrates does not disavow knowledge of how to learn about beauty. He tells Alcibiades that thought "begins to see clearly when eyesight begins to diminish" and urges Alcibiades to be patient since he is still far from that (219a).

In reply, Alcibiades avers that he, at least, is speaking candidly and urges Socrates to deliberate about what is best for the both of them. Socrates accepts this and promises to consider what is best for both him and Alcibiades. In saying that he believed that in this exchange he had "wounded" Socrates, Alcibiades indicates that he saw through Socrates' cautious advice and promise to assist him. Fully expecting Socrates to make amorous advances, Alcibiades embraced the "daimonic" and "wondrous" Socrates. But Socrates merely dozed off, thus triumphing over, despising, and laughing at Alcibiades' youthful beauty. Noting that he took great pride in that beauty, Alcibiades accuses Socrates of committing an outrage against it (219c2–5). He speaks as a prosecutor, calling his listeners "men of the jury" and charging them to condemn Socrates' "splendid arrogance." Even now, he finds Socrates' refusal to have sex with him so astonishing that he swears by all the gods and goddesses that Socrates actually went to sleep.

Alcibiades says that since Socrates eluded him, he was at a loss. He could neither be angered at Socrates nor give up wanting to "be together" with him. He eventually escaped from Socrates because Socrates' indifference convinced him that he had no "resources" for acquiring Socrates' beauty (219d–e3)—thus affirming at least a part of Diotima's claim that eros will perish when we believe we lack the resourcefulness to acquire what we desire (203e1–4). But for the most part his account of what transpired appears to contradict Socrates' account of eros. For at heart Socrates appears to be moved less by a desire to know how to be noble and good than by a desire to display the extraordinary weakness of his erotic passion and the great strength of his powers of self-command. Instead of loving beauty or nobility,

Socrates loves to lure those who think themselves beautiful or noble by pretending that he loves and respects them, only to expose them to his utter contempt. Whereas others would acknowledge that they are moved by their needs to honor Alcibiades and the god Eros, Socrates refuses to acknowledge his neediness and weakness. Behind everything Socrates says and does lurks an abysmal, powerful, and even magnificent pride, a love of victory and of overcoming. He is a living, whole example of the ancient "circle-men" described by Aristophanes earlier in the *Symposium.*

In order to fill out his praise of Socrates' extraordinary moderation and self-command, Alcibiades goes on to recount Socrates' other impressive deeds. He says that Socrates is invulnerable to money and altogether praiseworthy for his nature, moderation, and courage (219d–e). In separating Socrates' nature from his moderation and courage, Alcibiades implies that these last two virtues are unnatural. When praising Socrates' nature, Alcibiades mentions specifically his extraordinary prudence, endurance, and self-control. He cites the military campaign at Potidaea, where Socrates showed enough self-control to endure hardships better than anyone and to take full advantage of the pleasures to be had under difficult conditions. Socrates can drink without suffering any ill effects, inasmuch as wine does not affect him. While other soldiers bundled themselves to protect against the cold, Socrates dressed as usual and marched barefoot on the ice better than the others—an act which led others to suspect that he despised them (219e5–220c1). Alcibiades then quotes Homer in calling Socrates a "real man" (cf. *Odyssey* 2.242) and praises him for the heroic endurance he showed at the battle of Potidaea. Socrates' first feat at Potidaea was to stand all night pursuing a thought. Alcibiades does not report which thought Socrates pursued or whether he ever found it, but he does say that some foreign soldiers watched him all night until he prayed at dawn to the sun and left (220c2–d5). During the fighting, Socrates rescued Alcibiades and his weapons. Alcibiades was so impressed with Socrates that he nominated him for a prize for virtue, a prize which Socrates declined and urged be given to Alcibiades (220d–e). Alcibiades concludes his praise of Socrates' inner virtue by stressing Socrates' uniqueness. He asserts that while Brasidas is comparable to Achilles and that Pericles is comparable to Nestor and Antenor, Socrates is like no ancient model of virtue. His earlier comparisons of Socrates to Ajax and Odysseus are inadequate. If he bears resemblance at anyone, it is to unnatural, nonhuman beings such as the sileni and satyrs (221c2–d6; also 214a, 214d–e, 215a, 219b–d, 220c–d, 221b; cf. Vlastos 1991, 1; Nussbaum, 1986, 191). This implies that Socrates is not a model of human virtue but a kind of freak, in keeping with the view of his great critics Aristophanes and Nietzsche. Socrates' battlefield heroics reflect the same uncanny inner strength and pride that Alcibiades found in Socrates' declination to have sexual relations with him. Just as Socrates refuses to show any sign of erotic neediness in order to show his contempt for the beautiful Alcibiades and for the god Eros himself, so Socrates refuses to give in to his hunger or pain or fear so that he may show himself to be superior to others. In the bedroom or on the battlefield, Socrates behaves like one of Aristophanes' proud, hubristic, ancient "circle-men."

## ALCIBIADES' LOVE OF LOVERS

Because Socrates does not interrupt Alcibiades' speech at any one point, it appears that Alcibiades says nothing false. Yet at the end Socrates says that he believes that Alcibiades has been only pretending to be intoxicated and that his whole speech has been a veiled attempt to make Socrates love him rather than the tragic poet Agathon (222c–d). Thus Socrates' failure to interrupt Alcibiades does not mean that Socrates agrees with Alcibiades' story. Socrates does not contest Alcibiades' memory of events and conversations but suggests that Alcibiades misunderstands and distorts Socrates' intentions. While it may be easy to think of respectable explanations of why Socrates declined Alcibiades' offer of sexual relations, it is less easy to understand why Socrates fails to fulfill his promises to educate Alcibiades to virtue. Even if he does not desire to humiliate and triumph over Alcibiades but is instead consumed by love of the ideas, his apparent indifference to Alcibiades' needs seems to reflect an inhuman coldness and failure to appreciate the worth of Alcibiades as a human being (Garagin 1977; Nussbaum 1986). Socrates' self-sufficiency prevents him joining in human community in general and in political community in particular (Rosen 1987, 294, 324; Saxonhouse 1992, 182–184).

If Alcibiades' criticism can be answered, the answer must come from an explanation of what Socrates said and did on the night in question. Alcibiades characterizes Socrates' response to his declaration that he was willing to gratify Socrates in order to become the best possible to be "ironic as always." But how does Alcibiades know that Socrates is not being serious and straightforward? If one did not suspect that Socrates was being ironic, there would be nothing suspicious about Socrates' first response congratulating Alcibiades on his determination to be as best as possible—particularly insofar as this entails Alcibiades' willingness to defy conventional opinions about what is noble and base in order to improve himself. In fact, to the extent that Alcibiades overcomes his shame before the "senseless many" and feels shame instead before men such as Socrates, an important aspect of Socrates' account of eros is once again confirmed. For the change in what Alcibiades cares for supports Socrates' claim that what we love depends on our opinions about what is noble. Socrates' subsequent remark that Alcibiades sees an impossible or unworkable beauty or nobility in Socrates seems to be a simple inference that Alcibiades would not give up something in exchange for such a beauty were he able to devise a way to acquire it on his own. Socrates' observation that Alcibiades hopes to trade "bronze for gold" appears to be both a compliment, insofar as Alcibiades has an accurate sense of the relative worth of physical and psychic beauty, and an admonition, insofar as Alcibiades' proposal relies on the presumably wise Socrates trading the most valuable of things, knowledge of excellence, for something of far less worth.[4] Similarly, Socrates' warning that Alcibiades may misunderstand or overestimate Socrates' beauty is perfectly consistent with the inference drawn from his speech that our initial understanding of beauty or nobility is misguided insofar as we fail to see that genuine beauty or nobility must also be good or a means to our truest happiness. Socrates does not know how to be beautiful or noble *in the way he hoped he could* prior to thinking through his own erotic longings. But, in keeping with what he learns from speaking with Diotima, he is able to say that it is possible to learn about and acquire a truer beauty as a result of long reflection. Thus, Socrates tells Alcibiades on this occasion that Alcibiades can learn the truth about beauty over a long period of time. Insofar as Socrates wants to learn whether he can educate Alcibiades about what is truly noble and good, he could be perfectly sincere in promising to deliberate with Alcibiades about what is best for them both. If Socrates' response was offered in all seriousness, if Socrates was drawing Alcibiades' attention to his failure to think very clearly about Socrates' beauty or nobility and was offering to help him think about what is best, the massive question is not, Why did Socrates frustrate Alcibiades? but, Why did Alcibiades ignore Socrates' warnings about the imprudence and illusions that might underlie his proposition? What, in short, keeps Alcibiades from taking Socrates' remarks with the greatest seriousness?

Perhaps Alcibiades ignores the content of Socrates' remarks because he is not primarily concerned with learning how to deliberate about the noble and the good with Socrates. Instead of questioning Socrates about what his response means or taking comfort in Socrates' promise to help him, Alcibiades looks for signs that he has "wounded" Socrates and induced him to give in to his erotic longings (219b). Alcibiades' single-minded desire to arouse Socrates' eros suggests that, even more than he wants to learn from Socrates, he wants to be loved by Socrates. More precisely, Alcibiades acts as if he believes that he *deserves* to be loved by Socrates. Alcibiades' belief that Socrates owes it to him to take him up on his offer indicates that underlying Alcibiades' actions is not a simple desire to meet the need for beauty or nobility that Socrates has made him feel, but a desire for Socrates to show that Alcibiades is, in fact, a very beautiful or noble human being. Alcibiades expects Socrates to love him because he understands being loved to be an acknowledgment of his worth. A "perfectly" erotic man would love because he is convinced that he is in need and, to the extent that he believes he lacks nobility or beauty, would not think that he merits love or honor. Despite having been shown his profound ignorance of noble virtue, Alcibiades still thinks he is a noble or beautiful human being and merits being loved. Contrary to Socrates' remark in the *Alcibiades Major* that Alcibiades seems to have the greatest eros that anyone has ever had for anything (*Alcibiades Major* 124c), Alcibiades does not appear to be simply or purely erotic.

Alcibiades' conviction that he is *kalon* apparently undermines Socrates' initial triumph. It seems that Alcibiades' painful awareness of his ignorance does not spark an erotic desire for knowledge of how to be noble and good. For even though Alcibiades says that Socrates seemed "all-beautiful," Alcibiades believes that he has a kind of "youthful" beauty which Socrates lacks (217a, 219c). We see him enter the banquet having crowned himself with wreathes, asserting through his actions that only he is qualified to bestow honors on Agathon for his recent victory in a dramatic competition. Even after he sees Socrates and is reminded of his neediness, Alcibiades still thinks that Socrates longs to capture him and boasts of his good nature (218a). Unlike a "true" lover, who, according to Diotima's description, cannot shake off his profound awareness of his needs (204a), it seems that Alcibiades never fully loses confidence in his own intrinsic beauty and nobility. This suggests that Aristophanes is correct that we always love what is our own and can never shake off our fundamental belief that we are, at bottom, noble and good. But Alcibiades' reluctance to accept what Socrates shows him about his ignorance does not disprove Socrates' thesis that Alcibiades is moved by an eros to know what is noble and good. For even as Alcibiades recounts his failure to seduce Socrates, he remains wounded by Socrates or, more precisely, by the awareness of ignorance that was brought about through Socrates' speeches. Alcibiades never fully overcomes the pain he feels when he is confronted with his ignorance about and lack of noble virtue. He is unable to overlook the evidence of his ignorance, but he is also unable to accept the full consequences of that evidence. Instead of seeking the knowledge he needs to redress his deficiencies, he recoils from what Socrates has shown him of his ignorance and tries to win some word or sign from the man who shows him his defects that he is, after all, still very beautiful or noble. He believes that were Socrates to lose himself in loving him, Socrates would by that very act efface the evidence of Alcibiades' ignorance that Socrates brought so painfully to sight. Thus, Alcibiades' apparently enduring self-confidence is belied by his enduring desire to loved by Socrates in particular. He is still moved by a needy, erotic longing for some evidence to help him believe that he is noble and good. Instead of being a simple lover of what is "noble and good," Alcibiades is, more precisely, a "lover of lovers" (213d). He desires to be loved so that he can silence the doubts that make him love in the first place.

The fact that Socrates declined to have sexual relations with Alcibiades does not so much refute Socrates' account of eros as provide us with a model of eros in a soul that is not simply erotic. Alcibiades' pride and anger recall to us what Socrates says in the *Republic* of the importance of *thumos*, "spirit" or "spiritedness," in the soul. According to Socrates, *thumos* can manifest itself in a variety of ways, as anger or moral indignation or love of victory or love of honor (Pangle 1976, 1062–1064). A crucial difference between eros and *thumos* seems to be that while eros focuses our attention on the object of our desire, *thumos* draws our attention toward those who thwart our desires and to our right to have what we believe we lack. *Thumos* reflects and supports our conviction that we are worthy of what we desire and thus our belief that we have been wrongly deprived of what is ours. In this sense, Aristophanes' account of our circular ancestors implies that we are fundamentally thumotic rather than erotic. But unlike those ancient men, Alcibiades is not driven by his spirited pride to act on its own. Rather, that pride lashes out defensively, responding to Socrates' refusal to retract his insight into Alcibiades' neediness.

Early in the *Symposium*, the various symposiasts are divided into two groups: "strong drinkers" and "soft" ones (176c). The strong appear to have the most physical and psychic endurance. Alcibiades' unruly drunkenness, together with his jealousy and tendency to blurt out what he says himself he should hold back, imply that he lacks the self-control and endurance he so admires in Socrates. Plato's dramatic presentation of Alcibiades suggests that Alcibiades' relative softness of soul prevents him from facing his own deficiencies squarely. Because Alcibiades is too soft to see his needs without squinting, he succumbs to the spirited conviction that he cannot be as needy or as ignorant as Socrates has led him to believe. Similarly, Aristophanes' hangover and relative lack of endurance (176b, 185c, 223d) suggest that he, too, is much softer than Socrates. Aristophanes, of course, would agree with this assessment but would argue that Socrates' great endurance is simply inhuman. Socrates, however, would presumably reply that were Aristophanes only a little tougher, were he only able to keep his gaze where he needs to keep it, he could see through once and for all the many things that continue to inspire him with fear, anger, and hope even though he debunks them again and again.

In response to Aristophanes' abortive rejoinder to Socrates' speech (212c2–4), Socrates would concede that a love of one's own plays a prominent role in our lives. We love kindred spirits and like minds. But this love is always shaped by and dependent on the erotic desire to be noble and good. Alcibiades does not love those who are like him but, instead, tries to induce someone who is most unlike him, Socrates, to undercut the painful insight that Alcibiades is a needy human being. At the root of the love of one's own, at the root of a spirited or willful pride in one's own nobility, lurks the conviction that we are in need. In loving those who are like us, we are moved by an erotic awareness of our deficiency. But instead of pursuing someone or something unlike ourselves, we tell ourselves that insofar as we are needy we are not quite ourselves, that we know only a part of ourselves, and that in being together with our true loves we shall become the complete, noble, and good human being we truly are but which at present, we are not.

In response to the Nietzschean criticism that Socrates never fully experiences the instincts that speak to and through Alcibiades, Socrates could reply that were Alcibiades the kind of being that Nietzsche takes him to be, he would, at some point, put Socrates entirely out of his mind and would never stoop to wanting to be loved (*Beyond Good and Evil* 261). Nietzsche would, presumably, respond in kind that Plato's account of what transpired between Socrates and Alcibiades cannot be trusted. To decide the issue, one would have to learn for oneself whether Plato captures the nature of men such as Alcibiades.

## SOCRATES' TRUE VIRTUE

Just as Alcibiades distorts his own nobility in order to cling to his conviction that he is noble, he inevitably distorts Socrates' virtue as well. Instead of regarding Socrates as someone who is consumed by a passionate, erotic need to learn how to be noble and good, Alcibiades sees Socrates as a man who is intensely proud of his supernatural self-command, endurance, and bravery. He thinks that Socrates acts of out pride in the strength of his power to resist the passions that ordinarily govern and humble us. But on one occasion in particular, Alcibiades says that he saw with great clarity how Socrates makes prudent use of his endurance. At the battle of Delium, Alcibiades was on a horse, less afraid than at Potidaea, and better able to perceive how Socrates acts. As the Athenians retreated, Alcibiades saw that Socrates was more sensible than the other soldiers, including the general, Laches, who was beside him on foot. Quoting a line from Aristophanes' *Clouds*, Alcibiades says that Socrates walked as he does in Athens, "strutting like a pelican, his eyes darting from side to side," quietly looking out for friends and enemies (cf. *Clouds* 362). Socrates showed everyone that he is a "real man" who would defend himself vigorously against anyone who attacked him. His conduct saved both Socrates and Laches, explains Alcibiades, for enemies avoid those who act like Socrates and pursue those who flee (220d5–221c1). At Potidaea, where Socrates rescued Alcibiades, Alcibiades considered Socrates' virtue to be so uncanny, so contrary to his own advantage, that it deserved the greatest rewards for heroism (220d5–6, e2–4). At Delium, however, he recognized how Socrates' admirable steadiness and bravery is perfectly consistent with what is prudent. On that occasion, he saw that Socrates' conspicuous bravery is the safest method of retreat.[5] When Alcibiades was in grave danger at Potidaea, Socrates bravely saved him—yet on that occasion Socrates also had the presence of mind or prudence to save both Alcibiades and his weapons (220e). While admiring Socrates' ability to overcome eros, pleasure, fear, and fatigue, Alcibiades does not seem to notice that Socrates uses his strength of soul for rational and prudential purposes.[6]

Socrates seems not only unnaturally courageous to Alcibiades, but also unnaturally invulnerable to the effects of wine (214a, 220a). But, as with Socrates' courage, there is a reason for his sobriety. Socrates never seems to be drunk, because his character never changes when he drinks. When others drink, they lose the fear, shame, and self-control that suppresses their deepest desires (*Laws* 649a–b). But having reflected on and thought through what he fears and what makes him ashamed, Socrates is far less subject to these things than others. When drink dissipates Socrates' self-control, he seems sober, for his deepest desires are the same as the ones he manifests when he is not drinking.

Most importantly, Alcibiades fails to do justice to the place of philosophy in Socrates' life. Socrates indicates in his own speech that careful deliberation about his own ignorance and neediness helps to unleash a powerful eros to know what is truly both noble and good. But in recounting Socrates' virtues, Alcibiades is amazingly silent about the role which wisdom, or love of wisdom, plays in his life. By including everyone at the banquet among those who have been bitten by philosophic speeches and have felt the pain and frenzied longing they induce (218a–b), Alcibiades suggests that philosophizing consists in listening to Socrates' moving speeches that reveal our ignorance about and lack of what is noble and divine. But Socrates' philosophic life is not limited merely to such speeches. It also includes private reflections (174d).

Were Alcibiades able to face his erotic needs, perhaps he would have been able to admire Socrates for his genuine virtues. He would have recognized that Socrates awakens in him the same erotic longings for knowledge of what is noble and good that Socrates finds in himself. He would have seen that Socrates was able to undermine his self-assurance by challenging his beliefs about his virtue, thus showing that we feel self-assured or erotic depending on whether we believe that we are in need. He would have acknowledged that Socrates was able to turn him from politics toward the pursuit of self-knowledge, thus showing that what we love depends on what we believe is noble and good. Alcibiades would have seen, in other words, that his own actions seem to affirm Socrates' "psychology" of erotic matters. Moreover, Alcibiades might eventually come to see that his own words and actions undermine his alternative, non-Socratic account of virtue. He would have seen that his dissatisfaction with himself and with his opinions belie his challenge to Socrates' virtue. He might even have recognized how his weaknesses highlight the strengths that permit Socrates to confront his ignorance, pursue his needs, and make progress in learning what is noble and good.

But whether or not Socrates is able to bring Alcibiades that far along in his education, Socrates would be gratified as he reflected on how his association with Alcibiades confirms his knowledge of the soul and of its virtue.

If Socrates' association with Alcibiades helps to vindicate and strengthen his eros to philosophize, then that association cannot be considered a failure. But Socrates' failure to educate Alcibiades to virtue raises grave doubts about the usefulness or applicability of Socratic philosophy for politics. In fact, since Socrates inflames but never satisfies Alcibiades' eros to be loved, one wonders if Socrates' "experiment" with educating Alcibiades does not do more harm than good to political life.

## POLITICAL EROS AND POLITICAL PHILOSOPHY

Plato's account of Socrates' association with Alcibiades helps us understand the motives, capacities, and dangers of "political men." According to Diotima, eros leads some who have good natures to enter politics so that they might "give birth" to their implicit notions of moderation and justice. She claims that eros is a kind of psychic pregnancy, in which we carry within us noble virtues. But, she says, we are unable to give birth to these virtues unless we "come together with" someone else of great beauty or nobility. In terms of political eros, it seems that we do not dare to act nobly until we have shared in the nobility of others so that our own virtues are perfected or completed. By ruling and especially by legislating, erotic politicians believe they can share in the particular nobility of their own city and together with the city give birth to their own nascent virtues. Moreover, an erotic politician finds the people loveable because in shaping them in his own image he can preserve something of himself long after his death (209e). In this sense, Alcibiades will love the Athenian people both because he hopes to share in their nobility and also because he hopes that by inducing them to share in his nobility he can achieve a kind of immortality.

Diotima's claim that the ambition to rule is rooted in an erotic desire to manifest noble virtue contradicts the view held by many liberal theorists that ambition emerges solely from a desire for preference or praise. In fact, liberal philosophers openly question whether it is humanly possible to love noble virtue for its own sake. Hobbes, Locke, and Montesquieu claim that we perceive nobility or beauty in those things which promise to benefit us and that the desire to *be* noble is, at bottom, a desire to be praised and thought powerful by others.[7] This view is echoed by liberal statesmen such as Hamilton, who writes that the ruling passion of the "noblest minds" is the "love of fame."[8] But according to Montesquieu, the desire for praise is especially dangerous to republics because it sets individuals against one another rather than uniting them as fellow citizens. Moreover, he says that what we praise is so variable and ineffable that it is frequently a matter of whim or caprice. The desire to be honored for something definite and lasting leads many ambitious men to go to war so that they might display their courage and daring.[9] In light of the volatility of the passion for renown, liberals tend to promote milder, more reliable virtues, such as promise-keeping, civility, moderation, industry, and prudence.[10] Diotima, on the other hand, helps us recognize that our love of noble virtue differs from a desire for mere popularity and thus need not be as contingent, erratic, and explosive as early liberals suggest.

Yet Plato's dramatic presentation of Alcibiades adds another dimension to his teaching about "political eros." For it shows that Alcibiades is moved not only by a desire to manifest his virtue, but also by a desire to be loved and honored so as to silence his doubts about his worth. This raises the possibility that Alcibiades will especially want to be loved for those qualities that he quietly, half-consciously suspects are incomplete and defective. In fact, he will want to be loved precisely for those qualities that he fears are tinged with ignorance and vice. Thus, according to Plato, the eros to give birth to noble virtue through ruling or legislating is dangerous, not because our opinions about what is noble are radically contingent and subjective, but because we may very well want to be admired for the qualities which we suspect, somewhere in our hearts, are most doubtful.

While Socrates may not be able to win people such as Alcibiades away from politics and toward a philosophic life, he may be able to place a "ceiling" or limit on their ambition. Although Alcibiades fails to follow Socrates' guidance, he nonetheless shows a lasting deference to Socrates that he feels for no other human being. Alcibiades' respect for Socrates provides a "ceiling" or limit to Alcibiades' beliefs about his own noble virtue. While Alcibiades believes that he has great virtue, he is, when in the presence of Socrates, aware that he does not possess the whole of virtue. He is always aware that there are standards of virtue beyond his own vision of human nobility and goodness. Knowing this, Socrates seems to have performed some conspicuous acts of endurance, self-control, and prudence to inspire Alcibiades to emulate him (219e–221c).

When men of Alcibiades' intelligence, assets, and burning ambition determine to enter politics to prove their virtue and refuse a Socratic education, Socratic philosophy may seem powerless to reform or protect political life. But Socrates' knowledge of people such as Alcibiades may give us valuable political guidance. For at least Socrates helps us recognize the extent to which Alcibiadean ambitions are present in human nature and a permanent political possibility. Now, some might say that this insight has been rendered superfluous by liberal democracy. Has not liberalism diffused or redirected such passions so as to make them relatively harmless? Yet it makes a great difference how liberalism accomplishes this. According to thinkers such as Richard Rorty, liberalism softens Alcibiadean passions by choking them off in an atmosphere of dull practicality and disenchantment. We gain peace and individual freedom at the cost of intellectual and moral seriousness (Rorty 1991, 193). By not merely reminding us of the possibility of Alcibiadean ambition, but also by rekindling that ambition, Socratic philosophy may serve liberalism in at least two ways. Firstly, by helping us to see that great political ambition is an expression (albeit incomplete) of our natural longing to be noble and good, Socratic philosophy could help revive that ambition and thus help reintroduce new notions of virtue to our political landscape. Having done this, Socratic philosophy could, secondly, show us the value, the genius, of liberal political institutions in keeping competing ambitions in check without necessarily undermining the love of noble virtue that drives them.

Socrates' inability to educate Alcibiades to virtue reflects a fundamental limit on the power of reason to reform political life. Yet the example of Alcibiades by itself does not prove that philosophers are unable to educate all non-philosophers to virtue. Perhaps Alcibiades represents a human type that is unusually resistant to education. On the one hand, Socrates must wonder whether a city governed by philosophy could instil habits and beliefs in many non-philosophers that would bring them close to genuine virtue. On the other, Socrates' success in examining Alcibiades' soul by itself does not prove that Socrates knows the soul and its virtue. For even if Alcibiades' eros resembles that of Socrates, this does not rule out the possibility that there are other kinds of human beings whose devotion to the noble things is rooted in something other than an eros to be noble and good. Alcibiades, after all, seems to have an especially self-serving and perhaps even attenuated sense of justice. Perhaps there are others who experience the nobility of justice or other virtues differently than do Socrates and Alcibiades. How can Socrates know whether others sense or know something about justice that he does not and that calls into question his identification of virtue with philosophic wisdom? In order for Socrates to confirm his knowledge of the soul and own nobility and goodness, he must examine and consider those who care deeply for justice.

# CHAPTER 8

# *The Civic Understanding of Virtue*

To confirm his knowledge of the soul and its virtue, Socrates cannot rest content with his examination of grandly ambitious and morally ambiguous political men such as Alcibiades. For Socrates is accused by Strepsiades in Aristophanes' *Clouds* and by his fellow citizens in Plato's *Apology* of doing grave injustices such as corrupting the youth and disbelieving in the gods of Athens. Indeed, Socrates concedes that his need to converse with fellow citizens and foreigners precludes him from bearing the common burdens and from fulfilling the ordinary responsibilities of citizenship (*Apology* 23b, 31d–e). In order to vindicate his belief that the philosophic life is virtuous, Socrates must show that his way of life is just. He must demonstrate that the philosophic life is just even in the eyes of those who are genuinely devoted to civic virtue. In the *Republic*, Socrates claims to have vindicated philosophy before the tribune of civic virtue. In fact, Socrates claims not only that the philosopher is just, but also that the justice of the philosopher transcends that of the non-philosophic citizen. The philosopher has all the virtues to the greatest degree possible for a human being. According to Socrates, the multitude of non-philosophers can acquire at best a "political" or "popular" form of virtue less noble than the virtue of the good individual or of the philosopher (*Republic* 401eff., 430c5–6, 442c, 473c–e, 497a, 500d, 544a). Socrates says that every city is a cave-like prison suffused in illusions about the virtues and that no philosopher would ever want to live in, let alone rule, one (*Republic* 489b–c, 514–521). He adds in this context that the philosophers' prudence may be the only true virtue of the soul and that other so-called virtues, including the civic virtues of non-philosophers, are mere habits or dispositions of the body (*Republic* 518d–519a6, 520c, 619c6–d1). It seems to be because the philosophers are necessarily more virtuous than non-philosophers that the former must rule over the latter as kings.

Such claims compel one to wonder exactly how Socrates distinguishes the virtue of the philosophers from the civic virtue of non-philosophers and why he seems so certain that the former virtue surpasses the latter. Moreover, it is not obvious to what extent or in what sense philosophic virtue ceases to be "civic." Nor is it clear what obstacle or obstacles could prevent the civic virtue of the non-philosopher from being transformed into the nobler and truer virtue of the philosopher. How close, in the best case, can civic virtue come to philosophic virtue? The purpose of this chapter is to examine Plato's account of the character of civic virtue, to understand the needs it serves as well as its limits. It argues that a careful, dramatic reading of the *Republic* reveals a powerful argument for the superiority of philosophic to civic virtue in a manner that remains respectful of citizenship and the civic understanding of virtue.

While one of the main themes of Plato's *Republic* is an elaboration and examination of civic virtue, Socrates avoids using this specific term. At one point, however, he speaks of one particular virtue, courage, as being "political" or "civic" (430c3).[1] It seems that what makes this form of this particular virtue especially "political" is not simply that it is manifested on behalf of the city but, more precisely, that it derives from what one learns from the city. According to Socrates, it consists in accepting and preserving the "correct opinions" about what is and is not terrible, opinions that are given to us by the laws in the face of pains, pleasures, desires, and fears. Yet Socrates indicates that this form of courage is not the noblest sort and promises a better treatment of that virtue later in the dialogue (430c5–6). Although he does not say specifically in this passage what prevents civic courage from being the noblest kind, he points to its chief defect when he subsequently describes the courage of a good individual. The key difference is that those with civic courage stand by correct opinions that they have absorbed from laws, while those with the nobler courage stand by what is proclaimed by reasoned speeches (429c2, 7–8, 430a1–3, 442c2). To have civic courage is to remember and act on correct opinions that one accepts as true on the authority of law, while to have the nobler sort is to remember and act on what one knows to be true for oneself. This virtue is civic, in other words, because it is instilled in us by legal, civic means rather than by reason alone. Thus, the citizen who believes that it is terrible to abandon one's post or wounded comrades in battle without thinking through for oneself why this is terrible has civic courage. For those of us who lack the rational capacity to know for ourselves what is and what is not terrible, civic courage seems to be the next best kind of courage as well as a crucial ingredient of the next best form of rationality (Reeve 1988, 239). And to the extent that civic virtue ultimately requires strict adherence to the law, civic courage would seem to offer powerful support to civic virtue as a whole (424e5–425a1, 380c, 383c, 417b, 425e, 461b–5b, 605b; *Laws* 653b, 659d, 643e–4a, 645b–c).

In saying that civic courage means steadfast adherence to "correct opinions" given to us by the laws, Socrates indicates that one has civic courage in the strictest sense only when the opinions one absorbs from the laws are in fact "correct." In Books VI and VII, however, Socrates raises serious questions about the educative power of law, about the reliability of the opinions it teaches, and hence about civic courage and civic virtue, as such. These questions emerge as Socrates explains that philosophers often seem vicious because most potential philosophers are corrupted by the many non-philosophers who dominate each city, leaving only impostors to claim the mantle of philosophy (492c ff.). Cities are in effect schools led by Sophists who define what is noble (*kalon*), good, and just according to whatever pleases the multitude of non-philosophers who always govern. In order to explain why the domineering multitude never know the things that they claim to teach, Socrates alludes for a second time to their inability to accept that the many noble (or beautiful) particulars that they perceive and love "are not." They regard these many different particulars as beautiful while denying that there is anything that is "beautiful itself," while philosophers envision and love the altogether separate and transcendent idea of the beautiful (476c ff., 493e–4a). To the extent that every actual city is ruled by those who cannot philosophize, it seems that every actual example of civic courage is in fact steadfast devotion to incorrect opinions about what is and is not terrible.

Yet the *Republic* raises the possibility of a city that educates its citizens in light of genuine knowledge of the virtues. This city would appear to be as rational as possible, insofar as it is shaped by reason with a view to reasonable ends (Bruell 1994, 267). It would minimize the great defect of the rule of law that follows from laying down the same, universal rules for everyone without discriminating according to the particular virtues and vices, capacities and needs, of each individual (*Statesman* 294a10–295a8; *Laws* 627e1–628a5, 666e, 713c–e, 756e–757e; Bruell 1994, 278–279; Klosko 1986, 190). While the city described in the *Republic* cannot provide the personal attention required for perfect governance (*Laws* 713c–e; *Statesman* 271e4–272a1), its rulers monitor each citizen's character and talents in order to place each one in his or her natural class. Its laws and institutions are offered as models to be modified as circumstances dictate (412c–414a; Annas 1981, 105–106).

Despite the optimism about the rationality of laws that is implicit in these reforms, Socrates' continuing account of the city and its laws deepens his criticism of the education we receive from cities and from law. According to the account of the cave at the start of book 7, we are raised as prisoners to a false perspective on the world, able to see only the shadows of artifacts as they are cast upon a wall rather than things as they really are. We are burdened with many chains that prevent us from recognizing the artificiality of the world as we are given to understand it. One of the most important aspects of this artificiality comes to sight as Socrates mentions that the shadows include images of human beings and of justice (514c, 516a, 517d, 520c; *Laws* 663c; Annas 1981, 256; Klosko 1986, 92). These shadows are images of what it means to be a just or noble or good human being, and these images are projected by the laws. From the specific commands of legal codes to works of poetry, the laws present us with models of how we should live, with images of virtue, against which we are to measure ourselves and others (602d). By referring to these images as shadows of artifacts, Socrates indicates that every model of a just and noble and good human being that we absorb from the law is somehow unnatural, exaggerated, distorted. In this context, Socrates goes on to say that a true, liberal education consists in turning entirely away from what we learn in the cave (518b–d) and in using "dialectics" to recognize the inadequacy of what the lawgiver teaches about the just, the noble, and the good (538d6ff.). What is especially striking in the account of the cave is that Socrates makes these criticisms not merely of all actual cities, but even of the rational city that is ruled by philosophers (Irwin 1977, 221). He says that philosophers regard even this apparently philosophic city as a cave which they are unwilling to rule or even to enter (514a–515c, 516d–e, 517d–e, 519c–d, 520b–c, 521b1–3, 540a). Even though its citizens are to be schooled in "correct" opinions, these opinions remain essentially "ugly" and "blind," rooted in something other than knowledge or intelligence (377b, 412e–3a, 429c, 478a–c, 506c). Thus grounded, civic virtues are not virtues in the strictest sense. Socrates says that prudence (*phronesis*) is the only true virtue of the soul while the other so-called virtues, presumably including civic courage and the rest of the law-induced civic virtues, are closer to virtues of the body that are instilled by habits and exercises (518d9–519a6; 619c6–d1). It is because the city's virtues are rooted in dubious beliefs that its teachings are threatened by exposure to Socratic dialectic (497d–8c, 537–538; Bruell 1994, 263 n. 3; Nussbaum 1986, 88; Reeve 1988, 109).

On the whole, the cave image suggests that the citizen, as such, is never educated to genuine virtue and that civic courage and civic virtue as a whole consist in preserving distorted images of what is terrible and what is not terrible no matter what. But why would even the rational city described in the *Republic* be merely a cave? Why are its "correct opinions" no better than the distortions that prevail in other cities? Is it because philosophers are unwilling or unable to recommend laws that reflect the truth about virtue? Socrates' willingness to devise laws and images of virtue for the city in the *Republic* (380c, 383c, 421a, 456b–c, 461a ff.), as well as the Athenian Stranger's willingness to do so in the *Laws*, indicates that the difficulty is not simply that philosophers are unwilling to suggest better laws. Perhaps the city in the *Republic* is a cave in the sense that its founders must win the allegiance of the guardians, or at least of the auxiliaries, by telling them "noble" lies about theology, the autochthonous beginnings of the city, divine sanctions for natural classes, and the marriage lottery (377 ff., 414–415, 459c). But it is not enough for someone to recognize that these are lies in order to be liberated from the cave, for otherwise individuals such as Glaucon and Adeimantus would have already been "turned around," led from the artificiality of the cave to the sight of the good itself, and become philosophers. What is it that non-philosophers are unable or unwilling to grasp? What is it that keeps non-philosophers imprisoned in the cave? Perhaps there is something about law as such that makes even the best laws unreliable guides to the learning the truth about human nature. Perhaps there is something in the soul that makes us unwilling to accept or prone to distort the truth about virtue even as it is conveyed by the best laws. But if there is such an obstacle, what connection, if any, does it have to the defective eroticism which Socrates attributes to non-philosophers (476a ff.)? Does Plato's Socrates regard all forms of civic virtue, all laws, all political orders as equally defective? Finally, on what basis does he make such judgments?

The least arbitrary and most revealing way of approaching these questions is by examining the drama of the dialogue, for even though Socrates is not a lawgiver (but *Gorgias* 521), his conversations with particular individuals enable us to see precisely what he can and what he cannot convey about virtue to non-philosophers. Socrates' most conspicuous interlocutor in the *Republic* is Glaucon, a young man who wants passionately to know the goodness of justice and trusts in Socrates' probity and insight. In the course of teaching Glaucon about justice, Socrates attempts to lead him to understand the virtue of the philosopher. Glaucon is unable to absorb this teaching in the course of this particular conversation. Such an education requires the "turning" of one's soul and cannot be accomplished in one conversation (518c, 533a). The drama helps us see the obstacles that hinder Glaucon from understanding Socrates' teaching about virtue during their conversation about justice. There are, moreover, suggestions from other dialogues that Glaucon is incapable of absorbing a Socratic education and of becoming a philosopher (Bruell 1994, 268). At the opening of the *Symposium*, Socrates' disciple Apollodoros berates "Glaucon" for failing to follow Socrates and to devote himself to philosophy (*Symposium* 172a–173b). While some scholars take this to be the Glaucon of the *Republic*, Bury disagrees, presumably because it is difficult to believe that he could have fallen away so completely from Socrates (Bury 1932, 3). Martha Nussbaum, however, observes that by naming the character in the *Symposium* "Glaucon" Plato expects readers to think of the Glaucon of the *Republic* (Nussbaum 1986, 170). By reminding us of the *Republic*'s Glaucon in this context, Plato wants us to consider whether he is able to follow through on what Socrates tries to teach him in the *Republic*. Consulting other dialogues, one finds no suggestion that Glaucon pursued philosophy further. Christopher Bruell notes that "the only interlocutor of Socrates in the *Republic* of whom Plato informs us that he turned later to philosophy is Polemarchus (*Phaedrus* 257b3–4)" (Bruell 1994, 268). In the *Parmenides*, Cephalus asks Glaucon and Adeimantus to take him to their half-brother Antiphon to learn from him what transpired during Socrates' first conversation with the philosophers Parmenides and Zeno (*Parmenides* 126b–c). Unlike Antiphon, neither Glaucon nor Adeimantus is expected to have committed Socrates' conversations with philosophers to memory. In the *Apology*, Socrates notes how the relatives of his companions do not accuse him of corrupting them. He specifically notes that Adeimantus does not blame him for his influence on Plato, but he says nothing to suggest that he had any significant effect on Glaucon (*Apology* 34a). Hints such as these do not, of course, prove that Glaucon lacks the capacity to become a philosopher; but they at least alert us to the possibility that what hinders his education to philosophic virtue is significant and may be the kind of obstacle that prevents non-philosophers as such from sharing in philosophic virtue. By examining the concerns, beliefs, and deficiencies that impede Glaucon's progress in the *Republic*, we may come to understand the kinds of obstacles that must be overcome in order to philosophize and thus better discern what distinguishes the non-philosopher from the philosopher and civic from philosophic virtue.

At the beginning of Book II, Glaucon prefaces his long speech about justice by listing three categories of good things and asking Socrates to say into which of these categories justice falls. The first category consists of those things that are good "in themselves" rather than those which we choose for "what comes from them" (357b4–8). This category would include any good in which we "delight for its own sake" such as "enjoyment" and "harmless pleasures that have no after-effects other than the enjoyment in having them." A second category of good things consists of those that are "good in themselves" as well as good for what comes from them. Glaucon cites as examples thinking, seeing, and health, things that are not only enjoyable or beneficial immediately but also useful for other good things that come from them (357c1–3). The third category consists only of goods such as exercise, medicine, and labor that are not enjoyable by themselves but are useful insofar as they bring about other goods which produce enjoyment (357c5–d2). The most obvious difference among these categories seems to be that the goods in the first and second categories are enjoyable immediately, while those in the third category are enjoyed only for what they subsequently cause.

Socrates answers Glaucon by saying that he considers justice to be in the "noblest" or most beautiful category (*en toi kallistoi*), which he identifies as the category of things that we enjoy both for themselves and as means to other good things (358a1–3). According to Socrates, justice is unlike drudgery because it is enjoyable all by itself and unlike harmless pleasures in that it is desirable not only itself but also for the other good or enjoyable things that it brings about, things such as thinking, seeing, and health. Glaucon, however, asks Socrates to prove that justice is "good in itself," by which he seems to mean that it is praised without regard to further consequences (358b6–7). After this exchange, Glaucon goes on to make his celebrated speech blaming justice in order to provoke from Socrates its proper defense. The speech presents justice as being legal rather than natural, as a contrivance made by the cowardly majority in order to seduce strong, courageous "real men" into believing that it is good to follow the law and care for the well-being of others when by nature we all care mostly about our own happiness (359b2, 359c1–6). Any real man who willingly submits to the law and bears the burdens of citizenship is a dupe. By asking Socrates to refute this thesis, Glaucon reveals his hope that his own sense of justice is the product of genuine courage and rationality. But in wanting Socrates' help, Glaucon shows that he suspects that his sense of justice is no more than the product of weakness and social conditioning. Socrates is to put these doubts to rest by convincing him that a "real man" would choose to remain just in the face of the greatest hardships and that justice is compatible with the greatest courage and rationality. At the conclusion of his speech, he invents an image of a man who is perfectly just but who suffers enormously because of his justice; in asking Socrates to defend justice, Glaucon asks him show that such a man would willingly endure even a terrible death for justice's sake.

In thinking through what justice would have to be to live up to Glaucon's expectations, the primary difficulty is that his implicit account of the goodness of justice does not quite resemble any of the examples of good things in the three aforementioned categories. It is unlike enjoyment and harmless pleasures, as well as unlike thinking, seeing, and health, for justice could cost a real man everything, even life itself. It is also unlike exercising or taking medicine or laboring, insofar as these things are painful experiences that we must endure because they produce other things that we enjoy having. In fact, justice entails a measure of pain, if only because it means obeying laws that require us to treat others "as equals" (359c5–6) or as if their happiness were as important as our own, which means that we would sometimes have to disregard our own needs to care for those of others. But if the pain of justice is not a price we pay for some separate, subsequent good, what is the relation between the pain one endures for justice and the goodness of justice? It is only by conceiving of a courageous man who is willing to die miserably because all he cares about is justice that we are able to recognize something essential to justice: that it is something more important than our own individual well-being or happiness. It is not like a bitter medicine that we take to gain glowing health, but like a bitter drink that we swallow because it is good to take it, regardless of its consequences for us. It would be good to take it even if it killed us.

Having requested, however, that Socrates praise justice strictly for its own sake, Glaucon also asks him to show that those who have nothing but justice are happier than those who have everything but justice (361d3). He wants Socrates to argue, in other words, that being just is a sufficient cause of more happiness than one can have without justice and that being just is a necessary condition of perfect happiness. This request seems to fly in the face of the rest of Glaucon's implicit account of justice—for if he thinks justice is *the* means to greater happiness than is available through injustice, it is difficult to understand not only how it could be said to be good regardless of its consequences, but also why it would require any more "manliness" or courage than our willingness to take a bitter medicine that we know will give us glowing health (*Laches* 192e). Perhaps Glaucon wants to be shown that it is possible for justice or citizenship to be good "for its own sake" in two discrete senses: It is good both because it is an object of dedication worth more than our happiness and also because being dedicated to justice makes us happier than we could otherwise be. A "real man" disregards his desire for happiness to pursue justice but nonetheless finds that he is happiest for having done so. In order to satisfy Glaucon, Socrates must affirm that we can separate in our hearts and minds our willingness to be just "for its own sake" from our belief that justice is the core of our happiness. He would have to show that our fundamental experience of justice is that it is so important that we would choose it even if it were at the cost of our happiness and, in addition to this, that those who care only for justice are happier than those who do not care for it at all. He must show that we can understand the goodness of justice without any essential connection to our own good and that it just so happens that the just become happy.[2]

After listening to Glaucon's requests (supplemented and complemented by Adeimantus), Socrates expresses amazement that the boys remain attracted to justice even though they offer such powerful critiques of justice. Socrates says that he fears that he does not know how to satisfy them, even though he had said to Glaucon that he thought he knew in what way it is good. Socrates goes on to explore what justice is in the soul by first clarifying its place in a city. While elaborating the good city in Books II through IV, Socrates indicates that we cannot simply rely on what he has said to that point about the virtues to learn about the goodness of justice but must contrast what comes to sight in the good city with what comes to sight in a good individual in the hope that the truth about justice will emerge, in the same way that flame bursts out from rubbing together two sticks (434d2–5a; *Seventh Letter* 341c5–d2, 344b3–c1; Bruell 1994, 271–272; Irwin 1977, 332 n. 32.3.5). We must look, in other words, for friction, for differences and tensions, between justice in the good city and in the good individual in order to understand what justice is and how it is good. According to the argument laid out by Socrates, the city is wise insofar as its guardians have good counsel about what is best for the whole city (428d). Its courage, as we have seen, lies in its warriors' capacity to retain the opinions instilled by law about what is and what is not terrible. Its moderation consists in each part agreeing to the hierarchy of parts of the city; its justice, in the willingness of each part to perform only its own, proper, specialized function (431d–e, 433d). By stating that the particular citizen who possesses these virtues is willing to subordinate his or her own inclinations, desires, and ambitions to the good of the city, firm in the conviction (*dogmatos*) that the happiness of the city is more important than that of any of its parts (412d–e, 420b–c, 428d, 433, 434c, 519e, 544d–e), Socrates apparently affirms the fundamental tenet of Glaucon's account of the goodness of justice. He implies that the core of virtue or of "goodness" lies in subordinating one's happiness to that of the city. In light of this, virtue is "civic," not only insofar as one adheres to the correct opinions about the good, the noble, and the just that are given to us by the law, but also insofar as one cares for the city or for justice more than for one's own happiness.

Yet as Socrates describes the soul of a good individual, a somewhat different image of human virtue comes to sight. The wisdom of the good individual is said to consist not in knowing what is good for the whole city but in knowing what is good for the whole soul (441e4–5). Its courage lies in remembering not what the law proclaims but what reasoned speech proclaims to be terrible and not terrible. Its moderation consists in each part of the soul agreeing to the hierarchy of parts; and its justice, in the willingness of each part to do only its own, specialized job (442c–443d). The chief difference between the accounts of virtue in the city and in the individual is that while the virtuous citizen cares primarily about the city, the virtuous individual is concerned above all with his or her own, individual, psychic harmony or health (Annas 1981, 132; Bruell 1994, 271; Irwin 1977, 210; Nichols 1987, 95; Sachs 1971, 46). Such an individual calls "just" the good order of the parts of the soul as well as whatever produces that good order (443c, 444d–e).[3] In identifying justice with whatever makes the soul more harmonious or healthy, Socrates says explicitly that justice need not involve acting in relation to others. He says that *if* a good individual acts, in politics or in some other way, it is always with an eye to the harmony of his or her soul (443e). This is not to attribute to Socrates the view that one who has "psychic justice" would be a bad citizen, for, among other things, Socrates says that only someone with psychic justice is never tempted to tyrannize others (619b–e; Reeve 1988, 263). But through his comparison of justice with psychic harmony or health, Socrates reaffirms his initial answer to Glaucon's question about which category of good things would contain justice. He quietly denies that justice is good in the "purely" self-transcendent, self-denying, and heroic sense to which Glaucon alludes in his speech. It may be good or desirable on its own, but it must also be a part of, a means to, and another name for the health of the soul, a good that is both immediately gratifying and useful for other things (444d–e, 591b). It is not merely like health (357c1–3) but is in fact the health of the soul. Only psychic justice is justice itself or justice "in truth" (443c9). Socrates says that he has discussed the good city and its justice solely because these things provide an "image" of the justice of the good individual (443c4–5) and later adds that it does not matter whether the good city and its justice come into being at all as long as one has justice in one's own soul (443c, 472c–d, 591d–e, 592a7, 592b3–4; cf. 361d4–6). But on what grounds can Socrates call this internal, psychic, individual condition "justice"? How can he know that it reflects the goodness of justice better than what Glaucon understands justice to be? And exactly what does this imply about Socrates' respect for the civic virtue that Glaucon so admires?

Socrates advances this alternative account because he finds support for it from those, such as Glaucon himself, who are passionately devoted to virtue. More of Glaucon's account of justice emerges in response to Socrates' further presentation of virtue in Books V through VII, especially where he describes the character and motivations of the philosopher (484dff, 501d, 544a). The first thing that Socrates says about philosophers is that they are moved by an eros of knowledge of "the whole truth." To explain how philosophers differ from lovers of mere spectacles, Socrates says that they are like lovers of boys and wine who find every sort of wisdom beautiful and also like lovers of honor who prefer the most beautiful and highest sort of wisdom. In particular, they love the idea of the *kalon*, the form or look of that which is "beautiful" or "noble" (474c–475e, 479a, 499b–c, 501d). In addition to possessing a single-minded love of the ideas, they have a courage that shows itself in not looking upon death as something terrible (486b1, 487a5). This courage appears to be a reflection of a steadiness of soul that somehow does not interfere with but rather sustains their fiery passion to know (503c–d). Because of this great passion and their imperturbable psychic strength, they are otherwise moderate and never tempted to injure nor to steal. Having apparently completed his account of the philosopher's "beautiful and good" soul (503d), Socrates adds that they are especially eager to know the idea of the good, which he identifies as the greatest and most fitting study and something which one must know in order to make sense of the beautiful and the just (504d, 505a, 506a). Although most consider the good to be either pleasure or prudence, it is in fact something like the sun, something that illuminates the beings, that causes truth and knowledge, and that is "beyond" these things in beauty. It is, moreover, the cause of "existence" and of "being" and exceeds them in venerability and power. Glaucon seems to be greatly impressed by this description, as he exclaims "by Apollo, what daimonic transcendence" (509c1–2). In seeking the good, philosophers may seem to devote themselves to something utterly beyond themselves. But they are not like the heroic "real men" whom Glaucon hopes devote themselves to justice rather than to happiness, for even though he says that their initial liberation may be painful, he also says that it may be accompanied by great pleasures (538d, 581dff.; *Apology* 33c). In fact, these lovers neither undergo great torments nor sacrifice anything they otherwise desire in their pursuit of the good (485d6–e1); those who finally encounter the good are said to dwell while still alive in the Isles of the Blessed and to achieve the greatest happiness (519c, 526e).

Immediately after alluding to their bliss, however, Socrates suggests that the founders of the good city must compel these lovers of wisdom to surrender their perfect happiness in order to rule the city. Glaucon challenges this, asking whether those who commune with the ideas are to be done an injustice by being deprived of their happiness (519d).[4] This dissent tells us that he believes that there is a "beauty and goodness" of the soul, a glowing, inner health that consists in a fiery, magnificent, steady passion to know what is beautiful and good (503c–d), that those who possess this achieve complete happiness, and that they have no further need of nor obligation to care for anything else beyond it. Even though Glaucon claims to be uncertain about the goodness of justice, as a just man he knows in his heart that whatever justice is, it cannot be something that destroys happiness (cf. 334b, 335a, 335d, 347e). Contrary to what he earlier asked Socrates to show him, even he cannot fully separate his belief that justice is of the greatest importance from his expectation that it is a part of complete bliss. His most fundamental belief is not that justice is good regardless of its consequences, but that no matter how unhappy one makes oneself for justice's sake, in the end it is unthinkable for happiness and justice to remain at odds. His devotion to justice is never fully sundered from, and thus depends upon, his belief that being just is fully compatible with his own happiness. He thus seems to devote himself to justice in the expectation, hidden even from himself, that the best way to achieve perfect happiness is to put that goal out of his mind while striving to care for something else. In fact, his willingness to forgo his happiness precisely for the sake of the city or justice rather than for other potential objects of devotion points to his ultimate expectation that devotion to these things will result in perfect happiness, for even though they present themselves as more important than any one person's good, they also are understood to be "common goods," goods through which the individual secures a happiness unavailable on one's own (420b, 421c, 465a; *Laws* 875a–d, 903c). In light of this, "civic" virtue means not simply adherence to correct opinions given to us by the law, nor even caring for the city or justice above all else, but more precisely caring for the city or justice while striving neither to notice that we expect this caring for the city or justice to make us happy nor to think about the means by which the city or justice can make us happy.

This is not to say that Glaucon is incapable of envisioning how virtue and perfect happiness might be reconciled, for he points to one such means in swearing by Apollo when Socrates describes the good itself. Never having heard of the "doctrine of the ideas," Glaucon apparently understands the good to be something like the god Apollo, a providential god associated with the sun, who might admit "beautiful and good" lovers of the good to the Isles of the Blessed (cf. *Symposium* 180b3–5). And near the end of the conversation, Glaucon readily agrees to Socrates' suggestion that the just are not neglected by the gods but are rewarded if not in this life, then in the next (612c, 613a–b). Yet Glaucon never seems to see how deeply and completely he expects justice to culminate in happiness. Because Socrates, however, recognizes how deeply those who love justice expect it to result in individual psychic health and even bliss, he classifies it not as a noble sacrifice but as one of the noblest good things, that is, as one of those beautiful or splendid things that are enjoyable and useful for other things (334c–d, 358a1–3).

Because Glaucon never fully recognizes how confident he is that justice is good for him, he unknowingly exaggerates the self-transcendence of his own dedication to justice and thus never draws upon all the strength or courage that such transcendence would seem to call forth. Rather than force Glaucon to confront the problem at the heart of his understanding of justice, Socrates seems to test whether Glaucon will recognize that problem and its implications. For immediately after Glaucon complains that it would be unjust to force lovers of the idea of the good to rule the city, Socrates reminds him that they are concerned with the happiness of the city rather than of its parts and therefore the lovers of the idea of the good must come back to rule the city (519e; cf. with 420b–c, 464e). One might expect Glaucon to restate and elaborate his objection that justice cannot require the virtuous to surrender their perfect happiness even for the sake of the good city. Indeed, Socrates quietly agrees with this objection a few lines later when he remarks that philosophers who grow up outside the good city, that is, all actual philosophers, are under no obligation to rule (520a10–b4). But instead of pressing his objection, Glaucon simply accepts Socrates' reminder that the happiness of the city is more important than that of its parts. Throughout the rest of the dialogue, Glaucon goes on to speak about the measures needed to bring about the good city. In placing such emphasis on establishing the good city, Glaucon continues to speak as if the happiness of the city were more important than that of its parts—thus apparently forgetting that the good city is only an "image" to be used for recognizing the importance of establishing harmony in one's own soul, which is justice "in truth" (443c–e, 472c–d, 592b). By continuing to speak as if it were important to bring the good city into being, Glaucon still seems to believe that the happiness of the city is more important than that of its parts and hence that civic justice is identical to justice in the truest sense.

After drawing Glaucon's attention back to his concern with the coming into being of the good city, Socrates describes what its guardians must study to become both warriors and philosophers. But in laying out their course of study, Socrates gradually places less emphasis on the martial education than on the philosophic (Bloom 1968, 408; Nichols 1987, 217 n. 30). After Socrates recommends the study of mathematics to discipline the mind, he asks if geometry should also be studied. When Glaucon suggests that it is useful in war, Socrates replies that it has virtually no practical use but must be encouraged as much as possible for the sake of knowing "what is always" (527b). Similarly, when Socrates asks if astronomy should be studied, Glaucon remarks that it is useful for farming, navigation, and the art of generals; yet Socrates reprimands him for even considering astronomy's practical application (527d, 528e). After describing how students will study dialectics to discern the good itself, Socrates asks Glaucon "will you let your young people rule without this and without establishing a law that they must study it?" Without noticing how Socrates distances himself from the political application of this education, Glaucon replies, "I agree and join you in establishing this law" (534e). A few pages later, Socrates says to Glaucon that, after the education is complete, the students will have to descend into the "cave" again "for you" (539e3–6). Despite these repeated suggestions, Glaucon never notices how Socrates presents the good city as Glaucon's rather than his own and thus distances himself from the civic understanding of justice. At the end of Book VII, Socrates adds that in order for that city to come into being, everyone over the age of ten would have to leave it. In response, Glaucon says that they have discerned the quickest and easiest way that such a city could come into being, if it can come into being (541a–b). In saying this, Glaucon seems much less insistent that the good city be proven possible than he had in Book V (cf. 541a–b with 471e). Yet it is striking that he does not note the apparent impossibility of such an exodus and even suggests that the city might come into being by other means.

By the end of Book IX, however, Glaucon finally seems to have absorbed Socrates' lesson and says explicitly that the good individual will not mind political things but will attend only to "the city in speech" that does not exist anywhere on earth (592a–b). But after Glaucon accedes to this, Socrates begins Book X by reconsidering the actual city's institutions (595a, 605b, 607a, 607c), speaking once again as if they were concerned with bringing an actual city into being. And once again, Glaucon joins in, speaking as if establishing the good city were crucial to being just in the truest sense. In the course of this discussion, Glaucon refers to the unjust, not as those whose souls are disorderly and unphilosophic, but as murderers (610e1). Apparently going along with Glaucon, Socrates adopts a similarly civic understanding of justice when he describes the rewards of justice and penalties of injustice, for he refers to the just not as philosophers, who always disdain ruling and who are customarily reviled, but as those who sometimes choose to rule and always win honors (cf. 613d–e with 487d, 495c, 521b, 539c). Yet in the concluding myth of Er, Socrates reverts to a philosophic understanding of justice and says that the just are those who "always philosophize," who choose a private rather than public life, and who "practice justice with prudence in every way" (619d, 620c, 621c). On the whole, Socrates does not confront Glaucon with the implications of his beliefs about justice but instead shows us how Glaucon readily accepts invitations to look away from what he has implied about the character of justice and of his love of justice. Socrates never declares once and for all that the good city is impossible (Strauss 1964, 129). One reason why Socrates avoids saying explicitly that the good city cannot come into being may be that he wants us to observe how Glaucon remains eager to believe that it can and thus to observe how resolutely he adheres to a civic understanding of justice. Socrates does not, however, allow Glaucon to return to a merely civic understanding of justice that fails to admire the "private" philosopher as a just human being. For an important part of Socrates' purpose in the *Republic* is to provide Glaucon and others with a better image of philosophic virtue.

Glaucon's failure to understand fully the difference between merely civic and philosophic virtue during the action of the dialogue does not prove that he is incapable of going further on his own. He may, in fact, reflect on his statements and actions and recognize his own dissatisfaction with the proposition that the happiness of the city is more important than that of its parts. He may recognize that he exaggerates the selflessness of his own concern with justice and denies himself the opportunity to discern exactly how justice might be a means to his psychic health and happiness. Yet literary hints from other dialogues give us little reason to believe that he went back to and reflected on this or other Socratic conversations. The question of Glaucon's future compels us to ask more precisely what it is that hinders human beings like him from thinking through their understanding of justice.

In order to understand the obstacles that prevent non-philosophers from sharing in philosophic virtue, we need to consider why morally serious citizens such as Glaucon would be inclined to regard the goodness of justice and the happiness of the city as something separate from their own happiness. We need to ask why citizens like Glaucon would want to remain in the cave, resisting what a Socrates might teach them about the goodness of justice. Furthermore, we need to understand how and why lovers of wisdom are able to transcend the cave to the extent this is possible. Because Socrates' account of the cave is admittedly only an image, one must look to other parts of the dialogue, and not least to the drama, to understand the "chains" that are said to bind young men such as Glaucon in the cave. In the *Republic*, Socrates characterizes Glaucon as being both courageous and erotic (357a, 474d–475a). Glaucon's courage comes to sight when he challenges Socrates' account of justice at the opening of Book II, even though Socrates has just finished humbling Thrasymachus, the celebrated rhetorician. In his speech, Glaucon belies his erotic character when describing the perfect freedom of the man who wore the "ring of Gyges's ancestor"; for the very first thing he imagines that man doing is having sexual intercourse with the queen (357a). Similarly, in Book V, he delights at the prospect that the most valiant guardians will be permitted to kiss whomever they wish (468b–c). Socrates offers further evidence of Glaucon's eroticism by twice mentioning that Glaucon has lovers

(362, 402e). As we saw in Socrates' speech in the *Symposium*, erotic desire is not simply a sexual desire but is a needy longing for that which is beautiful or noble (*kalon*) (*Symposium* 203b). Socrates distinguishes eros of the good from eros of the beautiful on the grounds that we love good things in the expectation that they will make us happy while we love beautiful things in the expectation that they will make us immortal (*Symposium* 203b, 204c6–205a7, 206b1–207a4). Insofar as we desire only what we believe we need and lack (*Symposium* 200a1–e9), eros for the *kalon* reflects an awareness that we are mortal and an aspiration that beauty or nobility might somehow enable us to overcome or make up for our deaths. In that speech, heroes are singled out as examples of erotic human beings. They are said to be moved by eros to manifest a beautiful or noble courage by dying bravely, in part because this act endows their lives with something intrinsically splendid or "good in itself" and in part because it provides them with immortal glory that will survive their deaths (*Symposium* 208). Near the end of his speech, Socrates describes a further link between erotic love of the *kalon* and immortality: He suggests that those lovers who devote themselves to "the beautiful itself" seek to manifest thereby a "true virtue" that might win them the immortality they seek from loving gods (*Symposium* 212a2–7).

Bearing this psychology of eros in mind, Glaucon's love of justice comes more clearly into focus. Even though his erotic love for beautiful things tempts him to live beyond the law, he is at the same time deeply enamored by the beauty of justice. He is especially moved by the thought of a "real man" who overcomes deep and powerful needs for the sake of justice because this self-overcoming seems to call forth a prodigious and splendid inner strength, the very existence of which would provide such men with great solace for mortality. Glaucon's admiration and desire for nobility is even more explicit when Socrates goes on to describe a community that comes into being through mutual, economic self-interest and that is characterized by its practicality, gentility, and ease of life. As soon as Socrates mentions how its inhabitants will live and die in comfort, passing their tranquil lives on to succeeding generations, Glaucon calls such people "pigs" (372d). They appear to him to be less than human because they have only the "necessities" of life (369c, 372a, 373b). They exist without the need and even opportunity to make noble self-sacrifice and self-overcoming. There is nothing "noble" (*gennaias*) in the first city except its loaves of bread (372b). Recognizing that Glaucon longs for something beyond the mundane pleasures of "mere life," Socrates describes a second, "feverish" city that is more to his liking, a city filled with things that are beautiful rather than necessary (373a5). But Glaucon is far more pleased with the city that is "purged" of luxuries in Books II and III (399e) than with the feverish one because of the former's splendid public art and because of the noble, self-transcendent virtue that it requires of its citizens: Adeimantus, rather than Glaucon, objects to the sacrifices asked of the guardians (419a–b; 401e–403c, 416d–417b, 468e, 503a). Glaucon is attracted to the thought that by denying himself what is good for him, he will display the greatest, most shining, most noble strength of soul. Glaucon would find the moderate, practical, liberal virtues promoted by Locke and Montesquieu inadequate to satisfy his longing for the *kalon*.

By falling in love with the beauty of justice, Glaucon devotes himself to something that is not as radically and ultimately separate from his own well-being as he believes. He is not only convinced that justice cannot undermine perfect happiness, but also very pleased by Socrates' suggestion that by encountering the most beautiful of all beings one is able to live in the Isles of the Blessed when still alive and perhaps by the thought that one can thereby avoid death altogether. Moreover, in Book X Glaucon readily accepts Socrates' assertion that the gods do not neglect the just but reward them, if not in this life, then in the next (612c–613a). In fact, the last thing that Glaucon says in the dialogue is that there are few things more pleasant to hear than how the just are rewarded in the afterlife (614b). If Glaucon's love of justice is animated by the hope that it will ultimately provide him with perfect, lasting happiness, this in itself does not render him less noble. For it is disputable whether human beings will regard it as "noble" or virtuous to do things that fundamentally harm oneself (335c–d; *Laches* 192d). Socrates, at least, does not think that the noble things are utterly separate from those that are good for us, but includes them among things that are beneficial (358a1–3, 505a, 506a, 517c).

While both Glaucon and Socrates desire to be just and noble and good, only the philosopher pursues these ends successfully. Socrates' superiority to Glaucon is due not simply to his manifest intelligence, but also to his philosophic "courage," to his great steadiness of soul or endurance (503–504, 535a; *Symposium* 203d5, 219d2ff.; *Laches* 194a; Tessitore 1994, 131). According to Socrates' account of dialectics in the *Republic*, dialectics consists above all in thinking critically about what is just and noble and good and about the opposites of these things. But why must this prove so difficult that it requires great courage? What needs to be endured? The opening of the drama of the *Republic* offers us a concrete example of the importance of courage for dialectics and for transcending the merely civic understanding of justice and of virtue. Cephalus is a wealthy old man who loves to talk, especially now that his sexual longings have subsided. In the course of a few lines, the old man whose character has been shaped by eroticism reveals to Socrates that he is very afraid and hopeful about what will happen to him after he dies and now strives to be just to win a happy afterlife from the gods (330d–331b). But as soon as Socrates' questions lead Cephalus to see that he does not know precisely what it takes to be just, the old man flees the conversation, never to return. As important as knowing justice is to Cephalus, he is too fearful to endure examining it, too frightened of the possibility that he will discover that he will never learn how to be truly just in the eyes of the gods. Even if we do not consciously hope to use justice to win literal, individual immortality in the way that Cephalus does, our anxieties and wishes about death present obstacles to thinking clearly about what is just and noble and good. Because Glaucon hopes that the nobility of his concern with justice will console him for death or perhaps even provide him with immortality, he resists questioning the *perfect* selflessness and perfect nobility of his concern with justice. In describing a good education, Socrates recommends one that makes students tougher or hardier, especially regarding death and the death of loved ones (387c–e). But Socrates and Glaucon ultimately agree that it is too much to expect everyone to put entirely aside their grief at death (603eff.) and that this anguish makes it especially difficult to think clearly about what is good and bad (604b9–c1). In order to deliberate successfully in the face of our tribulations, we need a "medicine" or "education" that consists in both reason and habituation (604c1–d2, 606a8). In fact, even those with philosophic natures seem to find it difficult to overcome entirely their fears about death. Even a good individual needs a certain courage or steadiness of soul to recall what one otherwise knows is terrible and what is not terrible in the face of pleasure, pains, fears, and desires (430c5–6, 442c2, 535a). If death is not the terrible existence that Homer's Achilles says it is, it nonetheless casts so important a shadow over one's life that one cannot philosophize without thinking about it and brings on so great a loss that one needs to be stout of heart to think in light of it (386a–388c, 517c1; *Phaedo* 64a).

Because our anxieties about death lead us to exaggerate the selflessness of our concern with justice and to obscure the means by which we expect justice to make us happy, they are among the strongest roots of civic virtue. This helps us to understand why civic courage is singled out as the only virtue specifically called "civic," for it is precisely the lack of steadiness in the soul that leads us to understand virtue in a "civic" manner, that is, to be important without any regard to our own, individual well-being. Civic courage turns out to differ from the nobler courage, not because the former is grounded in thoughtless perseverance or habituation, but because it reflects a lack of endurance that succumbs to pains, pleasures, fear, and hopes about justice and the whole of virtue. To have philosophic courage is to have sufficient endurance to resist the very foundations of civic courage and to think through what the noble and good and just actually mean to us.

As an Athenian, Glaucon has not, of course, been subjected to the sort of civic education outlined in the *Republic*. But his eros for beauty or nobility causes him to admire the courage and rationality of the citizen who denies himself and submits to the law for the sake of justice (358e–359c). It seems that laws are able to promote civic virtue, not only by habituation (e.g., *Laws* 653a–c), but also by appealing to this natural erotic longing to be noble. One of the most significant natural differences between Glaucon and Socrates appears to be that the former lacks the steadiness of soul to scrutinize how his exclamation at 519d that it is unjust to destroy the perfect happiness of the lovers of the idea of the good calls into question his conviction that justice consists in devoting oneself to the city and its law. Glaucon is willing to question the goodness of justice but cannot, at least in the course of the dialogue, bring himself to consider the answer implied by his own beliefs. Socrates, on the other hand, is able to risk the thought that his own concern with justice is not as selfless and courageous as Glaucon wants to believe. Bearing the importance of steadiness of soul in mind, we may be able to explain why Polemarchus rather than Glaucon is said to be attracted to philosophy in the *Phaedrus*. Like Glaucon, Polemarchus is bold, even contentious (327b–c, 331d4–5); and like Glaucon, Polemarchus believes that justice must be beneficial (333a1, 334b7, 335d13). But Polemarchus is the only interlocutor who raises the question whether the good city is possible (449b1–450a2; Strauss 1964, 122–123). Polemarchus's willingness to question the possibility of what he fervently believes *should* come into being may reflect a toughness that Glaucon does not share. In light of Socrates' criticism of civic virtue, it seems that the best education, civic or otherwise, would help those with sufficiently good natures to master the fears that prevent us from recognizing what is problematic about our merely civic understanding of virtue.

Mary Nichols offers a rich, thought-provoking, and increasingly influential interpretation of the *Republic* as a critique of the longing for perfect justice. According to Nichols, the dialogue demonstrates how our political aspirations urge us to impose a single, universal vision on the city that inevitably obscures essential differences (Nichols 1987, 36–37, 95–96). In particular, she points to Glaucon as an example of those who are moved by this spirit. She attributes his demand to hear justice praised without regard to its consequences as a demand that justice be understood as something "pure or simple" and "unmixed with the complexity of relationships that characterize human life." At the heart of his desire for simplicity lurks a desire to find a world in which the just do not suffer but enjoy only "perfect goodness." According to Nichols, Glaucon is "ready to reject the world because he cannot find what is simply good there" (Nichols 1987, 60, 64–65, 69). She says that in response to Glaucon's demand for a simpler, more perfect world, Socrates describes the easy, bucolic goodness of the "healthy city" early in Book II. But Glaucon rejects this city because he knows "the world is not as harmonious as Socrates describes it, that the interests of men do not coincide, and that conflict among citizens and among cities necessitates rule." Glaucon desires harmony and simplicity, but he senses that "they cannot be found in the easy way Socrates prescribes" (Nichols 1987, 68). Socrates goes on to describe the good city at great length in order to expose how Glaucon's vision becomes manifestly inhumane and impossible. Despite the persuasiveness of Nichols's general thesis, it seems that she overlooks some important aspects of Glaucon's character. For even though Glaucon wants Socrates to show that the just ultimately find perfect happiness, he also wants him to show that justice is a test and sign of manly courage. Glaucon is less ready to reject the world because it is complex and imperfect than to reject *justice* because he suspects that we care about it out of weakness or simplemindedness. By admiring justice for the noble courage it calls forth, Glaucon expects it to entail sacrifices that are, in some respect, imperfections. He wants to know that justice is not only advantageous but also noble. In keeping with her presentation of Glaucon as desiring perfect goodness and deploring that the just suffer, Nichols argues that he "obviously dislikes tragedy" because it "reveals men's weakness, their inability to control their situation, and their vulnerability" (Nichols 1987, 60, 68, 111). But in Book X, when Socrates says that even the best of us enjoy and give ourselves to tragic poets who make us commiserate with mourning heroes, Glaucon replies, "Of course I know it" (605d; see also 607d). Glaucon joins Socrates in criticizing tragedy because it makes him enjoy public lamentations when, in fact, he takes pride in suffering quietly in accordance with the law (604a–b). Glaucon's admiration for the noble beauty of those who endure hardship is at the heart of his respect for the just. Furthermore, Glaucon's demand for such beauty or nobility gives rise to his objection to the healthy city in Book II. Glaucon does not directly question the possibility that the healthy city could come into being (Strauss 1964, 122) but instead denigrates its way of life, calling it a "city of pigs." As Nichols observes, Glaucon perceives a fundamental difference between "stronger" and "weaker" human beings (Nichols 1987, 68). At the root of Glaucon's inchoate complaint about the city of pigs is his conviction that "real men" who lived in that practical, healthy city would encounter nothing that is "useless but beautiful" and would never manifest nobility through struggle and sacrifice. Nichols makes a persuasive case that "political men" long to impose a partial and distorted vision on the city. But in at least one respect, the problem with Glaucon's vision is not simply that it simplifies complexities but that it mistakenly sees justice in two discrete ways: as something that is good for its own sake and also as *the* means to our happiness. He has, in this sense, a falsely bifurcated and falsely complex understanding of virtue. Plato's Socrates, on the other hand, seems to believe that genuine virtue has but one form (518e1–2; *Phaedo* 69b; cf. *Laws* 965d).

Having gained some clarity about the differences between civic and philosophic courage, we are in a better position to interpret Socrates' "formal" account of why non-philosophers are unable to understand *auto to kalon* near the end of Book V. Glaucon's central difficulty is not so much that he mistakenly believes that particular beautiful beings are beautiful without believing in the existence of "the beautiful itself" (476c) as that he mistakenly accepts an image or phantom of beauty or nobility for that which is genuinely beautiful or noble (479b11–d1). His belief that justice is good in two, utterly separate senses is only an image of justice, for even he will not maintain that justice can be good "for its own sake" unless it is also good for us. Moreover, as long as he steadfastly ignores potential frictions between the two aspects of justice's goodness, he will not begin to see how they might be reconciled. He will continue to admire the law-abiding, devoted citizen who never considers how civic justice contributes to his or her own happiness and psychic harmony. He now admires the philosopher as a just human being but will not recognize that *only* those who always consider the good order of their souls, who practice "justice with prudence in every way," are truly just (621c). More concretely, Glaucon will not see how the steadfast pursuit of knowledge of the just and noble and good provides Socrates with a harmony or health of soul that Glaucon himself would otherwise recognize as just and noble and good. Glaucon's "civic" understanding of justice remains incomplete and, to that extent, a mere image or phantom of justice (476c4–8; Dobbs 1994, 270).

Despite Socrates' many criticisms of civic virtue, the disdain for civic virtue reflected by his image of the cave is not, in itself, Plato's last word. For Socrates is apparently grateful for the physical protection and atmosphere of moral seriousness provided by the laws of Athens (e.g., *Apology* 41e–42a; *Crito*). Moreover, the *Republic* suggests how the moral education provided by laws might lend crucial support to philosophic investigation. In Book VII, Socrates acknowledges that spirited, young dialecticians often enjoy "tearing apart" what the law teaches about nobility and justice but fail to discern what is genuinely just and noble and good. In order to prevent dialectics from sinking into superficial skepticism, Socrates recommends that no one be allowed to engage in dialectics until they are moderated by age (537d, 539c); but this solution is problematic, since Socrates notes that the greatest and most numerous labors must be undertaken by the young (536d). In order to moderate the young dialecticians' fiery quickness so that they remain alert to evidence of what is genuinely just and noble and good, laws might be formulated that bolster their steadiness of soul and powers of self-command. In addition, Socrates' actions in the dialogue reflect an even deeper level of respect for civic virtue. Socrates' philosophic predecessors tended to dismiss the non-philosophers' beliefs about justice as mere convention unworthy of serious examination (*Laws* 889e3–890a2). Socrates, however, discovers that his lack of "divine wisdom" or definitive knowledge of the necessities that govern the whole compels him to reconsider whether philosophers have given adequate attention to what non-philosophers experience and say about justice and the gods who uphold justice (*Apology* 20eff.; *Phaedo* 99d–100c; *Republic* 506e, 509c). Unable to trust entirely his own subjective thinking, he determines to test and deepen his account of virtue against non-philosophic or non-scientific accounts. Throughout the dialogues, we find Socrates examining whether the words and actions of politicians, poets, sophists, priestesses, and others undermine or support his account of virtue. Thus, even as Socrates argues that most denizens of the cave can never be liberated from their shadowy understandings of virtue, in practice he relies on his fellow citizens' experiences and understandings of virtue to affirm his own (Irwin 1977, 38).

In the *Republic*, the understanding of virtue that Socrates encounters in men such as Cephalus, Polemarchus, Glaucon, and Adeimantus is the matrix out of which he demonstrates his own virtue. From among these men's understandings, Socrates focuses in particular on Glaucon's civic understanding of justice, treating it as the bar before which he must justify philosophic virtue. In the course of the dialogue, Glaucon does not fully grasp what is implied by his objection to the thought that justice can ruin the perfect happiness of those who love the good itself. But his words and actions signal his deeper recognition that justice cannot be more important than the harmony and happiness of one's own soul. Glaucon implicitly agrees with Socrates that only those who "practice justice with prudence in every way" are truly just human beings. Moreover, he agrees with Socrates that the noblest things are not those that we seek for their own sake but, rather, those that are *both* good in themselves *and also* useful for other things (358a1–3). Thus, by Glaucon's lights, the individual who cares primarily for the well-being of his soul by philosophizing possesses a more just, a nobler, a more complete version of civic virtue.

Glaucon's inability to recognize the philosopher's virtue helps us understand more precisely the relation between civic and philosophic virtue. On the one hand, philosophic virtue seems to be the completion of civic virtue and thus to differ from civic virtue as a matter of degree. Yet this seems at odds with Socrates' statements that the philosopher's nature differs decisively from that of the non-philosopher, that the soul of the philosopher is turned in a different direction from that of the non-philosopher, and that philosophers alone have prudence, which is the only genuine virtue of the soul. This difficulty might be resolved by considering more carefully Socrates' account of the philosophic nature. According to Socrates, one of the most important aspects of the philosophic nature is steadiness of soul. One needs this steadiness to turn away from the civic understanding of virtue and to scrutinize, clarify, and follow the implications of one's own beliefs. As we see in Glaucon, it is difficult to consider the relationship between civic justice and our own happiness in part because we long to understand our devotion to civic justice as utterly selfless and thus a display of perfect nobility; for we cherish our nobility as a consolation for death and possibly as a means to immortality. Throughout the *Republic*, Glaucon resists the thought that justice cannot be perfectly selfless and perfectly noble but requires us to be prudent or careful in seeking happiness and psychic harmony. By continuing to resist this thought, by trying to be perfectly noble rather than both noble and prudent, he forecloses the possibility that he will be just in the truest sense. Thus, Glaucon's words and actions point in the direction of a virtue that he does not possess. And this is of the utmost importance, to the extent that we are able to see in Glaucon concerns that animate all who can be said to love justice.

Socrates' examination of Glaucon is an impressive vindication of philosophic virtue. Yet Socrates' endeavor to examine how others experience and understand virtue is never complete. As we see in the *Euthyphro*, Socrates continues to conduct these investigations even at the end of his life. It seems that Socratic rationalism vindicates itself only to the extent that it remains open to the widest range of philosophic and non-philosophic experiences and understandings of virtue. For a Socratic philosopher to cease examining and thus respecting those with alternative notions of virtue would be to undermine the very foundations of philosophic virtue. For Socrates would lose the only solid basis of his respect for philosophy were he to disdain the civic understanding altogether.

Because Socrates never fully refutes every alternative account of virtue, he must continue to grant it the deepest possible respect and must not sweep it recklessly aside. Abstracting for the moment Socrates' desire to reform his fellow citizens, Socrates' *philosophic* need to confront his fellow citizens' deepest and most thoughtful accounts of virtue would lead him to exhort them to take their experiences and beliefs about virtue seriously and to defend them as best they can (e.g., *Apology* 28b–d, 41e2–42a2; *Symposium* 218d–219a). On the other hand, Socrates is sufficiently confident in the legitimacy of philosophy to defend it against its critics and to persuade his fellow Athenians that philosophers exemplify virtue. He displays a courage and self-command that citizens would readily find exemplary (e.g., *Symposium* 219e–221c). Moreover, he expects his manifest seriousness about virtue to merit not only tolerance of but even respect for philosophy among those who are most aware of the importance of virtue to themselves.

Contrary to both early modern critics of classical republicanism and postmodern critics of Platonism, the *Republic* endeavors to show that some are inspired to love the virtues of citizenship by longings within their own soul. Glaucon is moved by the virtue of the citizen out of a natural, erotic desire to share in what is noble and admirable. The *Republic* suggests that it is possible to promote civic virtue by drawing attention to how citizenship aims at satisfying this profound human longing. Plato's subtle drama is especially valuable insofar as it enables readers to enter into the thinking and experiences of interlocutors such as Glaucon so that we may come to feel the power and beauty of civic virtue. In fact, one of the main purposes of the dialogue may be to awaken skeptical readers to that power and beauty. After Glaucon and Adeimantus finish their long speeches at the start of Book II, Socrates claims that he is amazed that they are still attracted to justice despite having absorbed such powerful critiques of it (368a–b). But Socrates' professed amazement is puzzling, since he is already aware that Glaucon remains attached to justice despite having been exposed to powerful criticisms of justice leveled by Thrasymachus and many others (347e, 358c). Those who are likely to be genuinely amazed at Glaucon's persistent attachment to justice are those students of rhetoric, sophistry, and pre-Socratic philosophy who believe that our concern with justice is based on convention, on force and indoctrination, and who believe that it can readily be debunked and overcome. One purpose of the dialogue may be to alert such thinkers to their ignorance about the strength and complexity of justice, much as one of the purposes of Aristophanes' *Clouds* may have been to alert Socrates to the same phenomena.

Along with helping us to deepen our respect for civic virtue, the dialogue also offers us serious warnings. It teaches us that the lover of civic virtue resists considering precisely how civic virtue contributes to our happiness and harmony of soul. Yet, in the end, it does not so much condemn the virtue of the citizen as alert us to its tendency to be shortsighted about the virtue of human beings such as Socrates. By thinking through the potential limits of the love of citizenship, the dialogue as a whole helps us to deepen our respect for those who, like Socrates, devote themselves to the pursuit of what is genuinely "noble and good." In this manner, it allows us to be more just to the just.

# CHAPTER 9

## *Conclusion*

In the eighteenth century, the physicist Georg Christoph Lichtenberg wondered whether future generations would construct universities to restore the ignorance being swept away by the Enlightenment. Socratic education is not a simple return to ignorance, even though one of its purposes would be to debunk the Enlightenment's claim to have decisively debunked the love of noble virtue. Socratic education aims to restore not only the legitimacy of the most fundamental questions, but also the possibility of finding fundamental answers. Socrates' education culminates in knowledge of eros, which is to say in knowledge of what moves and gratifies and perfects the soul. This knowledge, he indicates, is the core of virtue and happiness.

Yet Socrates' knowledge of eros remains disputable (*Symposium* 175e, 216d, 219a) and in this sense remains knowledge of ignorance. According to Plato, Socrates' most prominent disputant is the comic poet Aristophanes. Taken with Aristophanes' critique of Socrates in the *Clouds*, Plato's presentation of Aristophanes in the *Symposium* elaborates powerful challenges and alternatives to Socratic claims to know the soul and to possess its virtues. In the *Symposium*, Socrates recounts how even he responded to his teacher Diotima's lessons in erotic matters with no less than seventeen questions and objections. Socrates' education culminates not only in an account of eros, but also in an awareness that he must supplement or confirm that account. At the end of Socrates' account of his education, Aristophanes' challenge to Socratic wisdom springs to life in Plato's portrait of Socrates' most notorious and problematic student, Alcibiades. The *Symposium* recounts for us how Socrates failed to give Alcibiades the education promised him in the *Alcibiades Major*.

Although Socrates is unable to lead every passionate, ambitious, noble-minded young man to virtue, his conversations with

Alcibiades in the *Alcibiades Major* and *Symposium*, as well as with Glaucon in the *Republic*, offer dramatic support for his thesis that by nature we are moved by an erotic need to know we are "noble and good." His interlocutors' responses to his arguments, their ultimate dissatisfaction with their own alternative understandings of virtue, and their own implicit respect for Socrates' nobility and goodness help to confirm Socrates' knowledge of erotic matters. By reflecting on Plato's subtle, dramatic portraits of particular human beings, readers are able to judge for themselves the success of his response to Aristophanes and, by extension, to modern critics of Socratic and Platonic philosophy—such as Nietzsche and Rorty.

Socratic education may serve liberal democracy by helping to restore the plausibility and dignity of the love of virtue. It can begin this service by questioning whether modern and some postmodern thinkers such as Rorty have exaggerated the contingency and subjectivity of what we believe to be virtue. For Socratic education offers evidence that our love of noble virtue is not simply the product of arbitrary historical movements and concealed wills to power, but an expression of natural, abiding needs to know we are "noble and good." Moreover, Socratic education could assist liberal democracy by encouraging us to reconsider the worthiness of reason as a guide in pursuing what is noblest and best. Socratics could call on theorists who charge that traditional, "Platonic" rationalism has flattened and narrowed our horizons to scrutinize the evidence in Plato's dramas that Socrates' dialectical inquiries illuminate our deepest and lasting needs. They could ask writers and other artists to reexamine whether their critiques of modern rationalism apply to the inquiries of the Platonic Socrates, who does not assume reason's authority but attempts to justify it on the basis of the experiences and understandings of a variety of particular interlocutors. Socratics could also challenge critics of modern science to reconsider their sweeping doubt of all forms of rationalism in light of Plato's account of the young Socrates' love of knowledge; recalling Plato's claim that the young Socrates was moved to study natural philosophy by an erotic desire to be "noble and good," they could help us to rethink the Nietzschean teaching that science is simply the expression of the philosopher's and modern democrat's will to power. Moreover, they could also challenge defenders of science to justify its goals and demonstrate its worth on "pre-scientific" political, moral, and religious grounds. Most directly and most importantly, Socratic education could help students of politics, of law, of philosophy, of literature, and of science to elaborate and think critically about their own, implicit beliefs about what is noble, what is good, what is just, and what is sacred. By encouraging us to elaborate and defend our various notions of what is noble and what is best, Socratic education promises to broaden and invigorate contemporary political debate. By rekindling the controversies about virtue that took place prior to and throughout the early stages of liberal democracy, Socratic education would help make liberal democracy once again the scene of serious reflection about virtue.

Some might object, however, that, by awakening the love of noble virtue in all its forms, Socratic education could encourage some to impose their own political or moral or religious vision on the whole of society. Were not, they may ask, the controversies that originally led to the founding of liberal democracy religious disputes about which Church is the true Church? And about the role of religion in politics? In fact, by introducing other, non-liberal and non-scientific accounts of virtue into public dialogue, does not Socratic education merely broaden the range of potentially intolerant notions of virtue? There seem to be several responses to such objections. Primarily, Socratic education lends philosophic grounds for remaining open to others in order to vindicate one's own knowledge of virtue. Socrates learns from reflecting on his own erotic love of wisdom that his thinking has been clouded by fears and hopes that he has not plainly seen. In order to be confident in his own knowledge, Socrates must remain as open as possible to the possibility that others experience nobility and goodness in ways that escape him. Dialogues that examine the eros for noble virtue such as the *Symposium*, *Alcibiades Major*, and *Republic* reflect Socrates' great attention to his interlocutors' non-philosophic and "civic" experiences and understandings of what is "noble and good." By reflecting on these dialogues, we can find reasons for resisting the temptation to believe that philosophy, or any other activity or way of life, has decisively answered the fundamental questions. Plato's Socrates awakens us to the need to remain respectful of and curious about alternative accounts of virtue for the sake of our own self-knowledge.

Yet we might understandably fear that some will conveniently disregard this Socratic lesson and try to impose their particular political or moral or religious visions on society as a whole. In response, supporters of liberal democracy might argue that this fear misunderstands and underestimates the strength of liberalism. For the founders of liberal democracy do not claim that citizens must become relativists or nihilists to be tolerant. Liberalism is intended to function amid disputes about virtue. Liberal forms and institutions are designed to channel and "check and balance" those who would impose an illiberal order on the whole of society. In fact, a revival of such ambitions may serve liberal democracy by reminding us of its institutional genius for controlling and moderating ambitions. Finally, while it is prudent to be wary of the love of noble virtue becoming intolerant, one should not overlook how the prevailing moral atmosphere is prone to its own forms of intolerance. Some regard the very attempt to justify one way of life as best as an affront to others and even as intolerance itself. By legitimating Socratic education, by holding up the erotic Socrates as a model of a truly liberal human being, we can at least become more tolerant of those who pursue genuine independence and excellence of mind.

# NOTES

## CHAPTER 1

1. Commenting on Nietzsche, Heidegger remarks that "implied in the essence of a creative establishment of goals and the preparation for such establishment is that it comes to exist and swings into action, as historical, only in the unity of the fully historical Dasein of men in the form of particular nations" (Heidegger 1979 [1961], 158).

2. While Strauss emphasizes the need for Socratic education, he does not promise that it could furnish the moral education once supplied by deep and widespread religiosity. At one point, he suggests merely that liberalism affords us the opportunity to "cultivate our garden" or, in other words, to pursue excellence on our own. But Strauss also raises the possibility of setting up "outposts" that "may come to be regarded by many citizens as salutary to the republic and as deserving of giving it its tone" (Strauss 1968, 24). By such outposts, Strauss apparently means not institutions that teach liberal education "in the highest sense" but simply political science departments and law schools that pursue the "more modest, more pertinent and more practical" goal of encouraging "whatever broadens and deepens the understanding" rather than "what in the best case cannot produce more than narrow and unprincipled efficiency" (Strauss 1968, 19; Bruell 1994a, 330). Strauss does not promise that liberal education, strictly understood, could ever become "mass education." But he at least raises the possibility that liberally educated men and women could become prominent enough in liberal society that "liberal education" itself might "acquire a hearing even in the marketplace" (Strauss 1968, 24).

## CHAPTER 2

1. One might expect Rorty's primary response to be that pragmatists will champion liberal beliefs that they know to be doubtful because they will welcome the opportunity to be courageous for its own sake (Rorty 1989, 47; 1991, 33). But since they are unlikely to take seriously any radical challenges to their civic beliefs, it is difficult to understand

how their steadfastness could be experienced as or called courageous.

2. Rorty also claims that Nietzsche's greatest interpreter, Martin Heidegger, was a thinker whose politics were contingent upon his philosophy. According to Rorty, Heidegger apparently loathed the Weimar Republic because he was a "Schwartzwald redneck" who hated "North German cosmopolitan mandarins" (Rorty 1989, 111). Heidegger dared to change the destiny of Europe because he wrongly imagined that he knew philosophic words that would resonate with and transfigure his fellow Europeans; but the vast majority of Europeans did not share his vocabulary and came to a different destiny (111, 118–119). In the end, his comments on technology and politics reveal him merely to be "resentful, petty, squint-eyed, obsessive—and, at his occasional worst (as in his praise of Hitler after the Jews had been kicked out of the Universities), cruel" (120).

## CHAPTER 3

1. While Brickhouse and Smith agree that the Oracle gives Socrates no specific command to interrogate others, they argue that Socrates found this command implied in the Oracle's answer. They claim that prior to Chaerephon's startling news that the god thinks no one is wiser than Socrates, Socrates knows that piety "requires one to serve the gods by promoting what is good" and that the oracle merely teaches him "the full extent to which his fellow Athenians had pursued and possessed only apparent goods" (Brickhouse and Smith, 1989, 97–98). After dedicating himself to understanding the Oracle's wisdom, Socrates arrives at his "understanding of what the god wanted most for men: the abandonment of their pretenses to wisdom and the comprehension that their material concerns profit them nothing until they have first achieved the most precious of all goods, human virtue" (99). But this fails to account for Socrates' claim to be ignorant of the greatest things, which presumably include what the gods require of human beings. Moreover, it does not account for Socrates' initial discovery of his own ignorance nor for the reliability of the course he chooses to test or refute the oracle. As Stokes observes, Brickhouse and Smith interpret Socrates' speech by taking for granted his innocence rather than by looking to the speech to explain his innocence (Stokes 1992, 30).

2. This knowledge consists not in reasoning deductively from hypotheses, nor in reasoning inductively up to them, but in knowing both the principles or causes that compel each being to be the particular being that it is as well as the principles or causes that compel each being to be. Plato *Republic* 511b, 533c–d, 534d; Aristotle *Metaphysics* 1051b–2a;

*Prior Analytics* 64b34–36; *Posterior Analytics* 71b3–4, 72b 3–4.

3. This account of Platonic philosophy applies to most of the Platonic *corpus*, but not to later works such as the *Phaedrus*, *Statesman*, and *Laws*, which are less Platonic for having been influenced by Aristotle (Nussbaum 1986, 291 n).

4. In the *Charmides*, Socrates feels competent to judge who is and who is not most wise in erotics. He says that he thinks Kudias most wise because Kudias said that one should beware going before a beautiful youth in the same way a fawn should beware going before a lion and "being seized as a portion of his flesh" (155d4–e1).

## CHAPTER 4

1. Unless otherwise noted, all subsequent citations refer to Burnet's edition (1901–5) of Plato's *Symposium*.

2. On the Socratic understanding of spiritedness, see Leo Strauss 1989b, 165–169.

3. According to Bloom (1992, 482), Aristophanes teaches that eros emerges entirely as a reaction against subjugating our natural sexuality to law. This would presumably account for the origin of both piety and eros in the ancient nature: After law is imposed on us for the sake of family, we understand the gods to have harmed us and want to be whole beings who can overcome the gods. There is some impressive support for this reading: The term *eros* is used to describe our weakness and separateness only after Aristophanes speaks of sexual repression. Were the sexual repression the sole cause of eros, it might also explain why eros is for only *one* other person and why sexual gratification offers a temporary relief from eros. And it gains further weight from the *Clouds*, which shows the reemergence of gods precisely where the family is threatened. But can sexual regulation explain the *entire* origin of resentment at the gods and eros? If the myth is to be followed strictly, pride and anger at the gods precede the subjugation of sexuality to the law of the family. Sexual repression exacerbates our erotic desires; but we are proud, angry, and impious before we are sexually regulated. If one resists taking the chronology of events in the myths so seriously, one must still ask why human beings would restrict our sexual longings in the first place. Why need the family at all? On the basis of Aristophanes' speech, the most plausible answer is that our primary orientation is toward whatever is our own, especially our own children. Moreover, Aristophanes says that we find relief from eros not only in sexual release but also in comedy and in thought, thus suggesting that the origins of eros extend to this deeper root.

4. The phrase "through injustice" is ambiguous, for it does not clarify whether we were split because of the gods' injustice or our own. The reference to what happened to the Arcadians suggests the latter. Saxonhouse says that "the Arcadians had been disloyal to the Spartans, as in effect had the spherical beings been to the Olympian gods" (Saxonhouse 1985, 30). See Xenophon, *Hellenica* 5.2.6–8.

5. Socrates' atheism seems qualified by his introduction of the Clouds, previously unrecognized goddesses whom he claims to worship. But there is reason to doubt that he considers them truly divine. Although he calls them his goddesses, he does so as a teacher of tricky rhetoric and in the same breath that he teaches that nothing rules but "vortex" or necessary, natural motions. He also presents them as indifferent to the law or justice (*Clouds* 434–435). After introducing them, he takes Strepsiades inside for a secret instruction which is never disclosed; but after that indoor instruction, neither Socrates nor Strepsiades ever refers to the Clouds as goddesses, just as Socrates' successful student Pheidippides never refers to them as goddesses at all. Prior to the private instruction Strepsiades refers to the Clouds as "queens of the whole" but afterwards gives this same title to Fraud (*Clouds* 357, 1150; Strauss 1966, 25). Socrates may initially present the Clouds as goddesses to displace the authority of Zeus and secondly to displace the gods altogether. As O'Regan says:

> There is no contradiction between his atheism and his subsequent introduction of the clouds. Rather, as suggested by *eis logous* here and later use of *epideixis*, or rhetorical display, in line 269, the clouds are introduced as arguments. Strepsiades will meet them in conversation: they are goddesses (*daimones*) because of their power as propositions. Using the clouds, Socrates can expose the reality of "divine affairs," namely that they are not divine at all. But the clouds themselves are not immune to the process. The sequence of arguments initiated by their entrance will end by stripping them of their independence and implicitly their divinity as well. (O'Regan, 1992, 44)

The Clouds, however, do not represent argument, as such. From the outset, Socrates is shown honoring not Clouds, but "air" or "ether." The Clouds, on the other hand, are neither ether nor water but a combination of these things. Their brilliant, dewey "nature" or "immortal form" can be cast off (*Clouds* 277, 289). Their ambiguity or variability reflects that they are the part of nature which can conceal or dissemble. They represent rhetoric, the form of argument which imitates and alters other, natural things, such as animals and human beings (*Clouds* 347–355; Nichols 1986, 14; Strauss 1966, 21). Poets can use them to conceal nature, inventing things such as centaurs (*Clouds* 346), or to reveal nature, using images to exaggerate or isolate characteristics so as to point to the essence of people and things.

6. One sign that even the Socratics concede that Aristophanes comes close to portraying the "historical" Socrates is that Plato, Xenophon, and Thucydides portray Alcibiades in ways that resemble Pheidippides (cf. Plato *Alcibiades Major* 110b–c with *Clouds* 25; Xenophon *Memorabilia* 1.2.40–46 with *Clouds* 1399–1400; and Thucydides 6.16 with *Clouds* 28).

7. At the conclusion of his speech, even the pedantic doctor who reproved him for his irrationality is pleased with the speech (193e4). Rosen goes much too far in saying that Aristophanes' patriotic opposition to the "enlightenment" makes him into a complete misologist (Rosen 1987, 137, 120–58 passim).

8. Consider, for instance, the remarkable distance between the traditional understanding of the origins of the human race and the account offered by the speech attributed to Aristophanes by Plato in his speech in the *Symposium*. Hesiod says that Earth was the first goddess and that the sun and moon are the children of the titans Theia and Hyperion (*Theogony* 371 ff.). But the natural philosophers claim that the earth is rock, that the sun is fire, and that the moon is earth that takes its light from the sun; and, as a result of such scientific explanations of celestial beings, they are charged with impiety (Diels 1985, Anaxagoras 18; Empedocles 42, 43; Parmenides 14, 15; Aristophanes *Clouds*, 225–233, 1506–1507; Plato *Apology* 26d). In saying that the moon is the offspring of the sun and the earth, Plato's Aristophanes accepts this most unorthodox, philosophic account.

## CHAPTER 5

1. Cicero *Tusculan Disputations* 5.10–11. Cf. *Academia* 1.15–6, *Brutus* 39; Xenophon *Memorabilia* 1.11–16; Aristotle *Nicomachean Ethics* 1141a20–b9, 1181b15; *Metaphysics* 987b1–2; Hobbes *De Cive* "Author's Preface"; Nietzsche *Birth of Tragedy* 15. See Guthrie 1971, 97–105; Strauss 1964, 13–18.

2. Unless otherwise noted, all subsequent citations refer to Burnet's edition (1901–1905) of Plato's *Symposium*.

3. If Diotima visited Athens ten years before the plague (201d) and Socrates spoke with her at that time, then their conversation took place in 440 B.C., seventeen years before the *Clouds* was first performed and approximately thirty years after the birth of Socrates.

4. Because these points have proven contentious, it is necessary to explain Socrates' apparent meaning. By consigning love of the father or mother, that is, incest, to the realm of the laughable and unimportant at

199, Socrates excludes eros of one's own from his discussion, thus implying that it is not one of the beautiful or praiseworthy aspects of eros. Socrates knows that human beings love "their own" things, meaning not only that some are tempted to commit incest, but also that we love our selves and those who are like us. But in limiting himself to telling the "most beautiful parts" of eros, he implies that these kinds of love are not as praiseworthy.

Socrates apparently identifies eros with desire and defines desire as a longing which follows from lacking and needing (200 ff.). If eros has or is a desire for something, then we will not love anything which we have or are. We would not love another person except to satisfy our desires. This apparent equation of eros with desire has been challenged on the grounds that it is too selfish or utilitarian an account of eros to be comprehensive or true (Dover 1980, 144; yet see Carson 1986, 3–11). But it seems that Socrates is aware that eros might be more than simple desire, for he asks if eros "desires and loves" its object, as if desire and eros were two different things. Again, even though eros may involve more than mere desire, whatever eros is in excess of desire, Socrates does not discuss it here because he denies that it is among the most beautiful parts of eros. Eros, insofar as it is praiseworthy, will be treated as a kind of desire.

Finally, Dover objects that one can possess some portion of a certain quality and yet desire more of it (Dover 1980, 135). Thus, we can love something without necessarily lacking it completely. But he does not seem to have thought through the implication of saying that eros is needy: Insofar as one loves, one lacks. A wholly erotic being would be a wholly needy being. Eros itself would be need itself.

5. Diotima seems to use the terms *wisdom* (*sophia*), *scientific knowledge* (*episteme*), and *prudence* (*phronesis*) interchangeably, as if she thinks that there is no wisdom that is not based on an empirical knowledge of causes and that prudence or practical wisdom is a part of wisdom. The translation of "prudence" or "practical knowledge" for *phronesis* in Plato may be controversial. Burnet, for example, argues that "in Plato the word *phronesis* is exactly equivalent to *sophia*" (1900, 261). But even if "Plato" is more reluctant than Aristotle to distinguish between practical and theoretical wisdom, "Plato" sometimes seems to use *phronesis* to mean wisdom or expertise concerning the use of good things (e.g., *Republic* 348b8–d9, 349e, 505bc, 518e–519b).

6. She says that daimons intercede between men and gods because the "daimonic realm" fills the interval between gods and men and that it binds up "the whole itself" (202e5–7). Man has access to the daimons through the "daimonic arts," which include "all divination and the art of the priests," which, in turn, includes "sacrifices, initiatory rituals, and

incantations" and every kind of "soothsaying and magic" (202e7–203a1).

7. While the Greeks had no term that is simply equivalent to our term *sexual desire*, the form of love called "Aphrodite" appears to come close to it. Whereas eros is associated with powerful desires that are not *simply* sexual, Aphrodite refers to the charming, mischievous, sexual allure of young love (e.g., Hesiod *Theogony* 203–206). Liddell and Scott translates *ta aphrodisia* as "sexual pleasures" and *aphrodisiaxō* as "to have sexual intercourse" or to "indulge lust."

8. Rousseau refers to childhood as the "peaceful age of intelligence" and adolescence as a "stormy revolution" which resembles "the roaring of the sea" which "precedes a tempest from afar" (1979, 162, 211).

9. Some deny that Socrates is even aware of the possibility that *to kalon* is not reducible to the good. Dover, for instance, claims that the substitution of "the good" for "the beautiful" here is a change in "mere terminology" (1980, 144). But Socrates' reaction to the change implies that he understands the terms differently. For further discussion of the distinction, see Arendt 1958, 13; 1990, 77; Aristotle *Eudemean Ethics* 1248b8–1249a17; Xenophon *Oeconomicus* 6.12–17.

10. It is possible that Socrates distances himself from Diotima's subsequent account of heroism and eros for fame by calling it "sophistic" (208c). Yet by calling it the speech of a *perfect* sophist, he may mean that he finds this teaching somewhat persuasive. Bury suggests that the phrase "like the perfect sophists" means "in truly professional style" or in the manner of a lecture (1932, 118).

11. Contrast this with Hannah Arendt, who says that the Greek acts virtuously to manifest his or her uniqueness and to be recognized by the public world (1958, 48–58, 160). Diotima, on the other hand, suggests that we act selflessly primarily because we want to be noble and that we seek fame as solace for having sacrificed our well-being.

12. Some commentators, such as Kenneth Dorter, readily discount Socrates' references to personal or providential gods on the grounds that they are merely ironic, intended to palliate the fears of "pious" and "unsophisticated" listeners; after stripping away the popular, mythic surface, one can discover the serious, philosophic teachings beneath (1981, 77); also Burger (1984, 205); Griswold (1986, 139ff.). This approach to these Socratic statements is, however, subject to at least two objections. Firstly, there is the interpretive difficulty presented by the nature of irony itself. As David Bolotin asks:

> How are we to avoid the dangers of arbitrary interpretation, such as that of regarding as genuine only those among Socrates' arguments that we happen to find congenial, while dismissing the others as Socratic irony? It seems to me that we can avoid such dangers, and that we can

> bring Socrates' innermost thought to light, but only if we approach the dialogue by beginning from the very surface of the text. This means that we must not presume to know in advance what Socrates could and could not have meant seriously; we must make a deliberate effort, if need be, to let the dialogue unfold for us as it did for the most docile of Socrates' interlocutors or listeners.

Bolotin argues that if we begin from the surface, we may recover the participants sense of what is at stake in the discussion; this, in turn, helps us discover which of Socrates' arguments are ironic or deficient and will alert us to the significance of Socrates' "anomalous expressions or seemingly casual remarks" which "will point us toward Socrates' deeper thinking" (1987, 39–40).

Secondly, it is striking that thinkers as divergent as Gregory Vlastos and Leo Strauss, taking two entirely different routes, arrive at the same conclusion that Socrates and Plato take seriously the possibility that there may be personal or providential gods: Strauss 1953, 150 n. 24; 1987, 4–5; 1964, 241; Vlastos 1971, 26; 1991, 158 ff.

13. Hanna Pitkin challenges Arendt's assertion that ambition for political glory is rooted in a desire for lasting recognition by stating: "It is one thing to hope for heavenly immortality, but the earthly immortal fame Arendt has in mind seems no good once one is dead. Why should I care—and care *so much*—about whether my name and deeds will be remembered after I am dead and gone?" (1981, 337). Plato's response appears to be that lovers of the noble do not seek mere recognition but half-consciously hope that their noble deeds will earn them genuine immortality from a providential god.

14. The Platonic Socrates will sometimes speak of the virtue justice in its ordinary sense; for example, see *Republic* 420b, 520a–b; yet *Republic* 430c.

15. The testimony of Xenophon (*Memorabilia* 4.7.5–6) also supports Plato's indication that Socrates studied natural philosophy, contrary to Vlastos (1991, 47–48, 161–162). For detailed comparisons between the Aristophanic and the Platonic Socrates, see Nussbaum (1980, 71–76 passim) and Strauss (1966, 8, 50–52, 313–314).

16. In fact, Bolotin (1987, 54) shows that Socrates performs a similar function for Cebes and Simmias in the *Phaedo*. While the *Symposium* portrays a young Socrates whose eros for *to kalon* and immortality lead him to discover his need to investigate noble virtue, justice, and the gods, it does not prove that the "historical" Socrates founded political philosophy in this manner. We do not know that he conversed with Diotima nor even that he loved the beauty of wisdom. But it does suggest that such concerns could have led a young lover of the beauty of wisdom to philosophize about "the human things."

17. Strauss 1989b [1963], 204.

18. Consider how Socrates recklessly encourages Alcibiades' ambition to rule the world (*Alcibiades Major*) and how he makes admittedly defective arguments in Book I of the *Republic* to elicit revealing outbursts from Polemarchus, Thrasymachus, and Glaucon.

## CHAPTER 6

1. Socrates' conversations with Diotima in the *Symposium* and with Parmenides in the *Parmenides* antedate the conversation recorded as the *Alcibiades Major*, since in these dialogues Socrates is said to be young and speaks as a student to teachers.

2. According to Schleiermacher, while the *Phaedo* as a whole celebrates Socrates' heroism as he died, Alcibiades' speech in the *Symposium* ennobles Socrates as he lived and is "manifestly the crest and crown of the whole dialogue" (1836, 278).

3. At the opening of the *Symposium*, there are many who do not know much about Socrates but who are eager to hear what they said to one another about the god Eros (*Symposium* 172a–c). The fact that Socrates is not eager to spread the story raises the possibility that he believes it might make him look guilty of something (173a–b).

4. E.g., Dover 1980 and Nehamas 1992.

5. The manuscript at 133c8–17 is bracketed by Burnet and appears to be corrupt.

## CHAPTER 7

1. All page references are to Plato's *Symposium* in Burnet (1901) unless otherwise indicated.

2. Gould 1963, 39–41; Nussbaum 1986, 194; Rosen 1987, 287.

3. Nehemas and Woodruff 1989, 64 n. 98.

4. Additionally, Socrates may have been reluctant to have sexual relations with Alcibiades simply because he was wary of the hopes and illusions that sometimes attend sexual excitement. According to Diotima, human sexuality is never a matter of mere physical pleasure or attraction or instinct. Aphrodite, she says, is beautiful and always attended by Eros (203c4–5). That is, the object of our sexual desires always appears to have a beauty that can generate erotic longings. Were Socrates to have sexual intercourse with someone whom he finds physically or sexually attractive, he might relapse into the uncritical attraction to the beautiful that he seems to have thought through after speaking with Diotima. Even after Socrates has "purified" his Eros for beauty, he

may have to rely on his prudence, endurance, and self-control to check his sexual longings (*Phaedrus* 256a7–b7; *Laws* 839aff.; Xenophon *Memorabilia* 1.3.10–14; Grube 1935, 90).

5. In the course of his praise, Alcibiades never claims that Socrates excels in assaulting the enemy; instead of risking all to display his heroic courage, Socrates has the courage that consists in keeping his wits about him when danger is at hand (*Laches* 193a; *Republic* 399a–b; Aristotle *Ethics* 1116b).

6. Socrates' great emphasis on prudence is in keeping with what Alcibiades says Socrates always says to him in the last part of Alcibiades' speech. In this latter passage, Alcibiades praises the inner beauty of Socrates' speeches and gives us a further account of their conversations. In the first part of his speech, Alcibiades said that no matter who makes Socratic speeches, everyone who hears them thinks that they are divine and extremely moving (215d1–e4, 216c4–5). But here he says that Socrates' speeches, like Socrates himself, are silenic and need to be opened up. According to Alcibiades, Socrates always sounds laughable as he speaks with words that are rough, like the "hide of a hubristic satyr." Always talking about pack-asses, blacksmiths, shoemakers, and tanners, Socrates is laughed at by those who do not know him. But Alcibiades assures us that if we open up and go inside Socrates' speeches, we will find that they are "the only speeches with sense," that they are the "most divine speeches," and that they have "the largest number of images of virtue within them." He says that these speeches allude to all that one must examine in order to become a gentleman (*kalos te kagathos*) (221d–222a). Consider how this differs from his initial presentation of the speeches: At first, Socrates' speeches are so musical and moving that, no matter who speaks them, everyone swoons in grief about their need for what is noble and divine. Now he says that the speeches seem prosaic and that only a few recognize their hidden meaning. The implication seems to be that Alcibiades attributes a hidden beauty to Socrates even where Socrates points to the importance of the useful or practical.

7. Hobbes *Leviathan* chap. 6; Locke *An Essay Concerning Human Understanding* bk. 2, chap. 28; Montesquieu *The Spirit of the Laws* bk. 4, chap. 2. Also Hume *Enquiries Concerning the Human Understanding* 276, "On the Independence of Parliament," in *Hume's Political Writings*, Library of Liberal Arts, p. 68.

8. *Federalist Papers* 72; also *Cato's Letters* no. 40.

9. Montesquieu *The Spirit of the Laws* bk. 3, chaps. 7 and 8; bk. 4, chap. 2; bk. 5, chap. 19; cf. Hobbes *Leviathan* chaps. 6, 10, 11, 13, 15 end. Pangle 1973, 67–68.

10. Hobbes *Leviathan* chap. 6, 15; Locke *Some Thoughts Concerning Education* secs. 133–145; Montesquieu *Spirit of the Laws* bk. 5, chap. 6; *Federalist Papers* 1, 3, 11, 37, 43, 78, 85.

## CHAPTER 8

1. Unless otherwise indicated, all subsequent references are to Burnet's edition of Plato's *Republic* (Burnet 1901).

2. Classical scholars have long disagreed over interpretations of Glaucon's account of the goodness of justice. The primary difficulty seems to be that Glaucon asks Socrates to show not only that justice is good without regard to its consequences, but also that those who are just are happier than those without justice. Some attempt to resolve this apparent contradiction by claiming that Glaucon thinks justice is a "component" of happiness (Irwin 1977, 188, 325–6 n. 8; Reeve 1988, 24–31). In calling justice a component, one avoids saying that justice is a cause of happiness, for that would, of course, imply that justice is praiseworthy for its consequences (Reeve 1988, 282 n. 19). But in fact Glaucon wants Socrates to affirm that justice *is* a necessary and sufficient condition of, that is, a cause of, greater happiness than is available through injustice. A more plausible way of reconciling Glaucon's demand that justice be praised without regard to its consequences with his demand that it be shown to be the source of the greatest happiness is that Glaucon wants justice to be praised on two separate and perhaps ultimately compatible grounds. One manifest objection to the suggestion that he wants justice to be praised both regardless of its consequences and also for its consequences is that the categories he lays out at the opening of Book II do not allow for something that is "good in itself" in the sense that it has nothing to do with some benefit or enjoyment. A second, alternative objection would be that in asking Socrates to show that justice makes us happy, Glaucon would contradict his stated desire to have justice praised without regard to its consequences. But these objections would be decisive only if we knew from the outset that Glaucon is incapable of confusion or inconsistency. But, in fact, we know that Glaucon is capable of such things, for he speaks at 359e–360a of acts of injustice and of justice being committed in the "state of nature," in a state which exists prior to the invention of the distinction between just and unjust acts. It seems that Glaucon's understanding of the goodness of justice is important, not because he represents Plato's understanding of justice, but because he brilliantly articulates a vision of justice that is very noble or "high-minded" but nonetheless still sub-philosophic and is a vision upon which one must reflect to understand justice itself (348c11; cf. Plato *Second Letter* 341c–d with Reeve 1988, 30–31, 249, 283).

3. This is not to attribute to Socrates the view that one who has "psychic justice" would be a bad citizen, for, among other things, Socrates says that only someone with psychic justice is never tempted to tyrannize others (619b–e; Reeve 1988, 263).

4. One does not have to resolve the issue of whether Socrates finally thinks philosophers would be made unhappy by ruling the city to grasp what Plato means to teach in this passage about Glaucon's understanding of justice. Socrates makes some statements that seem to qualify the philosophers' unwillingness to live in the cave; for example, his remarks at 465b–466d and 496d, which suggest that philosophers would prefer life in a rational city to life in cities governed by and for non-philosophers. But this does not prove that individual philosophers would want to *rule* the rational city (347c–d). As Reeve notes, philosophers would have to sacrifice some of their contemplative joy in order to govern (Reeve 1988, 202–203). Reeve, however, claims that philosophers would accept the burdens of rule in order to be "reliably happy" and lightens his account of those burdens by saying that Plato finds a life of "pure" philosophy is "too high for a human being" (Reeve 1988, 311 n. 10). Yet Socrates refers to philosophers who manage to philosophize without being politically active (496, 520a–b).

# BIBLIOGRAPHY

Ahrensdorf, Peter. 1995. *The Death of Socrates and the Life of Philosophy*. Albany: State University of New York Press.

Allen, R. E. 1992. *Plato's Symposium*. New Haven: Yale University Press.

Ansell-Pearson, Keith. 1994. *Nietzsche as a Political Thinker*. Cambridge: Cambridge University Press.

Annas, Julia. 1981. *An Introduction to Plato's Republic*. Oxford: Oxford University Press.

Anton, J., and A. Preus, eds. 1983. *Essays in Ancient Greek Philosophy*. Vol. 2. Albany: State University of New York Press.

Arendt, Hannah. 1958. *The Human Condition*. Chicago: University of Chicago Press.

———. 1990. "Philosophy and Politics." *Social Research* 57:73–103.

Bacon, H. 1957. "Socrates Crowned." *Virginia Quarterly Review* 35:415–30.

Barber, Benjamin. 1984. *Strong Democracy*. Berkeley and Los Angeles: University of California Press.

Bennet, William. 1994. *The Book of Virtues*. New York: Simon and Schuster.

Benson, Hugh H., ed. 1992. *Philosophy of Socrates*. Oxford: Oxford University Press.

Bernstein, Richard. 1978. "One Step Forward, Two Steps Backward." *Political Theory* 15:538–563.

Benardete, Seth, trans. 1986. "Symposium." *The Dialogues of Plato*. New York: Bantam.

Bloom, Allan. 1968. "Interpretive Essay." *The Republic of Plato*. New York: Basic.

———. 1992. *Love and Friendship*. New York: Simon and Schuster.

Bolotin, David. 1979. *Plato's Dialogue on Friendship*. Ithaca: Cornell University Press.

———. 1987. "The Life of Philosophy and the Immortality of the Soul: An Introduction to Plato's *Phaedo*." *Ancient Philosophy* 7:39–56.

Brickhouse, Thomas, and Nicholas D. Smith. 1992. "The Formal Charges against Socrates." *Essays on the Philosophy of Socrates*, ed. Hugh H. Benson. Oxford: Oxford University Press.

Bruell, Christopher. 1987. "Xenophon." *History of Political Philosophy*, 3d ed., ed. Strauss and Joseph Cropsey. Chicago: University of Chicago Press.

———. 1987a. "On the Lovers." *The Roots of Political Philosophy*, ed. Thomas Pangle. Ithaca: Cornell University Press.

———. 1994. "On Platonic Political Philosophy." *Review of Politics* 56 (2):261–282.

———. 1994a. "A Return to Classical Political Philosophy and the Understanding of the American Founding." *Leo Strauss: Political Philosopher and Thinker*, ed. Kenneth Deutsche and Walter Nicgorski. Lanham, Md.: Rowman and Littlefield.

Burger, Ronna. 1984. *Phaedo: A Platonic Labyrinth*. New Haven: Yale University Press.

Burnet, John. 1900. *The Ethics of Aristotle*. London: Methuen.

———. 1901–5. *Platonis Opera*. 5 vols. Oxford: Oxford University Press.

———. 1930. *Early Greek Philosophy*. London: A. & C. Black.

Bury, R. G. 1932. *The Symposium of Plato*. Cambridge, England: W. Heffer and Sons.

Carson, Ann. 1986. *Eros the Bittersweet*. Princeton: Princeton University Press.

Connolly, William. 1988. *Political Theory and Modernity*. Oxford, U.K.: Blackwell.

Cornford, F. M. 1971 (originally published 1950). "The Doctrine of Eros in Plato's *Symposium*." *Plato*, vol. 2, ed. Gregory Vlastos. Garden City, N.Y.: Anchor Books.

Dannhauser, Werner. 1968. *Nietzsche's View of Socrates*. Ithaca: Cornell University Press.

Detwiler, Bruce. 1990. *Nietzsche and the Politics of Aristocratic Radicalism*. Chicago: Chicago University Press.

Diels, Hermann, and Walther Kranz. 1985. *Die Fragmente der Vorsokratiker*. 3 vols. Hildesheim: Weidmann.

Dobbs, Darrel. 1994. "Choosing Justice: Socrates' Model City and the Practice of Dialectic." *American Political Science Review* 88 (2):263–277.

Dorter, Kenneth. 1982. *Plato's Phaedo*. Toronto: University of Toronto Press.

Dover, Kenneth. 1972. *Aristophanic Comedy*. Berkeley and Los Angeles: University of California Press.

———. 1980. *Plato: Symposium*. Ed. Cambridge: Cambridge University Press.

Edelstein, Ludwig. 1967. *Ancient Medicine*. Baltimore: Johns Hopkins University Press.

Ehrenberg, Victor. 1951. 2d ed. *The People of Aristophanes*. Oxford: Blackwell.

Elshtain, Jean Bethke. 1995. "Stories and Political Life." *PS: Political Science and Politics* 28 (2):196–197.

Euben, J. Peter. 1990. *The Tragedy of Political Theory*. Princeton: Princeton University Press.

Forde, Steven. 1987 "On the Alcibiades Major." *The Roots of Political Philosophy*, ed. Thomas L. Pangle. Ithaca: Cornell University Press.

———. 1989. *The Ambition to Rule*. Ithaca: Cornell University Press.

Foucault, Michel. 1984. *The Foucault Reader*, ed. P. Rabinow. New York: Pantheon.

———. 1985. *The Use of Pleasure*. Trans. Robert Hurley. New York: Random House.

Freud, Sigmund. 1977. "Three Essays on Sexuality." *On Sexuality*, trans. and ed. James Strachey. Harmondsworth: Penguin.

———. 1984. "Beyond the Pleasure Principle." *On Metapsychology*, trans. and ed. James Strachey. Harmondsworth: Penguin.

———. 1985. "Civilization and Its Discontents." *Civilization, Society, and Religion*, trans. and ed. James Strachey. Harmondsworth: Penguin.

Friedländer, Paul. 1964. *Plato: An Introduction*. Trans. Hans Meyerhoff. Princeton: Princeton University Press.

———. 1969. *Plato*. Vol. 2. Trans. Hans Meyerhoff. Princeton: Princeton University Press.

Galston, William. 1991. *Liberal Purposes*. Cambridge: Cambridge University Press.

Garagin, Michael. 1977. "Socrates' *Hybris* and Alcibiades' Failure." *Phoenix* 31:22–37.

Gomperz, Theodor. 1955. *Greek Thinkers*. New York: Humanities Press.

Gosling, J. C. B. 1960. "*Republic* Book V: ta polla kala etc." *Phronesis* 5:116–128.

Gould, Thomas. 1963. *Platonic Love*. New York: Free Press of Glencoe.

Griswold, Charles. 1986. *Self-Knowledge in Plato's Phaedrus*. New Haven: Yale University Press.

———, ed. 1988. *Platonic Writings, Platonic Readings*. New York: Routledge and Kegan Paul, Chapman and Hall.

Grube, G. M. A. 1935. *Plato's Thought*. Boston: Beacon Press.

Guignon, Charles, and David Hiley. 1990. "Biting the Bullet." *Reading Rorty*, ed. Alan Malachowski. Oxford: Blackwell.

Guthrie, W. K. C. 1971. *Socrates*. Cambridge: Cambridge University Press.

Hackforth, R. 1950. "Immortality in Plato's *Symposium*." *Classical Review* 64:43–45.

———. 1955. *Plato's Phaedo*. Cambridge: Cambridge University Press.

Havel, Vaclav. 1991. "Stories and Totalitarianism." *Open Letters*. New York: Knopf.

Heidegger, Martin. 1959 [1953]. *An Introduction to Metaphysics*. Trans. Ralph Manheim. New Haven: Yale University Press.

———. 1977 [1947]. "Letter on Humanism." *Basic Writings*. Trans. David Farrell Krell. New York: Harper and Row.

———. 1979 [1961]. *Nietzsche*. Vol. 1. Trans. David Farrell Krell. New York: Harper and Row.

———. 1982 [1961]. *Nietzsche*. Vol. 4. Trans. David Farrell Krell. New York: Harper and Row.

———. 1993 [1976]. "*Der Spiegel* Interview." *The Heidegger Controversy*. Cambridge: MIT Press.

Herzog, Donald. 1986. "Questions for Republicans." *Political Theory* 14 (3):473–493.

Hornsby, Roger. 1956. "Significant Action in the *Symposium*." *Classical Journal* 52:35–40.

Hubbard, Thomas K. 1991. *The Mask of Comedy*. Ithaca: Cornell University Press.

Irwin, Terence. 1977. *Plato's Moral Theory*. Oxford: Oxford University Press.

Jaeger, Werner. 1943. *Paideia*. Vol. 2. New York: Oxford University Press.

Kaufmann, Walter. 1968. *Nietzsche*. Princeton: Princeton University Press.

Kirk, G. S., and J. E. Raven. 1957. *The Presocratic Philosophers*. New York: Cambridge University Press.

Klein, Jacob. 1965. *A Commentary on Plato's Meno*. Chapel Hill: University of North Carolina Press.

———. 1968. *Greek Mathematical Thought and the Origins of Algebra*. Cambridge: MIT Press.

Klosko, George. 1986. *The Development of Plato's Political Theory*. New York: Methuen.

Kosman, L. 1976. "Platonic Love." *Phronesis* supplemental vol. 2:53–69.

Kraut, Richard. 1973. "Egoism, Love and Political Office." *Philosophical Review* 82:330–344.

———. 1984. *Socrates and the State*. Princeton: Princeton University Press.

Kymlicka, Will, and Wayne Norman. 1994. "Return of the Citizen." *Ethics* 104:352–381.

Lampert, Lawrence. 1986. *Nietzsche's Teaching*. New Haven: Yale University Press.

Levinson, R. B. 1953. *In Defense of Plato*. Cambridge: Harvard University Press.

Löwith, Karl. 1964. *From Hegel to Nietzsche*. New York: Columbia University Press.

Lyotard, Jean-Francois. 1985. "Discussion entre Jean-Francois Lyotard et Richard Rorty." *Critique* 41:581–584.

MacIntyre, Alasdair. 1984. *After Virtue*. 2d ed. Notre Dame: University of Notre Dame Press.

Malachowski, Alan, ed. 1990. *Reading Rorty*. Oxford: Blackwell.

——— . 1990a. "Deep Epistemology without Foundations (in Language)." *Reading Rorty*, ed. Alan Malachowski. Oxford: Blackwell.

Marcus, R. A. "The Dialectic of Eros in Plato's Symposium." *Plato*, vol. 2, ed. Gregory Vlastos. Notre Dame: University of Notre Dame Press.

Moravcsik, J. M. A. 1971. "Reason and Eros in the Ascent Passage in the *Symposium*." *Essays in Ancient Greek Philosophy*, ed. J. Anton and A. Preus. Albany: State University of New York Press.

Nehamas, Alexander, and Paul Woodruff. 1989. *Symposium*. Trans. Indianapolis: Hacket.

Neumann, Harry. 1965. "Diotima's Concept of Love." *American Journal of Philology*. 86: 33–59.

——— . 1966. "On the Comedy of Plato's Aristophanes." *American Journal of Philology* 87:420–426.

Nichols, Christopher. 1986. *Contest of the Faculties*. London: Methuen.

Nichols, Mary. 1987. *Socrates and the Political Community*. Albany: State University of New York Press.

———. 1988. "Spiritedness and Philosophy in Plato's *Republic*." *Understanding the Political Spirit* ed. C. Zuckert. New Haven: Yale University Press.

Nietzsche, Friedrich. 1966. *Beyond Good and Evil*. Trans. Walter Kaufmann. New York: Vintage.

———. 1967a. *Birth of Tragedy*. Trans. Walter Kaufmann. New York: Vintage.

———. 1967b. *Genealogy of Morals*. Trans. Walter Kaufmann and R. J. Hollingdale. New York: Vintage.

———. 1967c. *The Will to Power*. Trans. Walter Kaufmann and R. J. Hollingdale. New York: Vintage.

———. 1968. *Twilight of the Idols*. Trans. R. J. Hollingdale. London: Penguin.

Nussbaum, Martha. 1980. "Aristophanes and Socrates on Learning Practical Wisdom." *Yale Classical Studies* 26:43–97.

———. 1986. *The Fragility of Goodness*. Cambridge: Cambridge University Press.

Nygren, Anders. 1953. *Agape and Eros*. Chicago: University of Chicago Press.

Oldfield, Adrian. 1990. *Citizenship and Community*. London: Routledge.

O'Brien, Michael J. 1984. "'Becoming Immortal' in Plato's *Symposium*." *Greek Poetry and Philosophy*, ed. Douglas Gerber. Chico, Calif.: Scholar's Press.

O'Regan, Daphne. 1992. *Rhetoric, Comedy, and the Violence of Language in Aristophanes'* Clouds. New York: Oxford University Press.

Orwin, Clifford. 1994. *The Humanity of Thucydides*. Princeton: Princeton University Press.

Pangle, Thomas L. 1973. *Montesquieu's Philosophy of Liberalism*. Chicago: University of Chicago Press.

———. 1976. "The Political Psychology of Religion in Plato's *Laws*." *American Political Science Review* 70:1059–1077.

———. 1983. "The Roots of Contemporary Nihilism and Its Consequences for Nietzsche." *Review of Politics* 45:45–70.

———. 1984. "Introduction." *Studies in Platonic Political Philosophy*. Chicago: University of Chicago Press.

———, ed. 1987. *The Roots of Political Philosophy*. Ithaca: Cornell University Press.

———. 1988. *The Spirit of Modern Republicanism*. Chicago: University of Chicago Press.

———. 1992. *The Ennobling of Democracy*. Baltimore: Johns Hopkins University Press.

Pitkin, Hanna. 1981. "On Relating Private and Public." *Political Theory* 9:327–352.

Rahe, Paul H. *Republics Ancient and Modern*. Chapel Hill: University of North Carolina Press.

Reckford, Kenneth. 1987. *Aristophanes' Old and New Comedy*. Chapel Hill: University of North Carolina Press.

Reeve, C. D. C. 1988. *Philosopher-Kings*. Princeton: Princeton University Press.

Roberts, Jennifer Tolbert. 1994. *Athens on Trial*. Princeton: Princeton University Press.

Robin, Leon. 1929. "Commentaire" for "Platon: Le Banquet." *Ouvres completes*, vol. 4, pt. 2. Paris: Bude.

Rorty, Richard. 1979. *Philosophy and the Mirror of Nature*. Princeton: Princeton University Press.

———. 1982. *Consequences of Pragmatism*. Minneapolis: University of Minnesota Press.

———. 1987. "Thugs and Theorists." *Political Theory* 15:564–580.

———. 1988. "That Old Time Philosophy." *The New Republic*. Vol. 198. 14:28–33.

——— . 1989. *Contingency, Irony and Solidarity*. Cambridge: Cambridge University Press.

——— . 1991. *Objectivity, Relativism and Truth*. Cambridge: Cambridge University Press.

——— . 1991a. *Essays on Heidegger and Others*. Cambridge: Cambridge University Press.

——— . 1993. "Trotsky and Wild Orchids." *Common Knowledge* 1(3):140–153.

Rosen, Stanley. 1965. "The Role of Eros in Plato's Republic." *Review of Metaphysics* 18:452–475.

———. 1987. *Plato's Symposium*. 2d ed. New Haven: Yale University Press.

Ross, David. 1951. *Plato's Theory of the Ideas*. Oxford: Clarendon Press.

Rousseau, Jean-Jacques. 1979. *Emile*. Trans. A. Bloom. New York: Basic Books.

———. 1986. *Discourses and Essay on the Origin of Languages*. Trans. Gourevitch. New York: Harper & Row.

Sachs, David. 1971. "A Fallacy in Plato's *Republic*?" *Plato*, vol. 2, ed. G. Vlastos. Notre Dame: Notre Dame.

Santas, Gerasimos. 1988. *Plato and Freud*. Oxford: Basil Blackwell.

Saxonhouse, Arlene. 1984. "Eros and the Female in Greek Political Thought: An Interpretation of Plato's *Symposium*." *Political Theory* 12:5–28.

———. 1985. "The Net of Hephaestus." *Interpretation* 13:15–31.

———. 1992. *Fear of Diversity*. Chicago: University of Chicago Press.

Schleiermacher, F. E. D. 1836. *Introductions to the Dialogues of Plato*. Trans. William Hobson. Cambridge: Cambridge University Press.

Shorey, Paul. 1933. *What Plato Said*. Chicago: University of Chicago Press.

Solomos, Alexis. 1974. *The Living Aristophanes*. Ann Arbor: University of Michigan Press.

Stern, Paul. "Plato's Antifoundationalism." *Review of Politics* 51:190–217.

Stokes, Michael. 1986. *Plato's Socratic Conversations*. Baltimore: Johns Hopkins University Press.

———. 1992. *Socratic Questions*. Editor. New York: Routledge.

Strauss, Leo. 1953. *Natural Right and History*. Chicago: University of Chicago Press.

———. 1959. *What Is Political Philosophy?* New York: Free Press.

———. 1964. *The City and Man*. Chicago: Rand McNally.

———. 1966. *Socrates and Aristophanes*. New York: Basic Books.

———. 1968. *Liberalism Ancient and Modern*. New York: Basic Books.

——— . 1970. *Xenophon's Socratic Discourse*. Ithaca: Cornell University Press.

———. 1983. *Studies in Platonic Political Philosophy*. Chicago: University of Chicago Press.

———. 1989a. *On Tyranny*. Reprint. New York: Basic Books.

———. 1989b. *Rebirth of Classical Political Rationalism*, ed. Thomas Pangle. Chicago: University of Chicago Press.

Strauss, Leo, and Joseph Cropsey, eds. 1987. *History of Political Philosophy*. 3d ed. Chicago: University of Chicago Press.

Taylor, A. E. 1957. *Plato: The Man and His Work*. New York: Meridian Books.

Taylor, Charles. 1990. "Rorty in the Epistemological Tradition." *Reading Rorty*, ed. Alan Malachowski. Oxford: Blackwell.

Tessitore, Aristide. 1994. "Courage and Comedy in Plato's *Laches*." *Journal of Politics* 56 (1):115–133.

Thiele, Leslie Paul. 1990. *Friedrich Nietzsche and the Politics of the Soul*. Princeton: Princeton University Press.

Tocqueville, Alexis. 1969. *Democracy in America*. Trans. George Lawrence. New York: Anchor.

Vlastos, Gregory, ed. 1971. *Plato*. 2 vols. Garden City, N.Y.: Doubleday.

———. 1971a. "Introduction: The Paradox of Socrates." *The Philosophy of Socrates*, ed. Gregory Vlastos. Garden City, N.Y.: Doubleday.

———. 1981 (originally Published 1973). *Platonic Studies*. Princeton: Princeton University Press.

———. 1985. "Socrates' Disavowal of Knowledge." *The Philosophical Quarterly* 35:1–31.

———. 1991. *Socrates: Ironist and Moral Philosopher*. Cambridge: Cambridge University Press.

West, Thomas. 1979. *Apology of Socrates*. Ithaca: Cornell University Press.

West, Grace, and Thomas West. 1984. *Four Texts on Socrates*. Ithaca: Cornell University Press.

Williams, Bernard. 1990. "Auto-da-Fe: Consequences of Pragmatism." *Reading Rorty*, ed. Alan Malachowski. Oxford: Blackwell.

Wolin, Richard. 1992. *The Terms of Cultural Criticism*. New York: Columbia University Press.

———. 1993. *The Heidegger Controversy*. Cambridge: MIT Press.

Wood, Gordon. 1990. "Classical Republicanism and the American Revolution." *Chicago-Kent Law Review* 56 (1):13–37.

Woodruff, Paul. 1992. "Plato's Early Theory of Knowledge." *Philosophy of Socrates*. Ed. Michael Stokes. Oxford: Oxford University Press.

# INDEX